Our Moral Life in Christ

A Basic Course on Moral Theology

Aurelio Fernández-James Socías

Our Moral Life in Christ

A Basic Course on Moral Theology

SCEPTER PUBLISHERS, INC.
Princeton, New Jersey
MIDWEST THEOLOGICAL FORUM
Chicago, Illinois

Published in the United States of America by

Scepter Publishers, Inc.   Midwest Theological Forum
20 Nassau St.   712 S. Loomis
Princeton, NJ 08542   Chicago, IL 60607

Nihil Obstat
Reverend Patrick J. Boyle, S.J.
Censor Deputatus
July 14, 1997

Imprimatur
✠ Most Reverend Raymond E. Goedert, M.A., S.T.L., J.C.L.
Vicar General of the Archdiocese of Chicago
July 15, 1997

The Nihil Obstat and Imprimatur are official declarations that a book is free of doctrinal and moral error. No implication is contained therein that those who have granted the Nihil Obstat and Imprimatur agree with the content, opinions, or statements expressed.

ACKNOWLEDGEMENTS

Excerpts from the English translation of the *Catechism of the Catholic Church* for the United States of America Copyright © 1994, United States Catholic Conference, Inc. -Libreria Editrice Vaticana. Used with permission.

Excerpts from the English translation of the *Catechism of the Catholic Church: Modifications from the Editio Typica* Copyright © 1997, United States Catholic Conference, Inc. -- Libreria Editrice Vaticana. Used with permission.

Scripture quotations are adapted from the *Revised Standard Version of the Bible,* copyright © 1946, 1952, 1971, and the *New Revised Standard Version of the Bible,* copyright © 1989, by the Division of Christian Education of the National Council of the Churches of Christ in the United States of America, and are used by permission. All rights reserved.

Excerpts from the *Code of Canon Law, Latin/English Edition,* are used with permission, copyright © 1983 Canon Law Society of America, Washington, DC.

Citations of official Church documents from Neufner, Josef, SJ and Dupuis, Jacques, SJ, eds., *The Christian Faith: Doctrinal Documents of the Catholic Church,* 5th ed. (New York: Alba House, 1992). Used with permission.

Excerpts from *Vatican II The Conciliar and Post Conciliar Documents, New Revised Edition* edited by Austin Flannery, OP, copyright © 1992, Costello Publishing Company, Inc., Northport, NY are used with permission of the publisher, all rights reserved. No part of these excerpts may be reproduced, stored in a retrieval system, or transmitted in any form or by any means - electronic, mechanical, photocopying, recording or otherwise, without express written permission of Costello Publishing Company.

The editor would like to thank Fr. Aurelio Fernández, for giving permission to use his books *Teología Moral* (3 volumes), *Compendio de Teología* and *Breve curso de moral católica* (Madrid, 1993) as sources and references for this project. He also extends special thanks to all who have collaborated on the edition of this book and particularly to Emmet Flood, for doing so much to adapt its language, examples and tone for an American audience.

Contents

127   Chapter VII
      Sin and Conversion

Part II
Commandments and Beatitudes

ABBREVIATIONS USED FOR
THE BOOKS OF THE BIBLE

Gn	Genesis	Ob	Obadiah
Ex	Exodus	Jon	Jonah
Lv	Leviticus	Mi	Micah
Nb	Numbers	Na	Nahum
Dt	Deuteronomy	Hab	Habakkuk
Jos	Joshua	Zp	Zephaniah
Jg	Judges	Zc	Zechariah
Rt	Ruth	Hg	Haggai
1 Sam	1 Samuel	Ml	Malachi
2 Sam	2 Samuel		
1 K	1 Kings	Mt	Matthew
2 K	2 Kings	Mk	Mark
1 Ch	1 Chronicles	Lk	Luke
2 Ch	2 Chronicles	Jn	John
Ezr	Ezra	Acts	Acts
Neh	Nehemiah	Rm	Romans
Tb	Tobit	1 Cor	1 Corinthians
Jdt	Judith	2 Cor	2 Corinthians
Est	Esther	Gal	Galatians
1 Mac	1 Maccabees	Eph	Ephesians
2 Mac	2 Maccabees	Phil	Philippians
Jb	Job	Col	Colossians
Ps	Psalms	1 Th	1 Thessalonians
Pr	Proverbs	2 Th	2 Thessalonians
Ecc	Ecclesiastes	1 Tim	1 Timothy
Sg	Song of Songs	2 Tim	2 Timothy
Ws	Wisdom	Tt	Titus
Sir	Sirach	Phm	Philemon
Is	Isaiah	Heb	Hebrews
Jr	Jeremiah	Jas	James
Lm	Lamentations	1 P	1 Peter
Ba	Baruch	2 P	2 Peter
Ezk	Ezekiel	1 Jn	1 John
Dn	Daniel	2 Jn	2 John
Ho	Hosea	3 Jn	3 John
Jl	Joel	Jude	Jude
Am	Amos	Rv	Revelation

ABBREVIATIONS USED FOR
DOCUMENTS OF THE MAGISTERIUM

CA Centesimus annus (On the Hundredth Anniversary)

CCC The Catechism of the Catholic Church

CHCW Charter for Health Care Workers

CIC The Code of Canon Law

CL Christifidelis laici (The Lay Members of Christ's Faithful People)

DH Dignitatis humanae (Declaration on Religious Freedom)

DoV Donum vitae (Respect for Human Life)

DPA Declaration on Procured Abortion

DV Dei verbum (Dogmatic Constitution on Divine Revelation)

DVt Donum veritatis (Instruction on the Ecclesial Vocation of the Theologian)

EN Evangelii nuntiandi (On Evangelization in the Modern World)

EV Evangelium Vitae (The Gospel of Life)

FC Familiaris consortio (On the Family)

GS Gaudium et spes (Pastoral Constitution on the Church in the Modern World)

HV Humanae vitae (On Human Life)

IM Inter mirifici (Decree on the Means of Social Communication)

IOE Instruction on Euthanasia

LE Laborem exercens (On Human Work)

LG Lumen gentium (Dogmatic Constitution on the Church)

MM Mater et magistra (Mother and Teacher)

PH Persona humana (Declaration on Sexual Ethics)

ABBREVIATIONS USED FOR
DOCUMENTS OF THE MAGISTERIUM

PP   Populorum progressio (On the Development of Peoples)

PT   Pacem in terris (On Establishing Universal Peace)

RP   Reconciliatio et poenitentia (On Reconciliation and Penance)

RH   Redemptor hominis (The Redeemer of Man)

SC   Sacrosanctum concilium (The Constitution on the Sacred Liturgy)

SD   Salvifici doloris (On the Christian Meaning of Human Suffering)

SRS   Solicitudo rei socialis (On Social Concerns)

VS   Veritatis splendor (Splendor of the Truth)

FOREWORD
By
Augustine Di Noia, O.P.

"Christian, recognize your dignity and, now that you share in God's own nature, do not return to your former base condition by sinning. Remember who is your head and of whose body you are a member. Never forget that you have been rescued from the power of darkness and brought into the light of the kingdom of God." In these powerful words on the meaning of the incarnation (*Sermo* 21, 3) St. Leo the Great captures the very meaning of the Christian moral life. The dignity we have in Christ means that we must seek the things that are above: Christ makes it possible for us to seek and to live a life that is conformed to him who is our head.

Only by grasping the deep mystery of our life in Christ can we stem the tide of secularism and relativism that threaten to obscure the true dignity of the human person and to erode the social structures and moral values that safeguard this dignity. The objective of a sound education in Christian morality is to deepen our knowledge of this mystery of life in Christ. Precisely this purpose has guided the authors of *Our Moral Life in Christ*. This book offers to Christians an intelligent and profound preparation in the moral doctrine of the Catholic Church that will aid them in their own living in Christ and will help them to offer to others the fullness of Jesus' message, a fullness for which they hunger and thirst.

Only by first realizing the depth of God's mercy in rescuing us from the power of darkness can today's Christians be witnesses of the message of Christ. Every Christian, young and old, rich and poor, man and woman, must be prepared to bear witness by their example to the truth of Christ's message of salvation in the particular circumstances of his or her life. As Pope John Paul II has said on numerous occasions, the "culture of life" is struggling to be born anew in the culture of death. Now, on the eve of the third millennium of the Christian era, comes the summons to "renew all things in Christ." In order to contribute to this renewal, Christians need the kind of thorough intellectual formation in fundamental morality that *Our Moral Life in Christ* is designed to provide.

In these pages, the reader will learn that the Ten Commandments are God's gift to us to help us to reach the happiness he intends for us. The commandments provide us with an education of our desire, so that by observing them we learn to love God above all things and everything else in him. There is no place for a slavish servitude to the law in Christian morality. On the contrary, faithful observance of the commandments enhances the scope of the authentic freedom and assures the flourishing of our true humanity. The new life in the Spirit is the fulfillment and realization of the human good, which, by God's grace, is nothing less than participation in the divine nature and the communion of the life of the Blessed Trinity. By being transformed in Christ and conformed to Christ, we grow into the fullness of this life.

By offering the reader a solid foundation for the formation of his or her conscience, *Our Moral Life in Christ* provides a reliable summary of the Church's moral doctrine for those who seek to deepen their union with Christ and with one another in him. A spirit of prayer and reflection on the great truths of our faith pervades this text, and invites its readers to open their hearts to Christ and to obey his command to "let your light shine before men, so that they see the good that you do and give glory to God."

PREFACE

The concern for human conduct and the theoretical study of morality are at the center of the current "culture war" taking place in American society. Over the past several years, much has been written and said about public morals, character education and the need for a return to traditional moral values in the social and political life of U.S. society. Commendable as this concern is, much of the current discussion overlooks the fact that neither ethical theory nor the moral lives of men throughout history have been a consistent progression. For every period of moral excellence in human history, there have also been other eras of an evident decadence in doctrine and customs.

We should also point out another fact; namely, that those eras in which the moral life has deteriorated most have been the ones which most urgently call for a return to the study of ethical science. It is a fact that moral doctrine, when explained with rigor, helps to elevate one's conduct. The following three examples may be helpful in illustrating this point:

- When the Golden Age of Greek civilization ended, a kind of vacuum appeared in society. Pre-Socratic followers (in the 6th and 5th centuries B.C.) had achieved an expertise in the sciences which extended from Mathematics (Thales, Pythagoras), to Physics (Empedocles, Democritus) and, in general, what was later called Philosophy (Heraclitus, Parmenides, Anaxagoras etc.). All of this scientific knowledge of Ancient Greece was destroyed in the era of the Sophists. The declaration by Protagoras of Abdera (440-408), the greatest of the Sophists, that "man is the measure of all things," broke with the objective order. He taught that in the same way that objective and universal truth does not exist, neither does a universally valid moral law. This relativism created such confusion in Greek society that it caused the customs of the polis to crumble; it would naturally be difficult to maintain the authority of the state if there is no objective morality but only the ethical values created by man.

The challenge posed by this crisis was met by the moral teaching of Socrates (469-399 B.C.), who said: "We cannot be satisfied with only scientific knowledge: what is truly important to save society is the science about the conduct of man and this is called Ethics." Later, Socrates would teach that Ethics is the "science of sciences."

In summary, according to Socrates, neither history, nor play and entertainment, nor scientific knowledge, nor even medicine, can save man. What truly develops man's personality and helps him to be happy is ethical science.

- In the eighteenth century, the skeptical attitude represented by the Scottish philosopher David Hume coincided with a number of other problems in European culture which threatened society with universal skepticism. These crises were also overcome by a philosopher, Immanuel Kant, who advocated the application of "practical reason." Specifically, Kant called not for theoretical knowledge, but for a return to the moral life which will help man, in both his personal and his social life, to establish a sure ground for his existence. Kant declared that ethics is like the axis on which the life of man should revolve.

  This Kantian interpretation contributed effectively to creating a moral perspective based on such a rigorous sense of "duty" that a century later it was considered exaggerated. It was "formal ethics" or the morality of a categorical imperative, that is, "duty for the sake of duty."

- Finally, in our day, one hears much about the deplorable state of ethics and morality in today's world from many diverse sources. Not only the Church, but also men of science and even politicians speak of the loss of moral values in our culture. For that reason, they repeatedly denounce modern society as lacking in moral values. We are, they say, faced with a complete distortion and confusion of moral values. This confusion becomes particularly evident when the discussion of morality turns from the theoretical value of morality in human society to the question of which moral values should be adopted in the diverse cultures which have developed in many parts of the Western world.

  Evidently, if this process continues, the evils which could follow for our civilization would be immense. A society in which customs are not attuned to the dignity of man and which rejects the values of moral "good" and "evil," will eventually become so decadent that the evils which come from it will destroy society. According to the German scientist Heisenberg, what would follow in the moral order would be something similar to what followed the use of the atomic bomb and the inhumane life of those detained in concentration camps in the physical order (cf. W. Heisenberg, *Dialogues in Atomic Physics*, pp. 265-269).

For that reason, the call to renew the study of ethical science continues. It is necessary for politicians, philosophers, theologians, educators and artists alike to return again to the study of morality, because—as we said before—it is probable that an "im-moral" era will be followed by one that is "a-moral," quickly concluding in a general "de-moralization."

It is no secret that the deterioration of moral life also affects some sectors of the Christian world. Throughout this book, different texts of theologians, bishops and popes are quoted as proof of this situation. The crisis of the loss of moral direction demands answers, not only from the Church, but also from the same society which once rose to great moral heights under the influence of Christianity. We find ourselves in one of the most profound crises of morality since Christianity's inauguration of a new life in conformity with the ethical teachings lived and taught by Jesus Christ.

Nevertheless, the crisis cannot last indefinitely because the moral questions which confront society are of the greatest importance. Man cannot do anything less than ask himself: How can I be successful and triumph in life? How must I act to justify my existence? What should I do to be happy? These and other questions related with personal conduct cannot be avoided, since they imply the meaning of man's existence and point the way to the attainment of his happiness.

✳✳✳✳✳✳

Our Moral Life in Christ is a text in moral theology which approaches teacher and student from a christological point of view.

Historically, there are shifts which occur over the centuries in approaches to teaching a particular subject. Many of the classical texts tried to convince man to be moral by demonstrating that human beings could know the truth about themselves by learning how to distinguish right from wrong. Some of these texts also approached the problem by stressing the virtuous life in their presentation. In essence, the method was more rational than biblical in its approach.

This objective analysis of morality often led to an overly casuistic approach, i.e., one which too often emphasized the evaluation of particular individual cases while ignoring objective moral principles. Christian morality was in danger of being reduced to a morality of individual acts rather than a morality which engaged the total person. Far too many came to view this distorted morality of minimums as the morality of the Church, a morality which often lacked connection with Scripture or the life of grace established by Jesus.

The emphasis of this text on the application of biblical morality to contemporary moral concerns helps to align the teachings contained in this book with the revelation of God as contained in the teachings of Christ. Extensive use of recent Church documents such as the *Catechism of the Catholic Church, Evangelium vitae,* and *Veritatis splendor* throughout the text demonstrate the importance of the teaching authority of the Pope and the magisterium of the Church in determining matters of faith and morality.

Our Moral Life in Christ stresses the type of person that the Christian should be, a person who acts from the perspective of Christ himself, rather than a person who operates out of his own particular desires in making decisions. The goal is therefore to aid in the formation of Christians who desire to live a life of moral virtue at the service of love while striving toward ultimate perfection.

In short, this book tries to establish the foundations of Catholic morality with the intention of elevating the conduct of the believers. The following points serve as guidelines:

- Christian moral doctrine does not oppose all of the ideals proposed throughout history by the great ethical systems of humanity (cf. *VS* 94). At most, it only denies moral value to some very particular situations held by them, as it does when faced with the acceptance of polygamy in Islam or the defense of abortion, euthanasia or divorce by some moralists.

- It is clear that the morality preached by Jesus of Nazareth, who is the paradigm of human existence, is superior to all man-made moral systems. Even taking into account the difficulty that is involved in its fulfillment, it is necessary to recognize the greatness which the men and women whom the Church calls saints have achieved in their practice of Christian morality. When ethical problems are examined and an intellectual consensus is obtained, it is indispensable to take another look at the lives of those who personify the ideal of human existence. The *saints* are the prototype of that fully human existence which is the result of God's grace living in man.

- If a Christian wishes to be faithful to what he really "is," he should struggle to live the ethical demands presented and urged in the Gospel. In the opposite case, his life would proclaim the guilt of an evident incoherence between what he "is" and what he "proclaims."

- The believer in Christ not only must strive to personally live the style of life inaugurated by Jesus Christ, but he must also offer it to today's culture. In doing this, he gives to society the most efficient means to resolve the state of general crisis in morality which characterizes contemporary society.

- Catholic morality is not only for "knowing," but also for "practicing." This way of life contributes to improving the social, political and economic life of modern man, penetrating the world with the spirit of Christ and impregnating the different spheres of social life.

Part I

Principles of Moral Theology

Chapter I
PRELIMINARY NOTIONS

A few years ago the cry was, "Be like Mike", be like Michael Jordan. Those who took the slogan seriously wore Michael Jordan jerseys, kept track of his stats, practiced shooting in his style, cheered when he won and wept when he lost. Being "like Mike" meant being as much like him as was humanly possible. These fans used their freedom to imitate Michael Jordan in every way possible.

In a sense that is the call which Christ gives to all Christians: "Be like me". The difficulty is that many people view morality and discipleship as being exterior to themselves. The person sees himself as here, and the rules are over there somewhere. Yet, all Christians are called by the Sacrament of Baptism to use their freedom to "Be like Christ", to keep track of his stats (the Bible), practice his loving style, weep when his body (the Church) suffers and rejoice when it rejoices.

This can only be accomplished if a person sees that the only proper use of freedom is to be as "Christ-like" as possible.

Let us ask ourselves the following questions:

• What does it mean to be "Christ-like?"

• Did Jesus Christ establish a morality for his followers?

• Is personal freedom compatible with Christian morality?

Introduction

Throughout the second half of the twentieth century, the discussion of what role morality should play in the personal, political and legal framework of society has been heated. Today, there is open debate between the different political and philosophical traditions on this issue, and many distinct and contradictory ideas are proposed.

This chapter proposes an outline of Christian morality, a morality which aims to help the individual grow in the knowledge and love of God and to be as Christ-like as possible in all aspects of his personal and social life. To do so, it is necessary to first outline what makes Christian morality distinctive, and how the adoption of the moral life-style set forth by Jesus transforms the individual at the most fundamental level, so that he or she truly becomes a "new creation in Christ".

1. Christianity is not merely a morality

In order to clarify the meaning of Christian morality, the first task is to define its scope within the general meaning of Christianity, for Christianity is not merely a moral program.

Christian morality distinguishes itself from ethical systems and other religious beliefs in several areas. For example, Buddhism is essentially a morality, since its end is to provide man with a way of life that will help him reach happiness. But in regard to God the Buddhist keeps silent, for he does not know what to affirm.

Christianity, on the other hand, is the unveiling of the mystery of God as Father, Son, and Holy Spirit by Jesus Christ, who is the Son. Fundamentally, it is the communication of divine life and knowledge to man. Consequently, the acknowledgment and worship of a Triune God precede any moral consideration.

The risk of reducing Christianity to a set of rules to be lived, a kind of "don't do this and don't do that life," is constant. It is as easy for us to fall victim to this mentality as it was for many of the people in Jesus' time. In fact, the Old Testament revelation, which had presented so many aspects of God and his plan for man, was often reduced to a narrow, legalistic and hypocritical model of morality. This explains Jesus' critical attitude toward many aspects of the religious ideas of the Pharisees of his time (cf. Mt 12, 1-14, 22-30; 23, 1-33).

On the contrary, Jesus did not come as a moralist, but as the Incarnate love of God. He did not come to replace one set of rules with another but to promote a totally new way of living, the saving life of God. Christianity, then, is not merely a morality but a revelation that unveils the being of God as Father and his relation to human beings, who are his children.

2. But Christianity is also a morality

As is evident, Christianity is no stranger to a moral program and life. Jesus' saving message includes a moral system united to it in such a way that Christianity cannot be separated from morality.

> Faith also possesses a moral content. It gives rise to and calls for a consistent life commitment; it entails and brings to perfection the acceptance and observance of God's commandments (VS, 89).

Hence the title of this section, "Christianity is *also* a morality." No truly Christian life can be found which does not include the specific morality of Jesus Christ. An example can clarify this apparent paradox: man is not a brain, but is composed of different members which make up his body. Besides, the whole body is animated by the spirit. But man "also" has a brain. Furthermore, without the brain man ceases to exist as such. Such is the relationship between Christianity and morality: they are not identical; although Christianity involves other realities, a Christian life cannot exist without morality.

The *Acts of the Apostles* relates that on the day of Pentecost Peter announces the Christian message to the world. He speaks of the salvific plan of God accomplished by Jesus' death and resurrection. Upon hearing him, four thousand are converted, and immediately they ask: "Brethren, what shall we do?" (Acts 2, 37). They are baptized and believe in Jesus as God and Savior. Thus, the moral program comes after discovering the salvific message and believing in God and in Jesus Christ, his Son and messenger (cf. *VS*, 110).

3. Christianity is a religious morality

The Christian moral program is not limited to a rational ethics nor a morality established only on natural law; rather, *it is a morality which has its origin in God's self-revelation.* God revealed his ethical program when he created the first man and the first woman, and he reaffirmed it with the Ten Commandments which he gave to Moses on Mount Sinai. This moral program finds its highest perfection in the moral message taught by Jesus of Nazareth and in the unique and perfect fashion in which he lived it.

The fact that Christian morality is a revealed religious morality gives it two characteristics which set it apart from all other religious beliefs:

a. The concepts of good and evil are determined by God.

Original Sin left wounds in our human nature that can make it difficult to understand clearly the nature of good and evil. Since God has created man in his own image, human beings must act in accord with what their nature truly is, not in accord with what they would like it to be. The concepts of good and evil are determined and indicated by God himself, as the Creator. He dictates what is good for all creation, particularly for man and his social life.

Therefore, the ethical content or requirements for human conduct are not derived from what man *thinks is* reasonable, just or coherent, but from what God indicates to be so. Divine wisdom establishes the morality which contributes to complete human fulfillment in relation to human nature as God has made it. Whether man finds it reasonable has no bearing on the matter, but if reason is used properly, it will come to know about human nature as created by God.

This gives the Christian moral message both its divine origin and the conviction that what is prescribed as good and evil, sin and virtue, is precisely that which is *good and evil for man.* It is not a morality of the moment nor is it a self-serving one. Rather, Christian morality fulfills the human desire for happiness in this life and leads to the highest personal realization, life in and with Christ.

b. **The ethical requirements of the Gospel require the aid of God's grace.**

Since it deals with a life lived on the level of God, it will only be realized with the aid of his grace. Therefore, the fulfillment of the ethical requirements of the Gospel require the aid of God's grace since they are above human strength and beyond natural human accomplishment.

Morality was not imposed from outside of man and without help. On the contrary, the baptized person will fulfill the precepts of Christian morality to the degree that he cooperates with God, whose grace is never absent. If he does not live in a state of grace and is not faithful to his beliefs and practices, it will be impossible to live out the style of life posed by Jesus Christ.

What is the ultimate source of this inner division of man? His history of sin begins when he no longer acknowledges God as his Creator and himself wishes to be the one who determines with complete independence, what is good and what is evil. "You will be like God knowing good and evil" (Gn 3, 5): This was the first temptation, and it is echoed by all the other temptations to which man is more easily inclined to yield as a result of original sin.

But temptations can be overcome and sins can be avoided, because together with the commandments the LORD gives us the possibility of keeping them: "His eyes are on those who fear him, and he knows every deed of man. He has not commanded anyone to be ungodly, and he has not given anyone permission to sin" (Sir 15, 19-20). Keeping God's law in particular situations can be difficult, extremely difficult, but it is never impossible (*VS*, 102).

It is impossible to forgive one's enemies, to be just or to be truly chaste if one places one's trust in human strength alone. But it becomes possible—moreover in many circumstances easy—if the believer is faithful to the love of God and is united to his will.

In short, *to fully understand and live Christian morality one has to be Christ-like.*

4. Christian morality is a morality of following and imitating Christ

Christian morality assumes natural ethics, but it also surpasses it, since the moral precepts taught by Jesus form the basis of the Christian life. Life in Christ has the following elements, which were experienced by the first disciples and, according to *Veritatis splendor*, can be deduced from the dialogue between the rich young man and Jesus (cf. Mt 19,16-22):

a. **The call or vocation.**

The Christian life stems from a call from God. The Christian assumes that God calls every person. Hence, Christianity is defined as a vocation, or calling. In public life, Jesus goes out and occasionally calls individually, "Follow me," (Lk 9, 59) and other times collectively, "If any man would come after me . . ." (Mk 8, 34; cf. Mt 19, 16).

b. **The response.**

Man must respond affirmatively to this call from God. This response is essential, since faith, which begins with God's call, cannot flourish without this affirmative answer from man. Faith is like a conversation: God initiates the dialogue, but, if there is no response by man, then there can be no faith (Lk 18, 18-27; cf. *VS*, 10).

c. **The following.**

The call of Jesus is designed for the hearer to follow. This is why the understanding of morality as the following of Jesus is often found in Christian writings. This following is free, as expressed by Jesus in a conditional fashion: "If any man would come after me . . ." (Lk 9, 23; 14, 26; cf. VS, 11 and 19).

d. **Discipleship.**

The call of Jesus is ordered to being his disciple, since he is the teacher (Mt 23, 7-8). The relationship between teacher and disciple offers a description of the relationship between Christ and those who believe in him (cf. VS, 19-21). The word disciple indicates a taking on of a way of life, a particular type of discipline.

e. **The imitation.**

As is the case in the different human disciplines in which the disciple learns by imitating the teacher, the Christian also has to learn by imitating the life of Jesus. It is clear that the historical life of Jesus cannot be emulated.

- First, Jesus did things as the Son of God and was crucified for all people. No human being is capable of accomplishing what Jesus did on the cross even though some Christians have suffered this form of death.

- Second, Jesus himself did not assume all the circumstances that characterize human life; for example, Jesus was celibate, and this does not present an immediate model for spouses.

Because of this, the imitation of the life of Jesus is not to take the form of a literal copy of his life, but of a moral approach. That is, the Christian should assume the same attitudes—reflected in concrete acts—that Christ assumed. The goal is to act, in every situation of human existence, with the same disposition that Christ adopted or would adopt in our time. For example, in the face of power and service, money and poverty, pain and joy, life and death, the Christian should adopt the same fundamental dispositions that Christ did. Jesus affirmed: "For I have given you an example, that you also should do as I have done to you" (Jn 13, 15; cf. VS, 10 and 20).

That was the disposition and manner of acting that the close followers and the baptized embraced, after the Ascension. This why Jesus warns: "Truly, truly, I say to you, he who believes in me will also do the works that I do" (Jn 14, 12). The apostles advise the baptized to imitate Jesus, "because Christ also suffered for you, leaving you an example, that you should follow in his steps" (1 P 2, 21). Furthermore, Jesus showed us the way in his earthly life: "Jesus began to do and teach" (Acts 1, 1). As the encyclical *Veritatis splendor* points out:

> Following Christ is not an outward imitation, since it touches man at the very depths of his being. Being a follower of Christ means becoming conformed to him who became a servant even to giving himself on the cross (cf. Phil 2, 5-8). Christ dwells by faith in the heart of the believer (cf. Eph 3, 17) and thus the disciple is conformed to the LORD. This is the effect of grace, of the active presence of the Holy Spirit in us (*VS*, 21).

5. Identification with Christ: Life in Christ

New Testament morality does correspond to the *new being* acquired by man at Baptism. The Gospel of St. John and the writings of St. Paul, which expound on Christ's life and work, understand Christian existence as more than just an imitation of the life of Christ; rather, they describe it as a way of identifying with Christ.

The reason is profound. By Baptism, the Christian participates in the same life of Jesus, so much so that "the life of Christ is in him." The letter to the Philippians alone uses the phrase "in Christ" nine times, and six other times it uses a similar phrase, "in the LORD." "I in Christ and Christ in me" is a repeated expression in the writings of St. John and St. Paul.

The life in Christ is defined in graphic literary expressions by St. Paul. For example, he uses the verbs "*to put on* the LORD Jesus Christ . . ." (Rm 13, 14). These expressions are mentioned thirteen times with the sense of *putting on Christ interiorly*, not exteriorly.

In Baptism, Jesus is united to the life of man, and the transforming force of grace causes the Christian to turn to Christ and consequently to act like him. This is why it can be said that "every Christian is another Christ," and even, "the Christian is Christ himself."

Also the expression, "to be formed in Christ," is used regularly (Gal 4, 19). St. Paul explains this by means of Hellenistic art: the hollow space inside the mold shapes the molten metal into the statue. Similarly, Jesus is the mold into which the baptized are placed. The result is the reception of the *form* of Christ.

Consequently, the Christian moral life is by definition the imitation of Christ to the degree of identifying with him. And since the life of man is most properly of his soul—knowledge, thought, will, freedom—the Christian, then, ought to imitate Christ's thought, love, and actions (cf. *VS*, 19-21).

Paul gives the following ideal as a motto for the Christian life: "Have this mind among yourselves, which was in Christ Jesus . . ." (Phil 2, 5). And so, St. Paul gives the end of identifying with Christ in his letter to the Galatians, "It is no longer I who live, but Christ who lives in me" (Gal 2, 20). This formula represents the highest prize to which human existence is called, a life lived in God's presence.

However, this high goal cannot be reached by human strength alone. Christian life and morality are not merely exercises; the goal is only reached by the aid of the grace of the Holy Spirit. Prayer and the transforming grace of the sacraments are the normal ways through which Jesus and the Holy Spirit act, so there is no way to live a Christian morality that excludes them.

6. Characteristics of Christian morality

If we attempt to list the principal characteristics of Christian morality, they would be found in the following:

a. Christian morality first affects the person and then the *action*.

It is important to stress that Christian morality is addressed to the totality of man. Man's existence includes grace, by which the Christian becomes a new creature. Consequently, the idea is for the Christian to *be* a good Christian so that he may act accordingly.

This truth corresponds to the philosophical principle that "action follows being." If the Christian attempts to become a child of God, he will act in a humble, chaste, just and prudent manner. His life will be more than morally good; it will be genuine and make sense.

Jesus expressed this with the image of a tree and its fruits:

> For no good tree bears bad fruit, nor again does a bad tree bear good fruit; for each tree is known by its own fruit. For figs are not gathered from thorns, nor are grapes picked from a bramble bush. The good man out of the good treasure of his heart produces good, and the evil man out of his evil treasure produces evil; for out of the abundance of the heart his mouth speaks (Lk 6, 43-45).

Therefore, the Beatitudes, which express the heart of Christian morality, address more the being than the action, since the idea is first *to be* merciful, pure of heart, peacemakers, etc., and, consequently, to act as such (cf. *VS*, 15 and 21).

b. **Christian morality transforms both the inside and the outside.**

This characteristic is a result of the previous characteristic and is derived from it. In fact, when a morality primarily addresses every aspect of a person's existence —particularly when that person is touched by grace—it will then influence the deepest thoughts and desires of the person. Furthermore, it is self-evident that it is in the *interior of a person*—in the heart—that the moral life is forged.

Jesus expressed this in a striking manner:

> And he called the people to him and said to them, "Hear and understand: not what goes into the mouth defiles a man, but what comes out of the mouth, this defiles a man." Then the disciples came and said to him, "Do you know that the Pharisees were offended when they heard this saying?" He answered, "Every plant which my heavenly Father has not planted will be rooted up. Let them alone; they are blind guides. And if a blind man leads a blind man, both will fall into a pit." But Peter said to him, "Explain the parable to us." And he said, "Are you also still without understanding? Do you not see that whatever goes into the mouth passes into the stomach, and so passes on? But what comes out of the mouth proceeds from the heart, and this defiles a man. For out of the heart come evil thoughts, murder, adultery, fornication, theft, false witness, slander. These are what defile a man; but to eat with unwashed hands does not defile a man" (Mt 15, 10-20).

Every man knows that it is in the interior—in thought, will
and emotions—that moral battles are fought. Thus, a mere
dislike can quickly become a gesture of hate; a lustful thought
can lead to an impure action; the feeling of pride can be acted
out, and so forth.

This principle requires two things from man:

• The heart must be kept free from evil thoughts, desires,
  affections, for they can cause grave sins and can lead to
  bad actions.

• The mind must be kept under control since man sins first
  in his heart, even if his bad thoughts may not be realized,
  his twisted desires not executed and his evil feelings or
  desires not satisfied.

> Jesus brings God's commandments to fulfillment, particu-
> larly the commandment of love of neighbor, by internalizing
> their demands and by bringing out their fullest meaning.
> Love of neighbor springs from a loving heart which, pre-
> cisely because it loves, is ready to live out the loftiest chal-
> lenges (*VS*, 15).

c. **Christian morality considers the profound attitudes
   of the person.**

Man commits single acts, but such acts are the result of previous *attitudes*. In fact, some likes or dislikes, a disposition
to do good or evil, repeat themselves because the individual
has formed certain habits, good and bad ones, through his
past actions. It is evident that particular acts are important,
but it is necessary to analyze why they occur so frequently.

Educators insist that man—from infancy—should carefully
perform each one of his actions in order to create habits of
good conduct. They teach the significance of promoting a
deep awareness of the value of personhood and of life in man
which will make the correct choices easy and will accelerate
the formation of good habits.

If the person chooses the good and tries to acquire deep convictions in favor of Christian virtues, it will be easier to
change these convictions into good acts. As Jesus said, "If any
man would come after me, let him deny himself" (Mk 8, 34).

In fact, that firm and definitive decision *to be as Christ-like as possible* predisposes the believer so that all his actions are oriented towards Christ (cf. *VS*, 16).

This moral command to acquire Christian attitudes does not take away ethical value from the individual acts; on the contrary, each of those actions, precisely, demonstrates the results of the interior attitudes. On certain occasions, the deepest attitudes can be destroyed by a single act that is morally wrong. A man who abandons his wife and his children because he "is not happy with his life" cannot honestly claim that he is seeking the will of God above all other things.

d. **Christian morality is aware of what is forbidden, but stresses more what ought to be done than what is to be avoided.**

Christian morality is a *positive morality* that prescribes what a person, motivated by the love of God, ought to do. It can never be reduced to a merely *negative morality*, motivated by a fear of punishment, that says, "you can't do this and you can't do that."

It is true that the moral message preached by Jesus Christ includes many prohibitions—such as all those found in the Ten Commandments (theft, murder, adultery, deceit, etc.). In a word, all that goes against the love of God and neighbor *is forbidden*, and Jesus *does* warn that those who refuse to turn away from what is evil will be punished; nevertheless, the whole of Jesus' moral preaching stresses doing the good more than avoiding evil. It is about the type of person one should be rather than a list of *do's* and *don'ts*.

An eloquent example is Chapter 25 of the Gospel of Matthew. In it, the Evangelist summarizes the judgment that Christ will impose upon the conduct of each man. The condemnations of Jesus are towards those who have abandoned the good, and not to those who are doing evil deeds. In Jesus' parable, it is not just that the young and foolish virgins acted wrongly, but that they did not act wisely (Mt 25, 1-13). In the parable of the talents the men who received ten and five talents are rewarded because they increased them. The one who received only one talent is condemned because he refused to make use of the talent (Mt 25, 14-30).

Finally, the account of the goods and evils that Jesus demands of each person is about whether or not the good has been lived out: to feed the hungry and thirsty, to give shelter to the homeless, to visit the sick, to console the sad, to visit the prisoner, to teach the ignorant, etc. (Mt 25, 31-46). Thus, in the Last Judgment those will be saved who did the good and those condemned will be so because they did evil and failed to do the good.

Jesus also teaches this doctrine by use of parables. Among them, the parable of the rich man stresses the need to do the good, since the rich man is apparently condemned not for his evil acts but because he failed to care for his neighbor's needs (Mt 25, 31-46). The People of Israel, symbolized by the rich but sterile fig tree, are rejected because they failed to provide God with the fruits that were required of them (Mk 11, 12-14, 20-21).

We can draw two conclusions here:

* God is not the cause of the physical evils of humanity—hunger, misery, war, etc.—since they are the product of man's sin, but man has the moral obligation to avoid, and if possible, to prevent these evils.

* Sins of omission should be regarded seriously, as the apostle James teaches: "Whoever knows what is right to do and fails to do it, for him it is a sin" (Jas 4, 17).

e. **Christian morality requires not only just actions, but also holiness.**

When the New Testament is read, what is striking is the high level of morality required of Christians by Jesus and the apostles. The moral program of the Christian is not a morality of the minimum, but of the maximum; that is, it requires not a decent or honorable existence, but a saintly life.

In particular, the life of holiness which shines so brightly in the lives of so many of the people of God, humble and often unseen, constitutes the simplest and most attractive way to perceive at once the beauty and truth, the liberating force of God's love, and the value of unconditional fidelity to all the demands of the Lord's law, even in the most difficult situations (cf. *VS*, 107).

To emphasize the ethical content of the Beatitudes (Mt 5, 1-12; Lk 6, 20-26), Jesus places his moral program side by side with the Old Law. In fact, he repeats the juxtaposition six times: "You have heard that . . . but I say to you . . ." (Mt 5, 21-48). By it he revises the commandments, enriching and urging their ethical content.

> Thus it is evident to everyone that all the faithful of Christ of whatever rank and status, are called to the fullness of the Christian life and to the perfection of charity; by this holiness as such, a more human manner of living is promoted in this earthly society. . . . They must follow in his footsteps and conform themselves to his image seeking the will of the Father in all things (*VS*, 16).

"You, therefore, must be perfect, as your heavenly Father is perfect" (Mt 5, 48). Therefore Vatican II states as a condition for all the baptized the "*universal call to holiness*" (*LG*, 39-41).

f. **Jesus proclaims a series of moral laws, but Christian morality is not a rigid morality marked by multiplicity of precepts.**

This characteristic may seem inconsistent, but it is a consequence of Christianity being more a message of salvation than a morality. Besides, it helps clarify the difficult problem of the relationship between conscience and law (cf. pp. 86-87).

But the moral message is not a morality without laws. On the contrary, in Jesus' preaching there are concrete prohibitions, such as adultery (Mt 5, 27), avarice (Mt 6, 19-24), rash judgments (Mt 7, 1-6), divorce (Mk 10, 2-10), blasphemy against the Holy Spirit (Mk 3, 28-30; Mt 12, 31-37), scandal to the innocent (Mt 18, 1-5), etc.

Jesus himself fulfills the precepts of the law: he observes the sabbath (Mk 1, 21; 6,2; Lk 4, 16), the fast (Lk 4, 2; Mt 4, 1-2), the purification laws (Lk 2, 21-39; 2, 40-52; 3, 21-22), he attends Jerusalem as a good Jew to celebrate the feasts (Mk 11, 1; Lk 2, 41; Jn 5, 1; 7, 10; 11, 55), etc.

But the ethical norms in Jesus' morality do not constitute a morality of rules, rather a morality that includes laws. These exist in order to guide man to the good life. Laws point to what is good and evil; they show man the path he needs to follow if he wants to please God and save himself (cf. *VS*, 12-13; 95-97).

g. **The morality preached by Jesus is a morality that includes both reward and punishment.**

Lately, it has become a widespread conviction that an approach to morality which emphasizes reward and punishment should not be accepted by society. This false idea attempts to establish families, schools and a society in which these two realities have no part. This faulty conception is also applied to God and man.

Nevertheless, the New Testament leaves no doubt that the good behavior of man is rewarded, and his evil ways punished. While it is true that Jesus' preaching reflects God's habitual disposition of forgiveness and love, it is also a fact that punishment is often mentioned in the New Testament.

There are nearly ninety texts in the New Testament appealing to God's punishment for evil deeds, of which forty speak of eternal punishment. The rewards of heaven and the punishments of hell effect both the interior and exterior of man. Consequently, in the teachings of Catholic theology, heaven and hell as real ends of human existence, are two dogmas of the Church that correspond to the good or bad conduct of man during his life.

h. **Christian morality is morality for freedom.**

As will be explained in Chapter III, freedom is the greatest gift given to the human person by God, so much so that God himself will not force a man to do something contrary to his will. This implies that man has to use his free will for the good.

Since freedom is the indispensable condition of the moral life, the Christian moral message endeavors to cultivate true freedom so that man will not fall into the trap of sin. The message preached by Christ Jesus is an invitation to freedom: "for you were called to freedom, brethren" (Gal 5, 13). When the baptized misunderstood the freedom for which "Christ has set us free" (Gal 5, 1), St. Paul warned them not to use their freedom as an "opportunity for the flesh" (Gal 5, 13), but for the good (cf. Gal 6, 18). It is obvious that when the Christian practices the message preached by Christ Jesus, he acquires the highest degree of freedom. This is confirmed by the lives of the saints, who are models of living in freedom (cf. VS, 17).

Christian morality includes this warning of St. Paul to the Galatians: "For freedom Christ has set us free; stand fast therefore, and do not submit again to a yoke of slavery" (Gal 5, 1).

i. **Christian morality is fulfilled on earth, but it pertains to the next life.**

The Christian moral message states that "a close connection is made between eternal life and obedience to God's commandments" (VS, 12).

This characteristic of Christian morality overcomes two extremes: the one which presents an ethical program based solely on the need for a more just world, and the other which desires a moral life only for the salvation of one's own soul.

The first is espoused by those with a secular agenda who hope to formulate certain moral rules—whose only validity is acceptance by the majority—to establish a perfectly just and peaceful society in this world. The second can fall in the temptation of disregarding social duties and simply attending to personal struggles. Man is at the same time a citizen of this world and the next, so Christian morality attends to both of these realities: it cannot ignore the grave task of making a better world, according to God's will; and at the same time it is aware that the present moral state affects the eternal life in the future.

Vatican II summarizes this doctrine in the following statement:

> This council exhorts Christians, as citizens of two cities, to strive to discharge their earthly duties conscientiously and in response to the Gospel spirit. They are mistaken who, knowing that we have here no abiding city but seek one which is to come, think that they may therefore shirk their earthly responsibilities. For they are forgetting that by the faith itself they are more obliged than ever to measure up to these duties, each according to his proper vocation (GS, 43).

j. **Christian morality finds its beginning and end in love.**

The fact that this characteristic comes at the end of the list does
not mean it is of any less importance; on the contrary, it is the
crown of all. The Christian moral message begins with love and
culminates with the new commandment of love (cf. *VS*, 13-14).

The command to love is not only proclaimed by Jesus, who
calls it "my commandment" (Jn 15, 12) and "new" (Jn 13, 34),
but it is also stressed by the apostles in addressing the first
Christians. St. Paul praises love in the so-called "hymn of
love," that concludes: "So faith, hope, love abide, these three;
but the greatest of these is love" (1 Cor 13, 13).

And St. John, who relates the love of God with the love of
neighbor, teaches:

> Beloved, let us love one another; for love is of God, and he
> who loves is born of God and knows God. He who does
> not love does not know God; for God is love. In this the
> love of God was made manifest among us, that God sent
> his only Son into the world, so that we might live through
> him. In this is love, not that we loved God but that he loved
> us and sent his Son to be the expiation for our sins. Beloved,
> if God so loved us, we also ought to love one another (1
> Jn 4, 7-11).

The final lesson of Christian morality concerns the love of God
and neighbor: the love of God guarantees the authenticity of
love, and the love of neighbor shows that the love of God is
real. The good of the moral life is the practice of love and not
the fear of punishment, as St. John points out in his conclusion: "There is no fear in love, but perfect love casts out fear.
For fear has to do with punishment, and he who fears is not
perfected in love" (1 Jn 4, 18).

In this fashion, the acts of the believer, conforming to the
moral message preached by Christ Jesus, lead to trust and
hope in life. This attitude is full of expectation and is void
of any type of pessimism.

Conclusion

If, in light of this chapter, we examine the world around us, we can see how many people, including political and social leaders, are distant from Christian morality when speaking of "ethics" or "morality." Is this not due to a celebration of rights to the exclusion of obligations which come with rights? At one time this country operated on a Christian morality in its public life, but this has been replaced with a morality of individualism, which is merely an excuse to do as you feel. Is this not due to the lack of ethical principles which at the present time is visible in almost all nations?

It is obvious that modern states reject the principles of Catholic morality; but would it not be advantageous to embrace some principles of Christian morality to guide public life in government and law? Could not the world use a great outpouring of the love of Christ as manifested in his followers at the present time?

OUTLINE

I. Glossary

CHRISTIAN MORALITY:

The part of theology that specifies the moral norms derived from the *new being* which the Christian, because of his incorporation into Christ in Baptism, needs to follow, with the hope of imitating Jesus' life to the point of identifying with him.

CHRISTIAN VOCATION:

The call of God to man, by which he is incorporated into Christ through grace and becomes a member of the Mystical Body. As one of God's People, he partakes in the life of the Church.

HOLINESS:

The free dedication of oneself to the will of God and participation in the life of grace which he offers to the Christian. This dedication to God effects a moral transformation in the life of the individual.

THE LAW OF CHRIST:

An interior law which stems from grace—in connection with life in Jesus—and becomes a norm or impulse for imitating Christ and acting like him.

LEGALISM:

An approach to morality which emphasizes primarily the strict and precise observance of moral precepts, while tending to overlook the purpose for which the law exists.

LOVE (CHARITY):

The theological virtue by which a person loves God above all things for his own sake, and our neighbor as ourselves for the love of God.

NEW BEING IN CHRIST:

The supernatural condition of the baptized by which man participates in the life of Jesus.

NEGATIVE MORALITY:

A moral code that prescribes what ought not be done.

POSITIVE MORALITY:

A moral code that prescribes what ought to be done

SINS OF OMISSION:

Failure to do that which is known to be right, good, and required.

VIRTUE:

An habitual and firm disposition to do the good.

II. Summary of Principles

1. Natural moral precepts, including the most generic ones, have been perfected by Jesus Christ.

2. The law of Christ is not, essentially, a written law, but a vital interior and supernatural force which makes man act like Christ.

3. The law of Christ can be summed up as a law of love, as opposed to the many Mosaic precepts and natural law.

4. The law of Christ is found in many mandates, clearly formulated by Christ Jesus and by the apostles and interpreted
   by the Church, which help to fulfill the New Law.

5. Because he is a member of the Mystical Body of Christ, the
   Christian cannot carry out a moral life entirely of his own
   choosing. He needs the help of the Church and the grace of
   God.

6. The holy life of the Christian and the corruption of sin have
   good and evil consequences for eternal life.

7. To participate in the life of Christ Jesus, one needs to be in
   the state of grace. No one can identify with Christ without
   "living in him."

8. The sacraments of Reconciliation and the Eucharist are the
   most decisive means to "be identified with Christ." In Confession, grace is restored and the penitent "puts on Christ;"
   and in the Eucharist, "communion" is shared with the person of Christ Jesus.

9. In Christian morality the metaphysical principle is realized:
   action follows being. Consequently, the Christian needs to
   live according to his new being, that is, in communion with
   Christ.

SUPPLEMENTARY READINGS

1. In your life there are two things that do not fit together: your
   head and your heart.

   Your intelligence—enlightened by faith—shows you the way
   clearly. It can also point out the difference between following that
   way heroically or stupidly. Above all, it places before you the
   divine greatness and beauty of the undertakings the Trinity leaves
   in our hands.

   Your feelings, on the other hand, become attached to everything
   you despise, even while you consider it despicable. It seems as if a
   thousand trifles were awaiting the least opportunity, and as soon
   as your poor will is weakened, through physical tiredness or lack
   of supernatural outlook, those little things flock together and pile
   up in your imagination, until they form a mountain that oppresses

and discourages you. Things such as the rough edges of your work; your resistance to obedience; the lack of proper means; the false attractions of an easy life; greater or smaller but repugnant temptations; bouts of sensuality; tiredness; the bitter taste of spiritual mediocrity. . . . And sometimes also fear; fear because you know God wants you to be a saint, and you are not a saint.

Allow me to talk to you bluntly. You have more than enough "reasons" to turn back, and you lack the resolution to correspond to the grace that he grants you, since he has called you to be another Christ, *ipse Christus!*—Christ himself. You have forgotten the Lord's admonition to the Apostle: "My grace is enough for you," which is confirmation that, if you want to, you can.

(Blessed Josemaría Escrivá, *Furrow*, n. 166)

2. The Church's Magisterium intervenes not only in the sphere of faith, but also, and inseparably so, in the sphere of morals. It has the task of "discerning, by means of judgments normative for the consciences of believers, those acts which in themselves conform to the demands of faith and foster their expression in life and those which, on the contrary, because intrinsically evil, are incompatible with such demands." In proclaiming the commandments of God and the charity of Christ, the Church's Magisterium also teaches the faithful specific particular precepts and requires that they consider them in conscience as morally binding. In addition, the Magisterium carries out an important work of vigilance, warning the faithful of the presence of possible errors, even merely implicit ones, when their consciences fail to acknowledge the correctness and the truth of the moral norms, which the Magisterium teaches.

(*VS*, 110)

QUESTIONS

1. What is Christianity? Include in your definition an explanation of how Christian morality differs from secular ethics.

2. What happens to Christianity when it is reduced to being merely a moral program?

3. What are some characteristics of a "legalistic" approach to morality?

4. What do we mean when we say that Christianity is a religious morality?

5. What is the origin and the goal of Christian morality?

6. What five elements make up the morality of following and imitating Christ?

7. What does it mean to be Christ-like?

8. What are the characteristics of a Christian morality? How do these characteristics set Christian morality apart from all other religious beliefs?

9. What is the final lesson of Christian morality?

10. Where does Christian morality find its beginning and end?

11. Describe some elements of what the text speaks of as "life in Christ." Why is it that this life surpasses that of people who follow only a natural ethics?

PRACTICAL EXERCISES

1. Vatican II states that "a man is more precious for what he is than for what he has" (GS, 35). Explain how this sentence defines the Christian vocation and moral life in Christ.

2. The same document also says that "only in the mystery of the Incarnate Word does the mystery of man take on light." How does the Person of Christ make clear the truths of man's existence? (For example: the meaning of human existence, the nature of good and evil etc.)

3. Read and comment on Chapter 25 of St. Matthew's Gospel. What importance do sins of omission posses in relation to the understanding that the Christian moral life is a "following of Christ"?

4. Explain the consequences of Christ's words in Mt 15, 10-20.

5. Read Chapter 5 of the Constitution *Lumen Gentium* about the "universal call to holiness". What are the practical consequences that might arise from the principles laid out in this document?

6. According to the *Catechism of the Catholic Church* (nn. 1033-1037) what does the existence of hell reveal about humanity's destiny and proper end?

CHAPTER II
MORAL THEOLOGY

The creation of Man and Woman according to the Bible

God said, "Let us make man in our image, after our likeness; and let them have dominion over the fish of the sea, and over the birds of the air, and over the cattle, and over all the earth, and over every creeping thing that creeps upon the earth."

So God created man in his own image, in the image of God he created him; male and female he created them. And God blessed them, and God said to them, "Be fruitful and multiply, and fill the earth and subdue it; and have dominion over the fish of the sea and over the birds of the air and over every living thing that moves upon the earth." And God said, "Behold, I have given you every plant yielding seed which is upon the face of all the earth, and every tree with seed in its fruit; you shall have them for food. And to every beast of the earth, and to every bird of the air, and to everything that creeps on the earth, everything that has the breath of life, I have given every green plant for food." And it was so. And God saw everything that he had made, and behold, it was very good (Gn 1, 26-31).

The LORD God took the man and put him in the garden of Eden to till it and keep it. And the LORD God commanded the man, saying, "You may freely eat of every tree of the garden; but of the tree of the knowledge of good and evil you shall not eat, for in the day that you eat of it you shall die."

Then the LORD God said, "It is not good that the man should be alone; I will make him a helper fit for him." So out of the ground the LORD God formed every beast of the field and every bird of the air, and brought them to the man to see what he would call them; and whatever the man called every living creature, that was its name. The man gave names to all cattle, and to the birds of the air, and to every beast of the field; but for the man there was not found a helper fit for him. So the LORD God caused a deep sleep to fall upon the man, and while he slept took one of his ribs and closed up its place with flesh; and the rib which the LORD God had taken from the man he made into a woman and brought her to the man.

Then the man said, "This at last is bone of my bones and flesh of my flesh; she shall be called Woman, because she was taken out of Man." Therefore a man leaves his father and his mother and cleaves to his wife, and they become one flesh. And the man and his wife were both naked, and were not ashamed (Gn 2, 15-25).

Let us reflect on this passage of Scripture by considering:

- What does it mean that God created man in his image and likeness?

- What is the Christian concept of man?

- Is man a social being with rights and duties because of human solidarity?

Introduction

Before moral theology can be covered as a subject, it is necessary to explain the meaning of the basic concepts and principles which will ensure that there is an understanding of the subject by the reader.

In order to understand Catholic moral theology, it is necessary to be familiar with terms such as its definition, the determination of its specific object, the differences between its related parts, and the sources from which its principles are deduced.

1. Moral theology

> The Church's moral reflection, always conducted in the light of Christ, the "good teacher," has also developed in the specific form of the theological science call *moral theology,* a science which accepts and examines divine revelation while at the same time responding to the demands of human reason. Moral theology is a reflection concerned with "morality," with the good and the evil of human acts and of the person who performs them; in this sense it is accessible to all people. But it is also "theology," inasmuch as it acknowledges that the origin and the end of moral action are found in the one who "alone is good" and who, by giving himself to man in Christ, offers him the happiness of divine life (*VS,* 29).

Catholic moral theology seeks to reflect the new life in Christ as received in Baptism, and directed toward eternal salvation. It aims for the best life as lived by the Christian who wants to be a saint and is based on the ethical principles found in revelation which were lived by Jesus of Nazareth.

It also makes use of the so-called human sciences of medicine, psychology, sociology and law, where appropriate. This conversation between human knowledge and revealed teachings about man constitutes a guarantee that any moral science which takes into account God's own revelation will not be insufficient or erroneous. On the other hand, ethical systems based on reason alone are prone to all the errors so common in human thought.

This failure to take God's revelation into account can explain why so many ethical programs offered by different ideologies fall short of their goals. This failure is related directly to the desire to set up a system apart from God's vision which is the only true understanding of the dignity of man. Atheistic communism is the most recent example of these failed ideologies.

2. The moral conduct of man depends on the very concept of man

Each person has a standard of behavior by which he lives. If a person believes that he is nothing more than a highly-evolved animal, then the moral standards by which that person tries to live will be no more than biological rules; he will live as an animal. Man's morality in such cases is reduced to a morality of instinct (cf. *VS*, 4, 33, 84).

At the other extreme, if a view of man is stressed in which man is purely spiritual, the logical conclusion will be to defend ethical principles that favor a spiritual life. It would be an angelic morality which disregards man's physical side.

Throughout history there have been ethical systems which have exemplified these two radical extremes. For example, a popular ethic of today holds that "man proceeds from the animals and is indeed an animal." This type of *sociobiology* (the study of man as genetically determined) offers but one type of conduct making life easy and enjoyable. After all, if man's behavior is genetically determined, no moral demands can be made on him, since he has no real freedom to control his actions. By contrast, the Buddhist concept of man is totally spiritual, emphasizing the illusory nature of man's physical existence and the necessity of transcending that physical existence in order to achieve happiness.

3. The Christian concept of man and the effects of Baptism

The Christian conception of man shares some common aspects with humanistic concepts regarding man, but at the same time has elements that are not shared by them:

a. It separates itself from those theories that do not admit the existence of an immortal soul in man.

This element essentially differentiates him from the animals. The term spirit or soul is fundamentally a Western idea, though it is an undeniable reality in Eastern thought as well. It is Christianity, however, which confirmed and fully developed the Western understanding of an immortal soul.

In contrast to gross materialism manifested in the latter part of this century, many thinkers throughout history have reaffirmed the reality of the soul. Some use the word soul, while others use the word mind. Nonetheless, they all agree that there is an additional element in man superior to the brain, a plus that is not reducible to the brain, nor identical to the mind, but a profound and essential differentiating factor in relation to the animals.

b. The human soul is created directly by God.

The soul is not a product of generation, but is absolutely created by God (cf. CCC, 366). The soul is a spiritual reality, free and immortal. Through the soul, man is the image of God, since God is spirit and the soul is spiritual.

> "God created man in his own image, in the image of God he created him; male and female he created them."[1] Man occupies a unique place in creation: he is "in the image of God"; in his own nature he unites the spiritual and material worlds; he is created "male and female"; God established him in his friendship (CCC, 355).

c. To the being of man belong both the body and the soul.

Man, properly speaking, does not have a soul, but rather integrates the soul into his own being (he "is" soul), and similarly, man does not have a body; he is a body. Man is "one in body and soul."

> The human person, created in the image of God, is a being at once both corporeal and spiritual. The biblical account expresses this reality in symbolic language when it affirms that "then the LORD God formed man of dust from the ground, and breathed into his nostrils the breath of life; and man became a living being.[2] "Man, whole and entire, is therefore *willed* by God (CCC, 362).

d. Both realities constitute one radical unity.

The *Catechism of the Catholic Church* formulates this with the phrase: "the human person, created in the image of God, is a being at once corporeal and spiritual" (*CCC*, 362). Consequently, the unity of body and soul negates any interpretation of man as two separate entities. Man is a unity where both body and soul come together:

> The unity of soul and body is so profound that one has to consider the soul to be the "form" of the body:[3] i.e., it is because of its spiritual soul that the body made of matter becomes a living, human body; spirit and matter, in man, are not two natures united, but rather their union forms a single nature (*CCC*, 365).

The explanation for the profound unity of man, as in all created things, is found in Catholic theology under the ideas of matter and form. Just as in the physical order a statue is made up of matter, for example bronze, and a shape which gives it its particular characteristics, so are the body and soul the matter and form of the existing man. To separate the body and the soul would destroy man. And that is precisely death: the separation of body and soul. As St. Thomas Aquinas teaches, "the soul alone is not man." And a dead body is not, properly speaking, a "human body", but a corpse (St. Thomas Aquinas, *Summa theologiae*, III, q. 3, a. 2 a 2).

Given the fact that man is a spiritual and corporeal reality, morality affects both the body and the spirit, for, "in fact, body and soul are inseparable: In the person, in the willing agent and in the deliberate act they stand or fall together" (*VS*, 49).

e. **The novelty of Christian anthropology.**

The three previous basic statements belong to what is called natural anthropology, which is the study of man as he exists in himself. But Christian anthropology arrives at new truths. For our purpose, it is necessary to note three:

- The creation of man by God in his own image and likeness,

- The existence of original sin, and

- The redemption accomplished by Jesus Christ, which makes possible the life of grace given to man in Baptism.

It is through Baptism that man acquires a higher level of participation in God's life through grace. Theology teaches that in the baptized person the life of Christ is found, so much that one becomes a new being, a person-in-Christ:

> Incorporated into *Christ* by Baptism, Christians are "dead to sin and alive to God in Christ Jesus"[4] and so participate in the life of the Risen Lord (*CCC*, 1694).

This great reality elevates the baptized man to a higher state than the unbaptized man. The apostle St. Peter teaches that the baptized "become partakers of the divine nature" (2 P 1,4). Just as a child participates in the physical nature of his parents, so does—in a real, but spiritual fashion—the Christian participate by Baptism, in the nature of God. Hence the familiar quote of the Fathers: "Man is divinized." And this elevated condition requires of man a new type of conduct:

> Christian, recognize your dignity. For now you partake of divine nature; do not degenerate by turning back to your past state. Remember what Head you belong to and to what Body you are a member of. Remember that you have been snatched away from the power of darkness to be transported to the light of the kingdom of God (St. Leo the Great, *The Sermon on the Nativity*, 21, 2-3).

4. The specificity of Catholic morality

It can be asked: does the Christian, who is a new man, have the obligation to behave differently from the non-baptized? In other words, is there a specifically Christian morality superior to natural ethics and distinct from the other religious confessions?

Yes. In fact, it is clear that the believer in Christ has a new way of acting, since he has supernatural motives; that is, motives directly from God. Nevertheless, it is not just a new reason for doing good that Christianity offers. So, we find in the New Testament superior values and precepts that are not found in any other philosophical or religious system, nor explicitly in the Old Testament.

An example is Christ's statement: "A new commandment I give you that you love one another as I have loved you" (Jn 13, 33-35), which, apart from its richness, points to the measure of divine love and is a call to love even one's enemies. Jesus ended the law of retaliation (*lex talionis*) to return an evil for an evil, when he condemned vengeance; but he also said that it is not enough to forgive the enemy. Rather, he wants the enemy to be loved as he loves.

All people are obliged to cultivate the theological virtues (faith, hope and charity) and the need to avoid those actions which contradict them. Other examples have to do with the use of material goods, the demands of justice, and the realm of sexuality (Mt 5, 27-30). This new level of ethical duties points to the high moral program offered in the Beatitudes. In fact, the ethical code presented by Jesus in the Sermon on the Mount supersedes any known moral program (cf. *VS*, 12).

To indicate this, Jesus places the precept of the ancient law: "it was said to our ancestors," next to the new commandments given by him: "but I say to you" (Mt 5, 38-48; 6, 1-23). Hence, the need to have Jesus speak of his commandment (Jn 15, 10-11) and the apostles' plea to the newly baptized to "follow the precepts of the LORD" (1 Jn 2, 3-4; 3, 21-24).

Furthermore, the entire natural order has a new aid: grace makes human life meritorious because grace transforms human acts as a result of God's power. For this reason, the Christian exceeds the purely human, not by increasing on the outside, but by healing and perfecting the proper order in his soul.

The encyclical *Veritatis splendor* condemns the statement of those who assert that in revelation we find no "specific and determined moral content" (cf. *VS*, 37; 98).

5. Man is a social being. Moral requirements of human solidarity

The natural condition of being a person makes man both an individual and a social-being. The reason for this is derived from the very structure of the human person. Since Aristotle, it has been said that man is by his very nature a social being; sociability enters into the very definition of man (cf. Supplementary Readings 1 & 3).

> The human person needs to live in society. Society is not for him an extraneous addition but a requirement of his nature. Through the exchange with others, mutual service and dialogue with his brethren, man develops his potential; he thus responds to his vocation[5] (*CCC*, 1879).

A similar language is used in Vatican II: "The human person is by nature a social being." And the Council adds, "Life in society is not something accessory to man himself" (GS, 25).

Since man is by nature social, that same sociability requires that certain ethical demands be accomplished as part of his relationship to others in society, since from man's social nature originate rights and duties. As a result, Christian morality includes both personal and social obligations (cf. Supplementary Reading 2).

Moreover, since man is particularly inclined to ignore his social duties for personal gain, it is necessary to stress the importance of carrying out those social duties. Vatican II states the "need to transcend an individualistic morality" (GS, 30).

The *Catechism of the Catholic Church* dedicates a large portion to the exposition of doctrine according to the "human community". This is done after the presentation of the Christian idea of man (cf. CCC, 1877-1948).

The teaching of the Church attempts to safeguard Christian morality from being a purely individualistic approach, where little attention is given to social duties. This teaching is recalled and urged by Vatican II:

> The pace of change is so far-reaching and rapid nowadays that no one can allow himself to close his eyes to the course of events or indifferently ignore them and wallow in the luxury of a merely individualistic morality. The best way to fulfil one's obligations of justice and love is to contribute to the common good according to one's means and the needs of others, even to the point of fostering and helping public and private organizations devoted to bettering the conditions of life (GS, 30).

Veritatis splendor addresses this same point (cf. nn. 97-101).

6. Sources of moral theology

The different sciences not only make use of language and ideas directly ordered to arriving at their proper knowledge, they also use other sciences. For example, physics, which studies the nature and constitution of matter, will make use of mathematics to understand the laws governing matter.

Similarly, moral theology has its own sources, while making use of other sciences which assist it in recognizing essential Christian ethical values and their behavioral standards. The sources from which moral theology derives its doctrine are essentially the same as for theology in general: Sacred Tradition and Sacred Scripture, which form one sacred deposit of the word of God, and the Magisterium (the teaching office of the pope and the bishops teaching in unison with him), the authority which authentically interprets this sacred deposit.

a. Sacred Scripture.

Sacred Scripture is the written revelation that teaches what are the ethical values proposed by God. It also shows the moral precepts promulgated by God.

> . . . These are: the subordination of man and his activity to God, the one who "alone is good"; the relationship between the moral good of human acts and eternal life; and finally the gift of the Holy Spirit, source and means of the moral life of the "new creation" (*VS*, 28; cf. 2 Cor 5, 17).

In the Bible, Christian morality is mainly deduced from the New Testament. Here we find two basic criteria:

• The life of Jesus is the principal source from which the believer learns to live a Christian life.

• The moral doctrine which Jesus preached and taught— his words, his deeds and his precepts —constitute the moral rule of Christian life" (*VS*, 20).

> Besides the passing on of Jesus' teachings by the Gospels, a principal source of moral knowledge is found in the other writings of the New Testament. In fact, the apostles, besides recalling the moral teachings of the Teacher, expose other precepts which are derived from his doctrine, and are applied to the different circumstances of the first believers (*VS*, 26).

But not all biblical teachings are meant to be binding forever; in the Old Testament, many precepts had circumstantial value and were abolished by Jesus' preaching. Among them are ceremonial and permissible practices; chief among these is the practice of divorce, which was permitted by Moses but later prohibited by Jesus (Mk 10, 2-12; cf. Mt 5, 27-32; 19, 3-12).

Also, some New Testament teachings applied only to the early Church because of the particular situation of the first communities. An example is the abstention from certain practices as stipulated by the Council of Jerusalem (Acts 15, 19-21) or the case regarding the conduct of women in Corinth, as proscribed by St. Paul (1 Cor 11, 13-15).

b. Sacred Tradition.

Sacred Tradition constitutes the second source of Christian moral theology. The word tradition comes from the Latin *tradere,* which means "to hand on," and refers to those truths passed from generation to generation orally rather than in written form.

Tradition is the very life of the Church which preserves and guards the teachings of Jesus Christ. The writings of the Fathers (II-VII centuries), which systematize moral doctrine and apply the New Testament teachings to different times, are an important part of Tradition as is the teaching, life and worship practices of the Church, particularly those relating to penance and the forgiveness of sins (cf. *VS,* 27).

c. The Magisterium.

The Magisterium is the name given to the Church's teaching office. It derives from the Latin *magister,* which means "teacher" and refers to the authority of the pope and the bishops united with him in teaching matters of faith and morals.

> . . . But the task of authentically interpreting the word of God, whether written or handed on has been entrusted to the living teaching office of the Church whose authority is exercised in the name of Jesus Christ. This teaching office is not above the word of God, but serves it, teaching only what has been handed on, listening to it devoutly, guarding it scrupulously and explaining it faithfully in accord with a divine commission and with the help of the Holy Spirit; it draws from one deposit of faith which it presents for belief as divinely revealed (*DV,* 10).

The teaching of the hierarchy—of the popes, the councils and the bishops in their dioceses—occupies a distinguished place. In the final analysis, the Magisterium holds the right to interpret authentically the Christian moral message (cf. *VS,* 27, 30).

The ecclesiastical Magisterium defines both the truths of faith and the Church's moral teachings (cf. *VS*, 110). The phrase "faith and morals" is contained in many documents of Tradition.

> The Church's Magisterium intervenes not only in the sphere of *faith*, but also, and inseparably so, in the sphere of *morals*. It has the task of "discerning, by means of judgments normative for the consciences of believers, those acts which in themselves conform to the demands of *faith* and foster their expression in life and those which, on the contrary, because intrinsically evil, are incompatible with such demands." [*DVt*, 16]

> In proclaiming the commandments of God and the charity of Christ, the Church's Magisterium also teaches the faithful specific particular precepts and requires that they consider them in conscience as morally binding. In addition, the Magisterium carries out an important work of vigilance, warning the faithful of the presence of possible errors, even merely implicit ones, when their consciences fail to acknowledge the correctness and the truth of the moral norms, which the Magisterium teaches (*VS*, 110).

d. Ancillary sciences of moral theology.

Other sciences are also used to elaborate moral doctrine. Among them are:

- *Philosophical ethics* which aids in the understanding and posing of questions, as well as in providing a suitable language for expression,

- *Law*, especially *canon law*, which systematically studies the norms of the Church and

- The knowledge of other human sciences, i.e., *anthropology, psychology, medicine*, etc. (cf. *VS*, 111).

All of these sciences are only auxiliary, so they neither substitute for, nor diminish the authority of Scripture, Tradition, and the Magisterium, which constitute the sources of moral theology.

7. The Christian and the defense of truth

Plurality of opinion in matters of custom, politics and other relative matters is a legitimate exercise of human freedom. For example, in family life different ways of relating can exist between parents and their children, according to education, the times and social customs. But it is also evident that not every opinion or cultural expression is valid. A pluralism which does not admit of binding obligations in the parent-child relationship (because parents abandon their children—as in some instances of antiquity—or because the children fail to take care of their parents' needs) would not be considered a legitimate pluralism. A compromise in these principles could never be a Christian attitude, as it would involve renouncing the truth as revealed by God and accepting evil as compatible with Christian morality.

But while accepting a "healthy pluralism," Christians nevertheless have the obligation to acknowledge their beliefs and to preach the moral message given by Jesus. The believer in Christ possesses a qualified certainty about the content of natural law and other truths which help guide the conduct of man. Consequently, he must insure that Christian ethical principles inform human society.

This attitude is far from any kind of fanaticism or fundamentalism. The Christian cannot accept the sophism of those who declare that anyone who does not buy into a pluralism of opinions is a fanatic. On the contrary, the Christian ought to defend the truth in a positive manner, respecting others, living out charity, but proclaiming it without fear. This attitude is recalled at each moment by John Paul II. An example is found in the encyclical *Veritatis splendor*:

> The Church's teaching, and in particular her firmness in defending the universal and permanent validity of the precepts prohibiting intrinsically evil acts, is not infrequently seen as the sign of an intolerable intransigence, particularly with regard to enormously complex and conflict-filled situations present in the moral life of individuals and of society today; this intransigence is said to be in contrast to the Church's motherhood.
>
> The Church, one hears, is lacking in understanding and compassion. But the Church's motherhood can never in fact be separated from her teaching mission, which she must always carry out as the faithful bride of Christ, who is the truth in person. "As teacher, she never tires of proclaiming the moral norm. . . . The Church is in no way the author or the arbiter of this norm. In obedience to the truth which is Christ, whose image is reflected in the nature and dignity of the human person, the Church interprets the moral norm and proposes it to all people of good will, without concealing its demands for fervor and perfection."

In fact, genuine understanding and compassion must mean love for the person, for his true good, for his authentic freedom. And this does not result, certainly, from concealing or weakening moral truth, but rather from proposing it in its most profound meaning as an outpouring of God's eternal wisdom, which we have received in Christ, and as a service to man, to the growth of his freedom and to the attainment of his happiness.

Still, a clear and forceful presentation of moral truth can never be separated from a profound and heartfelt respect, born of that patient and trusting love which man always needs along his moral journey, a journey frequently wearisome on account of difficulties, weakness and painful situations. The Church can never renounce "the principle of truth and consistency, whereby she does not agree to call good evil and evil good;" she must always be careful not to break the bruised reed or to quench the dimly burning wick (cf. Is. 42, 3). As Paul VI wrote: "While it is an outstanding manifestation of charity toward souls to omit nothing from the saving doctrine of Christ, this must always be joined with tolerance and charity, as Christ himself showed by his conversations and dealings with men. Having come not to judge the world but to save it, he was uncompromisingly stern toward sin, but patient and rich in mercy toward sinners" (VS, 95).

Conclusion

The security offered by Catholic morality and the rigor of its doctrine is admirable. It incorporates a clear way of thinking based on sound philosophy and a solid idea of man discovered from a careful reading of revelation, while at the same time acknowledging a legitimate pluralism of opinion when such a pluralism does not conflict with God's revealed truth.

No other philosophical system offers such a high conception of the human person. Thus, Pope Paul VI stated, "The Church is rich in her humanity." The reason is obvious: Catholic anthropology is derived from God's conception of man. And the ultimate source of human dignity is man's relationship to Jesus Christ—God made man. "In reality it is only in the mystery of the Word made flesh that the mystery of man truly becomes clear" (GS, 22).

In addition, Catholic morality does not fall into the trap of elevating man to the point of making him faultless. Beginning with the dogma of original sin, the Church teaches about the precarious state in which man finds himself:

> Examining his heart, man finds that he has inclinations toward evil too, and is engulfed by manifold evils. . . . Therefore man is split within himself. As a result, all of human life, whether individual or collective, shows itself to be a dramatic struggle between good and evil, between light and darkness (*GS*, 13).

This Christian humanistic realism helps man aspire to high realms of moral life, but at the same time it warns him against the danger of separating himself from his true way of being. These two facts are always present in Catholic moral theology.

OUTLINE

I. Glossary

AMORALITY:

An attitude of man that lacks any moral orientation and acts at the margin, dispensing from all moral norms.

ANTHROPOLOGY:

The study of the nature of man.

THE BIBLE:

The name given to the books of Sacred Scripture.

CORPOREAL:

Synonym for bodily.

FUNDAMENTAL MORALITY:

The part of moral theology that studies the nature of the moral act and the conditions that make a concrete action moral.

GRACE:

The free gift of God's own life that God makes to the soul in Baptism; it is infused into the soul by the Holy Spirit to heal it of sin and to sanctify it.

IMMORALITY:

Behavior that goes against moral norms.

MAGISTERIUM:

The name given to the ordinary and universal teaching authority of the pope and the bishops in communion with him, who guide the members of the Church without error in matters of faith and morals by Christ.

MATERIALISM:

The belief that matter is the only reality and that everything can be explained only in terms of matter and that comfort, pleasure, and wealth are the only or highest goods or values.

NATURAL LAW:

The participation of human beings in the eternal law of God, it is the objective order established by God which determines the requirements for humans to thrive and reach fulfillment.

ORIGINAL SIN:

Adam and Eve's abuse of their human freedom and their disobedience of God's command. This sin separated man from God, darkened the human intellect, weakened the human will and introduced into human nature an inclination toward sin.

PHILOSOPHICAL ANTHROPOLOGY:

The part of philosophy that studies the specific nature of man.

PLURALISM:

The existence of a variety of opinions or ideas within human society, some of which may contradict or oppose one another. A pluralism in the application of moral principles and social customs is valid insofar as it does not contradict God's revelation and sound reason.

REVELATION:

The truths about himself and his will which God has freely communicated to humanity.

SACRED TRADITION:

The Word of God entrusted to the apostles and their successors by Christ and the Holy Spirit, and transmitted by their teaching to each generation of Christians.

SCRIPTURE:

The collection of books in the Old and New Testaments.

SECULARISM:

A system of doctrines and practices that rejects any form of religious faith and worship.

SOCIOBIOLOGY:

The study of man as genetically determined.

SOURCES OF MORAL THEOLOGY:

They are the same for the whole of theology, i.e., Scripture, Tradition and the Magisterium, the three in an indissoluble unity.

THEOLOGICAL ANTHROPOLOGY:

The part of theology that studies the nature of man according to revelation.

THEOLOGICAL VIRTUES:

Virtues infused in the soul at Baptism which place man in direct contact with God. In Catholic theology, there are three: faith, hope and charity.

II. Summary of Principles

1. Catholic moral theology is the science of applied faith. It is derived from Scripture, Tradition and the teachings of the Magisterium. It's role is to guide man's conduct in relation to good and evil.

2   Each person will act more or less morally, depending largely upon how well he or she understands what it means to be truly human. In other words, the meaning of humanness is the norm by which one judges the rightness or wrongness of one's actions.

3. The Christian conception of man includes belief in the existence of an immortal soul, created by God, which distinguishes man from the animals.

4. Christian anthropology includes these fundamental ideas:

   • human beings are created in the image and likeness of God;

   • Original Sin is real and is the source of the sinfulness found in human experience;

   • the human race has been redeemed by Jesus Christ.

5. Baptism raises a person to a supernatural existence by giving grace, which is a share in the life of Christ.

6. Sharing in God's grace transforms human life and gives human acts supernatural value.

7. Man is, by nature, a social being. Christian morality includes both personal and social obligations and excludes a purely individualistic approach to morality.

8. The Christian, while recognizing freedom of conscience and a "healthy pluralism" in matters of opinion, possesses certainty about the natural truths which guide human conduct. As a result, he must try to make Christian ethical principles inform society.

SUPPLEMENTARY READINGS

1. There are some also who, either from zeal in attending to their own business or through some sort of aversion to their fellowmen, claim that they are occupied solely with their own affairs, without seeming to themselves to be doing anyone any injury. But while they steer clear of the one kind of injustice, they fall into the other: they are traitors to social life, for they contribute to it none of their interest, none of their effort, none of their means.

(Cicero, *De officiis*, Bk. I, 9)

2. It is in accordance with their dignity that all men, because they are persons, that is, beings endowed with reason and free will and therefore bearing personal moral responsibility, are both impelled by their nature and bound by a moral obligation to seek the truth, especially religious truth. They are also bound to adhere to the truth once they have come to know it and direct their lives in accordance with the demands of truth. . . . In availing of any freedom man must respect the moral principle of personal and social responsibility; in exercising their rights individual men and social groups are bound by the moral law to have regard for the rights of others, their own duties to others and the common good of all. All men must be treated with justice and humanity.

(DH, 3-4)

3. Hence it is evident that the state is a creation of nature, and that man is by nature a political animal. And he-who by nature and not by mere accident is without a state, is either a bad man or above humanity; he is like the "Tribeless, lawless, hearthless one," whom Homer denounces—the natural outcast is forthwith a lover of war; he may be compared to an isolated player of chess.

Now, that man is more of a political animal than bees or any other gregarious animals is evident. Nature, as we often say, makes nothing in vain, and man is the only animal whom she has endowed with the gift of speech. And whereas mere voice is but an indication of pleasure or pain, and is therefore found in other animals (for their nature attains to the perception of pleasure and pain and the intimation of them to one another, and no further) the power of speech is intended to set forth the expedient and inexpedient, and therefore likewise the just and the unjust.

(Aristotle, *Politics*, Bk. 1, Ch. 2, 1253a 1-15)

4. A time will come when people will give up in practical existence those values about which they no longer have any intellectual conviction. Hence we realize how necessary the function of a sound moral philosophy is in human society. It has to give, or to give back, to society intellectual faith in the value of its ideals.

(Jacques Maritain, *On the Use of Philosophy*)

APPENDICES

1. Catholic morality and civil ethics in modern society

It is indisputable that today's society distinguishes itself by a pluralism in all fields of knowledge. Different philosophical and political systems are professed, several ways of understanding the moral life compete with one another, and diversity is found in religious beliefs.

In view of this situation, the assertion is made that it is impossible to provide a single manner of conduct for the whole of society because its citizens cannot agree on a single moral program. Therefore, it is necessary to come to a consensus with the hope of finding those ethical values that can be applied to each and every citizen.

Disagreement arises, however, when an attempt is made to delineate the common factor to which all wills must converge. In the first place, the advocates of secularism ask that it be free of any philosophical and religious considerations. Furthermore, many pretend to improve the concept of a morality based on natural law by substituting it with a secular morality.

These limitations, however, present some difficulties. Can we disregard some concepts, such as the spiritual understanding of man or the understanding of a universal law of good and evil? Moreover, are not those who demand complete separation of religion and law already starting with philosophical and political preconceptions?

In any case, it should be noted that the moral demands should not be excessively reduced. Civil ethics ought not to be an ethics of minimums. On the contrary, it should aspire to give and demand values that favor a social order worthy of man. It should at least cover two levels: the defense of the individual as a person and the protection of the rights of the social order. Consequently, the lowest level ought to demand respect for and juridically protect the fundamental rights of man.

Hence, civil ethics cannot be a permissive ethics which favors the whim of citizens, nor can it exclusively have its foundation in a majority vote. The social agreement cannot be reached at any cost by means of fundamental concessions, or by submitting grave matter solely to a voting process.

More can yet be said. With errors in wide sectors of the present culture (cf. *VS*, 28-34), the search for immediate solutions in a secular ethic, in the long run, will only yield new and greater evils in the social order.

2. "New morality"

> "The 'new morality' means different things to different people, but the general idea is that traditional morality placed too much emphasis on inflexible general rules, on obedience, and on abstract ideals of right and wrong; whereas the emphasis of the new morality is on the concrete situation, on love, and on the person" (Germain Grisez and Russell Shaw, *Beyond the New Morality*, p. xviii).

According to those who adhere to the philosophy of the new morality, there is no need to categorize levels of action and types of goods, or to consider factors such as the object, intention and circumstances which surround an action. The only important consideration is the question of love—what is the most loving response that I can make in this or in any situation? What is the choice which increases the amount of good for my neighbor, while diminishing the amount of harm to him and anyone else?

This sort of moral philosophy is appealing to many people, especially many Christians, precisely because it appears on the surface to match exactly what Jesus spoke of as the greatest of all the commandments: "'You shall love the LORD your God with all you heart and with all your soul, and with all your mind, and with all your strength.' And the second is this, 'You shall love you neighbor as yourself'" (Mk 12, 30-31).

Attractive as this philosophy is to so many, it is nevertheless flawed and bears only a superficial resemblance to Jesus' command to his followers. Why?

The first difficulty encountered with followers of this philosophy is the difficulty in defining precisely what is "love" and "the good." For many people today, love is an emotion or a sentiment, while the good is equated with pleasure and happiness. The notion of self-sacrifice seldom enters into the picture when speaking of love, and any sort of action which requires difficult choices resulting in unhappiness or pain for any party involved cannot possibly be good.

The idea that loving another person may occasionally involve doing or saying things which cause that person distress or hurt, or which angers them is rejected as unkind, judgmental or cruel. Further, the idea that I may be required to sacrifice my good (i.e., happiness or pleasure) for the good of another is also unacceptable. What sort of God would ask me to be unhappy? Finally, the idea that what is pleasurable may not necessarily be good is frequently met with scorn and derision.

The second problem is that the question of God and his will is left aside entirely, or included only insofar as asserting that he wants us to do no harm to others. But the definition of what constitutes harming another is often broadened to proportions which make it difficult to find any way of acting that does not in some way involve harming another (i.e., psychological or emotional harm), and the idea that loving God could possibly involve giving assent to his will as expressed in specific commandments is rejected altogether. Thus the proponents of the new morality make no room for objective moral guidelines which are binding on the consciences of every individual in all circumstances.

A final observation about this approach to morality is that it reverses the real relationship between the individual and the situation which calls for a moral response. In asserting that the moral thing to do in every situation is the most loving thing to do, proponents of situation ethics believe that the situation imposes a morality on us.

But the opposite is actually true; it is our choices and actions in response to the situation which creates the morality. If this were not true, then there could only ever be one right response to any given situation, thus eliminating the need for individual judgments of conscience. An individual's conscience would in fact have no role to play in determining the morally correct response to any situation.

Situations do exist in which two people can reach radically different moral conclusions while acting out of a genuine desire to do what is morally right, with concern for the good of others foremost in their minds, and having access to the same information.

Therefore, while it is true that people can be blinded to reality by their preconceived notions of right and wrong, and can be unwilling to examine or revise these notions, it is not possible to use this as the basis for a moral philosophy which eliminates the reality of moral judgments based upon individual conscience.

QUESTIONS

1. What is moral theology?

2. What are the foundations upon which Catholic moral theology is built?

3. What does Catholic moral theology aim to do?

4. What is necessary to guarantee that a moral system will be correct?

5. What two realities form a radical unity for the human person?

6. What is the final goal of each person according to Catholic moral theology?

7. What are the sources of Catholic morality? What are the two sources from which the Magisterium draws its teaching on faith and morals?

8. True or false: Moral theology is more certain than philosophical ethics because moral theology is based upon truths revealed by God and philosophical ethics is based on the conclusions of human reason.

9. Who systematized the Church's moral teaching?

10. Why is it impossible for moral theology and philosophical ethics to truly contradict one another? What can we say must be true whenever there appears to be a contradiction between the two?

PRACTICAL EXERCISES

1. Adolf Hitler is considered one of the greatest tyrants of history. He is often referred to as the archetypal incarnation of evil. *Without reference to any moral precepts,* demonstrate why he was evil and ought to be condemned as such. In other words, without reference to the notions of "right" and "wrong" prove that Hitler and what he did are criminal. Is such a proof possible? How does this show that almost everyone, even those who deny

it, believe that there are some principles of morality which exist objectively?

2. Point out the differences between philosophical ethics and Christian moral theology.

3. Outline and summarize the principle ideas expressed by Aristotle in Supplementary Reading 3.

4. Compare the ideas of Aristotle and the political and philosophical thoughts of the Roman orator Cicero in Supplementary Reading 1. What are some of the similarities and differences in their thoughts?

5. What are some of the moral principles expressed in the New Testament? Name some of the principles proposed by Christ himself in the following passages:

—Mt 5, 21-48,

—Mk 9, 42-48; 10, 1-12,

—Lk 17,1-4,

—Jn 14, 34-35.

Can you identify others?

6. Compare and contrast the moral precepts of the Old and New Testament. Begin with the Ten Commandments in Exodus 19, and the Beatitudes in Matthew 5, 1-22. What is the relationship between the Law of God as expressed by Moses on Mt Sinai and Jesus in this Sermon on the Mount? Are they compatible? Some people believe that Christ's teaching contradicts the Law of Moses. Are there any contradictions between the two? (If so, can you reconcile these differences?) What are the similarities?

7. This chapter speaks of the social obligations which one must fulfill in order to live a moral life. What are some of these social obligations?

8. Christian humanistic realism helps man aspire to high realms of moral life, but at the same time it warns him against the danger of separating himself from his true way of being. Could you give an example?

Chapter III
Freedom and the Moral Act

Tom and John are old friends, schoolmates and later students in the same law school. At present they work in law offices in different parts of the country. Since Tom is in Chicago and John is in Pittsburgh, their meetings over the past two years have only been occasional, and they talk only about their graduate studies, for both are candidates for doctorates at different universities.

Tom spent his summer vacation in California, where he was doing research for one of his classes. From there he wrote to John and mentioned that he had met a professor whose specialty was in the area of John's research; Tom advised him to get in touch with that professor. John did write to him, and after several letters they agreed to meet in California at the end of the summer. With that meeting in mind, Tom and John met shortly before it to exchange impressions of their respective jobs. When Tom took John to the airport for his flight to California, he asked him to return a library book which he had neglected to return during the summer. Tom then called a friend in California and asked him to meet John's plane. He pressed him, too, to make sure the book got returned. Meanwhile John would be looking for Tom's friend with the intention of giving him the book.

The plane arrived on time, and John quickly found Tom's friend. But while they were greeting each other, two plainclothes detectives approached and placed them under arrest. John was unable to conceal his astonishment, and he protested their innocence of any wrongdoing. But at the police station, the package John was carrying was opened, and he was even more astonished to discover that instead of a library book the package contained a half pound of cocaine.

John was an excellent student, an honorable person, and a good Christian who was hoping to attend Mass that very day before meeting with the professor he had come to see. Now, at the police station, he found himself in utter confusion. Naturally, he expects to be put on trial and will have to try to prove his innocence in court. Yet it will not be easy to convince the judge of that since he and Tom have been close friends for so long; it won't be easy to prove that he was completely unaware of Tom's private life. He even wonders whether he might be morally at fault and guilty of a sin that will need to be mentioned in Confession—at least a sin of omission.

The present case raises certain issues. Certain fundamental principles need to be clear. But it also raises other questions; for example:

- Can John be seen as an accomplice in this situation?

- Are his actions punishable in the eyes of either civil law or morality?

- Concretely, what answer can John be given about his actions in this time of confusion?

Introduction

If, indeed, morality is peculiar to man, when does an act become good or evil? What is the role of freedom in the moral life? When does a person take full responsibility for a particular act?

From his conduct it is obvious that a Christian has reasons which justify his moral life that are different than those of a non-Christian. He accepts right conduct because he knows that man is created by God and has been redeemed by Christ Jesus. As a result, he rejoices in knowing that he is a son of God. If man is the only creature loved by God for its own sake, then God also gives man a proper way of acting (CCC, 1700 ff.).

The believer knows that God set down what ought to be done or avoided. Since this view is not accepted by all, the believer, apart from the teaching of the Bible, needs to know the rational principles of the moral life which are taken for granted. They are:

a. **Freedom, which makes man a moral agent.**

b. **Conscience, which gives man the capacity to discover God's plan as written in his soul.**

c. **Law, which does not limit freedom but allows it to function properly.**

Besides these three preconditions, the Christian cannot ignore this radical and definitive principle: Jesus clearly set out what is good or evil for man by his words and the conduct of his life. Hence, Christian morality is the most effective means of acquiring the dignity proper to man because it is a morality of imitating Jesus Christ.

In this chapter we propose that an authentic human existence, worthy of the person, can only be reached when one lives as a human person. This supposes a development of all of his potentialities, of being intelligent, free, and, in consequence, responsible for his actions. With this end in mind, the conditions for true human and moral actions are studied.

1. Importance of the moral life

Right moral conduct perfects man and wrong moral conduct degrades him. The morally good and evil are the most revealing descriptions of human life. Other terms, such as wealth, poverty, success, failure, health, illness, or any other conditions which may exist in a man's personal life are certainly important, and at times decisive, but they do not touch human life as profoundly as the effects of good and evil do.

If morality affects man deeply, then it follows that the study of ethics, which shows where true values lie, is of significant importance to the human being. As was stated by Socrates, "the science of good and evil" is the most important of all the forms of knowledge, since it places man on the road to true happiness. Thus, Plato also wrote: "but still I should like to examine further, for no light matter here is at stake, nothing less than the rule of human life" (Plato, *Republic*, I, 352d).

2. Man can choose good and evil

Every man is a moral being, capable of doing good and evil, of being just or unjust, honorable or dishonorable. Moral good and evil cannot be attributed to the animals, only physical good and evil. Thus, for example, an animal is either healthy or sick, or an animal may be able to skillfully accomplish its proper end which is instinctively ingrained in its genes. A horse is said to be good or bad in a horse race; a dog can have a better or worse nose for hunting; but neither the horse nor the dog can sin or practice virtue, nor can they be just or unjust. In no way are they morally responsible.

Man, on the other hand, is morally responsible for his actions. He acts with thought and deliberation. The reason is that he alone has knowledge and a will. *Intelligence* gives meaning to things and *free will* allows for the fulfillment or omission of actions the intellect has determined to be good or bad.

The human person, therefore, can lead an exemplary existence, striving for sanctity, or committing the most evil actions. This reality is often evident, and was noted by Aristotle:

> For man, when perfected, is the best of animals, but, when separated from law and justice, he is the worst of all; since armed injustice is the more dangerous, and he is equipped

at birth with arms, meant to be used by intelligence and virtue, which he may use for the worst ends. Wherefore, if he have not virtue, he is the most unholy and the most savage of animals, and the most full of lust and gluttony. But justice is the bond of men in states, for the administration of justice, which is the determination of what is just, is the principle of order in political society (Aristotle, *Politics*, Bk. 1, Ch. 2).

With these two options, the good that perfects and the evil that degrades, human existence is lived out. Morality is the science that teaches man how to choose the good and avoid evil and offers him the means, so that, besides living with the dignity proper to him, he may accomplish his end, eternal salvation.

People today need to turn to Christ once again in order to receive from him the answer to their questions about what is good and what is evil. Christ is the Teacher, the risen One who has life in himself and who is always present in his Church and in the world. It is he who opens up to the faithful the book of the Scriptures and, by fully revealing his Father's will, teaches the truth about moral actions (cf. *VS*, 8).

3. The human act, a moral act

While it is true that every man can act morally, moral good and evil cannot always be attributed to every man in all circumstances. This calls for some distinctions. A moral or immoral act is truly human when a man brings it about with *knowledge* and *free will*. Consequently, those actions which lack knowledge or freedom do not fall under the realm of morality, as may be the case with the insane or when a person is semiconscious (sleepwalking). Along with human acts, classical literature speaks of the *acts of men* which are acts accomplished without knowledge or deliberation, and so are considered differently than human actions.

While intellect and free will are the spiritual powers which human beings possess, they are not separate from the rest of a man's life. In other words, the human act involves the whole person and not just the intellect and will. It is man, with all his virtues and vices, his character and his interactions with others who is moral or immoral, good, or evil. "Human acts are moral acts, because they express and determine the goodness or evil of the individual who performs them" (*VS*, 71).

4. Knowledge is a condition for morality

Man, from the beginning of Western culture, has been defined as a rational animal, and therefore thinking needs to be understood as a necessary element of morality. So, the first requirement for a moral act is that it be done with knowledge.

There are different degrees of knowledge however, and how clearly one thinks through his actions affects the seriousness of sin or the degree of reward that is due the person's action. Here a distinction can be made between *full* and *partial knowledge*.

a. Full knowledge.

Full knowledge involves clear and deliberate knowledge of the morality of the action being considered. Concretely, to commit a mortal sin, full knowledge is needed: a mortal sin does not come about as a surprise. Full knowledge, presumes two things:

- *That the agent knows clearly what he is doing.* Hence, mortal sins do not occur in the state of sleep or semiconsciousness.

- *That the agent be aware of its serious moral dimension;* he needs to know the act as good or evil. He does not need to know that this act "offends God." It is enough to know that this act is prohibited or seriously sinful. For example, there is full knowledge when someone slanders another knowing it is not true; but there is no sin when someone clearly knows he is discussing information that was shared with him by a co-worker, but is not aware that he is discussing confidential company information that was obtained in an unethical manner. The same can be said for good acts: there is no need to know that this pleases God; it is enough to know that it is a good act.

b. Partial knowledge.

Partial knowledge involves the presence of some obstacle which interferes with correct judgment, as may be the case in the use of prescribed medications or psychological alterations due to fear or depression.

5. The human act is a free act

Freedom is man's greatest quality. Inorganic creation is ruled by material properties and animals by the constant inclination of their instinct. The instinctive force of animals is replaced in man by his creative capacity for freedom.

> Freedom is the power, rooted in reason and will, to act or not to act, to do this or that, and so to perform deliberate actions on one's own responsibility. By free will one shapes one's own life. Human freedom is a force for growth and maturity in truth and goodness; it attains its perfection when directed toward God, our beatitude (CCC, 1731).

> *Imputability* and responsibility for an action can be diminished or even nullified by ignorance, inadvertence, duress, fear, habit, inordinate attachments, and other psychological or social factors (CCC, 1735).

The existence of freedom is a basic premise in Catholic morality, but its improper use may lead to serious difficulties. In fact, in freedom good and evil are forged. Moreover, to the degree that man reaches high levels of freedom, he becomes capable of high levels of morality. On the other hand, the sinful man ends up being a slave to his passions, and loses his freedom. Thus, freedom is one of the central themes of moral theology, since in it the two specific operations of man are found: intellect and will. In fact, free acts demand the use of the intellect and will.

In dealing with the subject of freedom, in the present culture, it is necessary to understand the concept of freedom:

a. Existence of freedom.

It is worth noting that no other historical period has so strongly claimed the role of freedom in the personal and social spheres of life as the present age (cf. *VS*, 32). Moreover, the feeling for freedom is the loudest cry of our times. And despite all of this, there are still those who deny it; man, it is said, lacks freedom, and is dominated by circumstances.

> Side by side with its exaltation of freedom, yet oddly in contrast with it, modern culture radically questions the very existence of this freedom. A number of disciplines, grouped under the name of the "behavioral sciences", have rightly drawn attention to the many kinds of psychological and social conditioning which influence the exercise of human

freedom. . . . But some people, going beyond the conclusions which can be legitimately drawn from these obser-
vations, have come to question or even deny the very reality of human freedom (*VS*, 33; cf. Supplementary Reading 1).

The reason may be found in not distinguishing enough between the existence of freedom and its limitation. In fact,
human freedom is limited, precisely because man is a limited being. While we are willing to admit the limitation of our
intelligence and strength, we are not willing to admit to a limited freedom.

> Rational reflection and daily experience demonstrate the
> weakness which marks man's freedom. That freedom is real
> but limited. . . . Human freedom belongs to us as creatures;
> it is a freedom which is given as a gift, one to be received
> as a seed and cultivated responsibly. It is an essential part
> of that creaturely image which is the basis of the dignity
> of the person. Within that freedom there is an echo of the
> primordial vocation whereby the Creator calls man to the
> true good, and even more, through Christ's revelation, to
> become his friend and to share his own divine life. . . . Free-
> dom then is rooted in the truth about man and is ultimately
> directed towards communion (*VS*, 86).

In other words, man is not free to be who or what he wishes
for God has chosen man for himself. The freedom man has
is the freedom to establish a loving relationship with Jesus
Christ. When man chooses to reject this call, he becomes a
slave to his passions, and that is why some men are called
animals for they have lost the freedom to choose by entan-
gling their lives in sinful habits and have become instinctively
sinful.

The existence of freedom can be proven by Scripture and by
reason. In fact, the Old Testament presents the relationship
between man and God in terms of freedom; so that, already
in the beginning of humanity, man made bad use of his freedom, and risked his destiny.

God certainly gives man some precepts, but man has the
ability to reject them. As we see in the book of Sirach:

> It was he who created man in the beginning, and he left him in the power of his own inclination. If you will, you can keep the commandments, and to act faithfully is a matter of your own choice. He has placed before you fire and water: stretch out your hand for whichever you wish. Before a man are life and death, and whichever he chooses will be given to him (Sir 15, 14-17).

The history of God with his people develops in a climate of freedom. The history of salvation is the joining of two wills which seldom agree: that of God and man, constituted by the People of Israel. Hence, the promises and chastisements of God to the People of Israel. Many misfortunes of man derive from his misuse of freedom:

> Do not say, "It was he who led me astray"; for he has no need of a sinful man. The LORD hates all abominations, and they are not loved by those who fear him (Sir 15, 12-13).

b. Freedom and knowledge of the truth.

There is a fundamental dependence of freedom upon truth. In fact, freedom supposes knowledge of the truth, so that ignorance is an obstacle in choosing.

> According to the Christian faith and the Church's teaching "only the freedom which submits to the Truth leads the human person to his true good. The good of the person is to be in the truth and to do the truth" (VS, 84; cf. Pius XII, *Address to the International Congress on Moral Theology*, 970).

Furthermore, freedom raises the capacity of man to love the truth and to grow in the knowledge of moral values. Here we see that "the truth will make you free" (Jn 8, 32). But truth is not identical to opinion or to what one wants, rather it corresponds to an objective reality. The intimate relationship between freedom and truth is broken when man determines what is right and wrong for himself.

> In this way the inescapable claims of truth disappear, yielding their place to a criterion of sincerity, authenticity and "being at peace with oneself," so much so that some have come to adopt a radically subjectivistic conception of moral judgment (VS, 32).

c. Freedom and the good.

Human freedom is ordered toward good and not evil. To do evil is not freedom, nor a part of freedom, but only a sign that man is free. In fact, freedom is not rooted in the physical ability to do evil, but in the moral duty to do the good. It is obvious that a teacher, for example, has the physical ability to insult a student, but he ought not to do so. Similarly, a strong student can abuse a weaker one, but he ought not to do so. Every man has the physical ability to do a great number of morally objectionable things, but he has the moral duty of avoiding them.

> It is, however, only in freedom that man can turn himself towards what is good. The people of our time prize freedom very highly and strive eagerly for it. In this they are right. Yet they often cherish it improperly, as if it gave them leave to do anything they like, even when it is evil. But that which is truly freedom is an exceptional sign of the image of God in man. For God willed that man should "be left in the hand of his own counsel" so that he might of his own accord seek his creator and freely attain his full and blessed perfection by cleaving to him.

> Man's dignity therefore requires him to act out of conscious and free choice, as moved and drawn in a personal way from within, and not by blind impulses in himself or by mere external constraint. Man gains such dignity when, ridding himself of all slavery to the passions, he presses forward towards his goal. By freely choosing what is good, and, by his diligence and skill, effectively secures for himself the means suited to this end.

> Since human freedom has been weakened by sin it is only by the help of God's grace that man can give his actions their full and proper relationship to God. Before the judgment seat of God an account of his own life will be rendered to each one according as he has done either good or evil (GS, 17).

Thus, a person increases his freedom to the degree that he rejects evil and does good. To the contrary, evil enslaves. This is the meaning of St. Paul's words:

> Do you not know that if you yield yourselves to any one as obedient slaves, you are slaves of the one whom you

OUR MORAL LIFE IN CHRIST

obey, either of sin, which leads to death, or of obedience, which leads to righteousness? (Rm 6, 18).

To understand freedom as the possibility of doing evil is to set it on the wrong path of caprice, passions and vain desires, all of which lead freedom on its way to becoming an animal instinct.

To summarize then, the intimate relationship between freedom and truth is reiterated by the Catechism of the Catholic Church:

> The more one does what is good, the freer one becomes. There is no true freedom except in the service of what is good and just. The choice to disobey and do evil is an abuse of freedom and leads to "the slavery of sin"[1] (CCC, 1733).

d. Freedom implies responsibility.

Each man is responsible for his actions and their consequences, and society simply responds according to what those actions merit. There is no such thing as an irresponsible freedom. The way to acquire and grow in freedom is by exercising responsibility.

> Freedom makes man *responsible* for his acts to the extent that they are voluntary. Progress in virtue, knowledge of the good, and ascesis enhance the mastery of the will over its acts (CCC, 1734).

> Some of you listening to me have known me for a long time. You can bear out that I have spent my whole life preaching personal freedom, with personal responsibility. I have sought freedom throughout the world and I'm still looking for it, just like Diogenes trying to find an honest man. And every day I love it more. Of all the things on earth, I love it most. It is a treasure which we do not appreciate nearly enough (Blessed Josemaría Escrivá, *Christ is Passing By*, 184).

e. God respects human freedom.

God will not enslave the freedom of the individual because to do so would reduce that person to the sort of existence lived by the animals. Therefore, we cannot blame God for the human evils which find their origins in the abuse of freedom. War, hunger, crimes, drugs, AIDS—none of these are desired by God. The abuse of human freedom is to blame.

Man's freedom is limited and capable of error. In fact, man failed. Adam freely committed the Original Sin. By refusing God's plan of love, he deceived himself and became a slave to sin. This first alienation engendered a multitude of others, first in the family and then in society. From its outset, human history attests the wretchedness and oppression born of the human heart in consequence of the abuse of freedom.

f. **Freedom and divine grace.**

All the aid that God offers to man with all its graces and gifts does not diminish his freedom; rather it helps him to see the truth more clearly, and it gives him more strength to conquer his passions. So, the Christian—contrary to many opinions—is more free than the man who lives by his instincts or desires:

> The grace of Christ is not in the slightest way a rival of our freedom when this freedom accords with the sense of the true and the good that God has put in the human heart. On the contrary, as Christian experience attests especially in prayer, the more docile we are to the promptings of grace, the more we grow in inner freedom and confidence during trials, such as those we face in the pressures and constraints of the outer world. By the working of grace the Holy Spirit educates us in spiritual freedom in order to make us free collaborators in his work in the Church and in the world (*CCC*, 1742).

g. **Freedom and law.**

Freedom and law cannot truly oppose one other. There exists a true harmony between just laws and man's conscience. Freedom therefore presupposes—and even demands—the law of God. As Pope John Paul II teaches:

> God's law does not reduce, much less do away with human freedom; rather, it protects and promotes that freedom. In contrast, however, some present-day cultural tendencies have given rise to several currents of thought in ethics which center upon an alleged conflict between freedom and law. These doctrines would grant to individuals or social groups the right to determine what is good or evil. Human freedom would thus be able to "create values" and would enjoy a primacy over truth, to the point that truth itself would be considered a creation of freedom. Freedom would

thus lay claim to a moral autonomy which would actually amount to an absolute sovereignty (*VS*, 35).

Freedom is the power that man has over his own acts with the end of accomplishing God's will. Consequently, freedom should not signal a neutral attitude of the human will towards choices. On the contrary, freedom ought to demand what conforms to the divine will (cf. Supplementary Reading 3).

The key that opens the door to freedom is prudence, which is the ability to make and carry out correct moral acts. This virtue is acquired in the choices one makes on a daily basis and requires planning. To be free one must plan to make the correct choices and carry them through in addition to examining on a daily basis the results of all his moral choices.

6. Man is responsible for the good or evil of his free acts

For an act to be good or evil there needs to be consent: only an act that results from consent and freedom can be attributed to man. Ordinarily, this is easy to see. However, situations occur where it is difficult to determine whether true freedom is present, but both will be examined as one. The Catechism proposes a similar reasoning:

> An effect can be tolerated without being willed by its agent; for instance, a mother's exhaustion from tending her sick child. A bad effect is not imputable if it was not willed either as an end or as a means of an action, e.g., a death a person incurs in aiding someone in danger. For a bad effect to be imputable it must be foreseeable and the agent must have the possibility of avoiding it, as in the case of manslaughter caused by a drunken driver (*CCC*, 1737).

Conclusion

Freedom—which is our free will, our power to choose between different alternatives, our power to say yes or no—characterizes man and forms the basis of his dignity, enabling him to bear personal responsibility. Man is free and responsible because he can choose. Imprisonment is a great indignity because it deprives a man of choice. It is very evident that to the extent to which a man has no real choice, he is not free. He is only free when he can choose this or that, when he can say yes or no. If he can only say yes, he is not free.

In addition, some of our free choices develop us more; some develop us less. Others thwart our growth. We are not static personalities. We are changing all the time, whether we want it or not, or like it or not. In part, circumstances force us to change. Nonetheless, what fundamentally affects our changing personalities is our own free choices—whether we say yes when we could have said no, whether we say no when we could have said yes.

We are like men constantly on the road, coming to crossroads all the time and choosing. Very clearly, therefore, it is important to know what sort of things one chooses, and how they affect one's own development as a person. Because choices, like roads, are not indifferent. They tend to lead you somewhere—toward the goal (if you have one) or away from it.

Is a person less free because he accepts restrictions? Not all restrictions necessarily involve a loss of freedom. Certain restrictions are in fact a safeguard of freedom. A man may accept them because he is personally convinced that they help to make or keep him free; and is also convinced that if he does not observe them, he can lose his freedom.

A road is a restriction. It has a certain paved width; it has curves and guardrails. But the man who suddenly decides he will no longer be a "slave" to these restrictions and who, instead of following the next curve, drives straight on, will probably find that his "freedom" leaves him at the bottom of a ditch or wrapped around the nearest tree.

> The kingdom of Christ is a kingdom of freedom. In it the only slaves are those who freely bind themselves, out of love of God. What a blessed slavery of love, that sets us free! Without freedom, we cannot respond to grace. Without freedom, we cannot give ourselves freely to our LORD, for the most supernatural of reasons, because we want to (Blessed Josemaría Escrivá, *Christ is Passing By*, 184).

OUTLINE

I. Glossary

CONCUPISCENCE:

The inclination of the sense appetite (of the passions) that demands and seeks the sensual good.

FEAR OF EVIL:

The fear of evil which can overcome one's reason and diminish full responsibility for a sin.

FREEDOM:

The internal capacity of the person by which the will is able to choose between wanting or not wanting.

FULL KNOWLEDGE:

The clear and deliberate knowledge of the sinfulness of an action which is required as a condition before a person can be guilty of sin.

HUMAN ACT:

An act which is performed with both *knowledge* and *free will*. Human acts, depending upon the degree of knowledge and freedom involved in their commission, are considered either morally good, morally evil or morally indifferent.

IGNORANCE:

The lack of required knowledge.

INDIFFERENT ACTS:

Actions which have nor moral value in themselves, but which depend upon the intention of the person performing them and the circumstances which surround their commission for their moral value.

INDIRECT RESPONSIBILITY:

The attribution of the effect that secondarily follows a free act.

INVINCIBLE IGNORANCE:

Ignorance required to make a moral choice which cannot be overcome by ordinary and reasonable diligence.

PARTIAL KNOWLEDGE:

Knowledge that is obscured by the presence of some obstacle interfering with a moral judgment.

RESPONSIBILITY:

The demand for an account for one's acts before oneself and before a superior authority; it includes accepting the consequences of one's actions.

VINCIBLE IGNORANCE:

Ignorance which can and must be overcome before a moral choice is made.

VIOLENCE (EXTERNAL):

The coercion of an external force against a person's will.

II. Summary of Principles

1. Only free acts merit reward or punishment.

2. All acts, internal or external, can become good or evil, when they involve deliberation.

3. The free and voluntary act excludes ignorance, concupiscience, fear and violence.

4. Moral responsibility can be diminished or removed by ignorance, violence, fear and other psychological and social circumstances (cf. CCC, 1735).

5. Man has the obligation to love, defend and form his personal freedom, and to respect the freedom of others.

6. Man is morally responsible for a secondary effect which could have been easily foreseen.

7. Invincible ignorance is not imputed as a fault and takes away responsibility.

8. The law does not exclude freedom, but rather guides it in a manner proper to man.

9. Merit confers upon man a certain suitability so that God may grant him "an increase in grace and the prize of glory."

10. Good acts done in a state of mortal sin do not merit a supernatural reward.

SUPPLEMENTARY READINGS

1. I deny that freedom exists at all. I must deny it—or my program would be absurd. You can't have a science about a subject matter which hops capriciously about. Perhaps we can never prove that man isn't free; it's an assumption. But the increasing success of a science of behavior makes it more and more plausible.

(B.F. Skinner, *Walden Two*, p. 257)

2. Yes. Free choice is inescapable. We are "condemned to freedom," as Sartre put it.

   Why the negative language ("condemned")? Because there is something in us that fears freedom. If we are free, we are responsible. We can't pass the buck to others and blame our society, or our parents. Or the government. Our problem is laziness. . . .

   . . . Most people love freedom when it means being able to do whatever they feel like doing. But they don't love freedom when it means the responsibility of making moral choices and living with the results. Freedom is not easy. But today we want everything to be easy. That's why our political freedom is currently in great danger. Freedom is not in danger in places like Poland today, because it is not easy there. Poles know the value of freedom. They had to struggle for it, and pay for it.

   But whether or not we have political freedom, everyone has moral freedom. Every human being has the free will to choose between good and evil, and the responsibility to do so. That's essential to human nature. That's why we are all "condemned to freedom."

(Peter Kreeft, *Making Choices: Practical Wisdom for Everyday Moral Decisions*, pp. 13-14)

3. A certain type of man feels, on every conceivable occasion, that his rights are threatened, or trespassed upon. He always keeps on his guard lest some impairment of his rights should escape his attention. Dominated by his fear of such an injury or encroachment, he seldom stops to consider whether a thing is valuable in itself or not, whether it glorifies God or offends him. Hence, his vision of various situations is obscured; his capacity of adequate judgement

is blunted. He is incapable of a free, an unwarped response to values. In his mind, the theme of his rights overshadows the question of the objective value involved; thus, instead of a disinterested love of truth and of right he is likely to develop a bitter and cantankerous attitude. Indeed, his inordinate insistence on his rights may sometimes tempt him to ride roughshod over those of others. Such people, in their cramped egoism, are as far remote from true freedom as it is possible to be.

(Dietrich von Hildebrand, *Transformation in Christ*, p. 207)

QUESTIONS

1. Why is it that only human beings, and not animals, are able to act morally?

2. What are the rational principles of the moral life?

3. What is the radical and definitive principle of moral life?

3. Define a human act. When is an action a truly human act?

4. Toward what end do the highest levels of freedom lead man?

5. Is freedom limited? How?

6. Upon what does freedom fundamentally depend? Why?

7. Toward what is freedom oriented?

8. What is the effect of evil?

9. What is freedom?

10. What is prudence?

11. Why must freedom and responsibility go together?

12. Does grace diminish freedom? Explain your answer.

PRACTICAL EXERCISES

1. What is St. Paul's understanding of human freedom as evidenced in the following passages of Scripture:

   — Rm 6, 11-23; 7, 2-12; 8, 1-5;

   — Gal 4, 21-23?

2. Liberty can lead to licentiousness, an excessive enjoyment of human freedom which respects no moral precepts or standards. What is the significance of the following scriptural texts which address this danger? Rm 6, 15; 1 Cor 6, 12; 10, 23; Gal 5, 13.

3. Are you convinced by Skinner's arguments in Supplementary Reading 1 that deny human freedom? Why or why not? What arguments can be used to refute Skinner?

4. According to Supplementary Reading 3, what concerns ought to be of greater importance to a man than just "his rights?"

5. What relationship exists between freedom and responsibility?

6. Of what kind of freedom is Blessed Josemaria Escriva speaking in the quotation contained in the Conclusion to this chapter? What does he mean when he speaks of that "blessed slavery of love, that sets us free!"?

7. To what degree does God respect our freedom as human beings? Are there ever instances in which he will act directly to interfere with man's freedom? Why or why not? Do you ever wish that God would act differently? What would be the positive and negative consequences of his doing so?

CHAPTER IV
THE MORAL CONSCIENCE

In the following passage of Scripture, the prophet Nathan confronts King David. King David had committed adultery with Bathsheba, the wife of Uriah the Hittite, who was a soldier in the King's army. In order to conceal his sin and to take Bathsheba as his wife, the king had arranged for Uriah to be sent to the front line of battle on a suicide mission, thus adding murder to his sin of adultery.

And the LORD sent Nathan to David. He came to him, and said to him, "There were two men in a certain city, the one rich and the other poor. The rich man had very many flocks and herds; but the poor man had nothing but one little ewe lamb, which he had bought. And he brought it up, and it grew up with him and with his children; it used to eat of his morsel, and drink from his cup, and lie in his bosom, and it was like a daughter to him. Now there came a traveler to the rich man, and he was unwilling to take one of his own flock or herd to prepare for the wayfarer who had come to him, but he took the poor man's lamb, and prepared it for the man who had come to him."

Then David's anger was greatly kindled against the man; and he said to Nathan, "As the LORD lives, the man who has done this deserves to die; and he shall restore the lamb fourfold, because he did this thing, and because he had no pity." Nathan said to David, "You are the man. Thus says the LORD, the God of Israel, 'I anointed you king over Israel, and I delivered you out of the hand of Saul; and I gave you your master's house, and your master's wives into your bosom, and gave you the house of Israel and of Judah; and if this were too little, I would add to you as much more.

'Why have you despised the word of the LORD, to do what is evil in his sight? You have smitten Uriah the Hittite with the sword, and have taken his wife to be your wife, and have slain him with the sword of the Ammonites. Now therefore the sword shall never depart from your house, because you have despised me, and have taken the wife of Uriah the Hittite to be your wife.'

Thus says the LORD, 'Behold, I will raise up evil against you out of your own house; and I will take your wives before your eyes, and give them to your neighbor, and he shall lie with your wives in the sight of this sun. For you did it secretly; but I will do this thing before all Israel, and before the sun.'"

David said to Nathan, "I have sinned against the LORD." And Nathan said to David, "The LORD also has put away your sin; you shall not die." (2 Sm 12, 1-13)

In light of this reading, let us ask ourselves the following:

• What is conscience?

- How does conscience aid the person who seeks to live a truly Christ-like life?

- How does a person develop his conscience so that he can be confident of its judgments?

Introduction

The concept of conscience is fundamental to Catholic theology. This is because man, in all his actions, ought to conform his conscience to the will of God. Even popular wisdom often equates the value of man with his conscience. Thus, the most negative judgment passed on a person's character is "That man has no conscience," or even worse, "He has a perverted conscience." Both cases illustrate the value of conscience. The uprightness of one's conscience determines the degree of one's moral perfection.

It is also noticeable how often men appeal to their personal consciences: "I ask that my conscience be respected," "Your conscience may say this is wrong, but my conscience tells me it's all right;" "My conscience allows me to do this." So, we defend and protect it when someone tries to violate those decisions made "in good conscience." Thus, society defends "freedom of conscience." There is a general recognition that conscience exists, but there is no agreement on what it is or how it functions.

In the Christian tradition, conscience receives the highest respect. The Fathers of the Church (Christian writers from the 2nd to 5th centuries after Christ) call it "the spark of the Holy Spirit," "the sacredness of man," and "the sanctuary of God." It is considered sacred for in it God speaks to man. Origen affirms that conscience is the quintessence of the spirit of man ("the soul of the soul is conscience") and he assures that it can be seen as "a corrective spirit and teacher of man" (cf. Supplementary Readings).

Legal recognition by the state for the right of the person to object in conscience is necessary in modern times because civil law sometimes permits and even requires morally evil actions. A society is said to be just when its laws defend the freedom of right conscience of each and every one of its citizens within due limits.

1. What is conscience?

Conscience is not a feeling, nor a theoretical judgment on whether something is good or evil but a practical judgment: *It judges whether a particular act is right or wrong from an ethical point of view.*

> Conscience is a judgment of reason whereby the human person recognizes the moral quality of a concrete act that he is going to perform, is in the process of performing, or has already completed (*CCC*, 1778; cf. also 1796).

Conscience is capable of judging moral and immoral situations, so it is capable of judging *concrete acts.* Its purpose is to evaluate whether or not this particular act is good or evil, and to act accordingly.

Since it is a *judgment of reason* it must be made with the intellect. So man is held responsible for what he does, since he knows the good and evil involved. Man can receive either punishment or reward (cf. *VS*, 57-59).

The new life brought about by Baptism gives special light to the conscience. The new Christian receives special graces that help him understand and live the moral demands of the Christian life. This can be seen with regard to two points, as outlined in Chapter 5: to interpret the precepts of natural law and, above all, to know and fulfill the requirements that the "life in Christ" demands. That is, the "New Law" which the Holy Spirit communicates to the baptized, with the hope that he may be able to realize his specifically Christian life (cf. *CCC*, 1777).

> Conscience is man's most secret core, and his sanctuary. There he is alone with God whose voice echoes in his depths. By conscience, in a wonderful way, that law is made known which is fulfilled in the love of God and of one's neighbor. Through loyalty to conscience Christians are joined to other men in the search for truth and of the right solution to so many moral problems which arise both in the life of individuals and from social relationships.
>
> Hence, the more a correct conscience prevails, the more do persons and groups turn aside from blind choice and try to be guided by the objective standards of moral conduct. Yet it often happens that conscience goes astray through ignorance which it is unable to avoid, without thereby losing its dignity. This cannot be said of the man who takes little trouble to find out what is true and good, or when con-

science is by degrees almost blinded through the habit of committing sin (*GS*, 16).

2. Conscience and truth

It is necessary to state that conscience is rooted in truth: there is a truth about man, law, and what is good and evil. Because truth is prior to conscience, conscience must respect truth. When fundamental truths are ignored, there is error in practical judgments. That is, the conscience will make false judgments when it fails to acknowledge the truth about things. John Paul II states:

> Ethical Goodness is only another name for the truth, when it is sought by the practical intellect. One cannot obscure or harm the practical dimension of the truth without, to a large extent, injuring its theoretical aspects (Pope John Paul II, *Discourse to Scientists*, May 8, 1993).

And, the encyclical *Veritatis splendor* shows the reason why conscience is subordinate to truth:

> As is immediately evident, the crisis of truth is not unconnected with this development. Once the idea of a universal truth about the good, knowable by human reason, is lost, inevitably the notion of conscience also changes. Conscience is no longer considered in its primordial reality as an act of a person's intelligence, the function of which is to apply the universal knowledge of the good in a specific situation and thus to express a judgment about the right conduct to be chosen. . . Instead, there is a tendency to grant to the individual conscience the prerogative of independently determining the criteria of good and evil and then acting accordingly.

> Such an outlook is quite congenial to an individualistic ethic, wherein each individual is faced with his own truth, different from the truth of others. Taken to its extreme consequences, this individualism leads to a denial of the very idea of human nature (*VS*, 32).

Therefore, conscience ought to freely embrace truth, since truth is a permanent light, which never fades away. Conscience shares an innate capacity to come to the truth. Insofar as man has the use of reason he can discern the good and evil. Conscience is an inextinguishable light which is given to us by nature. Thus, the obligation to follow our judgment when truth is present in it.

3. The formation of conscience

Because a sound conscience is necessary in order to make correct moral judgments, every man has the obligation to apply the means to correctly form his conscience.

Keep in mind that the individual is born without the knowledge of good and evil. These concepts are acquired through education and built upon by reason, which elaborates on them by the light of natural law and, above all, by the law of the Holy Spirit and Christian reflection. In fact, just as man is born without ideas and acquires them throughout his life, so can this process of conscience be described, in regard to the categories of good and evil.

Nonetheless, just as the child who has no innate ideas has great capacity to acquire them via reason, so too conscience is an inextinguishable light that enables one to acquire the moral concepts.

Furthermore, a child's reason takes its knowledge from different sources. Those most immediate would be other people (parents, teachers), or it can be acquired by personal experience (he learns that fire burns by its effects), or it is a product of theoretical reflection, truths derived by other truths (the intellectual life).

Similarly, then, the child—with the law which God has planted in the center of his heart already present—builds his moral criteria, either because he is taught by his parents and teachers, or because good and evil resonate within himself, or by reflecting on the requirements of natural law; but above all because the Spirit assists him in finding the internal law given at Baptism.

4. Means to the formation of conscience

To form a right conscience there are specific means, which also share similarities with those employed in the education of the intellect (cf. *CCC*, 1783-1785).

a. Acceptance of moral teaching.

A child needs to be docile to the moral lessons being communicated to him by his parent and teachers. An adult needs to be attentive to the moral teaching being offered by the Magisterium of the Church. It is a serious obligation to form one's conscience according to the teaching of the Magisterium. For the Church possesses the fullness of truth, and one is guilty of sin and responsible for the consequences if he ignores the truth.

b. Knowledge of the Christian life and doctrine.

Right conscience tries to configure its moral criteria to the patrimony and style of the Christian moral life which is transmitted by the teaching of the Bible, Tradition and the Magisterium.

c. Prayer and meditation.

It is important to attend to the dictates of one's conscience, and to carefully consider the particular moral choice in our prayer:

> Faced with a moral choice, conscience can make either a right judgment in accordance with reason and the divine law or, on the contrary, an erroneous judgment that departs from them (*CCC*, 1799).

d. Personal examination.

As a way of *internalizing*, the best means is an examination of conscience. Just as intellectual objectivity is reached by critical intellectual evaluation (examination), so can moral rightness be accomplished by a serious examination of conscience. An essential consequence of the *examen* is the practice of *sacramental confession*. A further comparison with the intellectual life may shed light on the subject: In the academic world there is a preference for comprehensive examinations or final course examinations over simple tests; the same would hold true for the moral life (conscience), where *confession* and the *examen* are seen as a more complete form of moral examination.

e. Spiritual direction.

Finally, conscience can acquire a more objective moral judgment when one enters into dialogue with another person, who helps one overcome subjectivism or caprice. Just as the student gains further and deeper intellectual insight by consulting with his professor, the person who sees a spiritual director can reach a higher degree of moral rectitude.

5. Division of conscience

a. When a judgment of conscience is given, it can be:

- *Antecedent*, which precedes action; before acting, one deliberates and concludes that an action is good or evil.

- *Concomitant,* a judgement which accompanies the action as it takes place.

- *Consequent,* a judgement which follows the act.

b. If conscience is understood in relation to the law that it seeks to fulfill, one can distinguish between:

- *True conscience* objectively coincides with the application of the law. For example, the eighth commandment forbids lies; my conscience judges truly when I am convinced that it is never permissible to tell a lie.

- *Erroneous conscience* does not correspond with what the law or norm requires because an error in judgment has occurred. When a person does not know what the moral law requires, his ignorance is either *vincible* or *invincible.*

    — *Invincible ignorance* is ignorance of what is required by the moral law that is not the fault of the person acting. He has no reasonable way to know the truth. He who acts with *invincible ignorance* does not sin, if he has taken the necessary and reasonable steps to learn what is permitted and prohibited.

    — *Vincible ignorance* is ignorance of the truth which results from a person's failure to find out what is required of him. It is important to note here that this failure can be either willful (as in the case of a person who knows that he is in error but refuses to take the necessary steps to find out the truth) or the result of neglect (a failure to discover the truth because of laziness or disinterest). To act with vincible ignorance is to risk committing a sin.

c. In reference to the judgment of conscience, it is necessary to remember that conscience is not an infallible guide; there is always the possibility of error in one's judgments. Therefore, in order to act in "good conscience," a man must first seek to know what is truly good. The man who has become blind to the truth through habitual sin, or who refuses to seek what is good, is culpable for the evil of his actions, for his ignorance is vincible.

6. To act always with right conscience

Man is obligated to follow his conscience. When he is in error, his personal freedom to choose must be acknowledged. Vatican Council II speaks thus, regarding an erroneous conscience:

> On his part, man perceives and acknowledges the imperatives of the divine law through the mediation of conscience. In all his activity a man is bound to follow his conscience in order that he may come to God, the end and purpose of life. It follows that he is not to be forced to act in a manner contrary to his conscience. Nor, on the other hand, is he to be restrained from acting in accordance with his conscience, especially in matters religious (*DH*, 3).

Since conscience is the instrument with which man must judge his actions, such judgment should always be made with a true or correct conscience. This requires knowledge of the general principles of morality, and their application, by conscience, to concrete acts.

> The dignity of the human person implies and requires *uprightness of moral conscience*. Conscience includes the perception of the principles of morality (synderesis); their application in the given circumstances by practical discernment of reasons and goods; and finally judgment about concrete acts yet to be performed or already performed (*CCC*, 1780).

Conduct modeled on right principles, then, is needed to overcome ignorance, since it is pointless to make judgments of conscience without knowledge of the law or its precepts (cf. *VS*, 63).

Nevertheless, in rare cases, man is obligated to act immediately. In this circumstance, since he is unable to secure an informed moral judgment, he may do what he believes would correspond with God's will. To act rightly in this circumstance, he needs to be conscious of the following:

a. **Never do evil for good.**

b. **Love for God and neighbor overrides any other consideration.**

c. **Act towards others as we would like them to act towards us** (cf. CCC, 1789).

When asked why should man, in the final analysis, listen to his conscience, the Christian rightly affirms: conscience always obliges in the name of God. God wants us to follow his law. Hence, conscience is obliged to follow the divine will. Even the case of the invincible erroneous conscience does not give us an exception: in this case, conscience desires an evil, because it judges it to be a good and hopes to fulfill God's will. This capacity to err is one more reason to form our conscience correctly.

7. The Bible appeals to the conscience of man

The existence of conscience, besides having rational proofs, is also a fact proposed by revelation.

In fact, the Old Testament states that God seeks man's conscience: "He searches out the abyss, and the hearts of men" (Sir 42, 18). It teaches that the evil man, "distressed by conscience, . . . has always exaggerated the difficulties" (Wis 17, 11). Moreover, according to Eastern sensibilities, the Old Testament stresses the intimacy of conscience to the point of identifying it with the *heart*. So it counsels: "Let not loyalty and faithfulness forsake you; bind them about your neck, write them on the tablet of your heart" (Pr 3, 3).

In the New Testament the term "conscience" is mentioned thirty times in reference to the need for proper behavior. Thus, St. Paul blames the pagans for all their corruption, as "their conscience also bears witness" (Rm 2, 15). St. Paul encourages the Christians to carry out good conduct, "not only to avoid God's wrath but also for the sake of conscience" (Rm 13, 5), for they will have to give an account to God for their conscience (2 Cor 4, 2).

8. Proofs for the existence of conscience in every man

It is important, then, to give some arguments that prove the existence of moral conscience. The specific nature of the rational being, man, includes conscience. In fact, an essential characteristic of the person is his capacity to reflect, that is, to be conscious of his life and actions. This capacity is reflected in man in three ways:

a. Sense experience.

By it man is conscious of his own sensations of pleasure, pain, cold, heat, and so forth. At this primary level there exists, already, a difference between man and animal. As the Spanish philosopher Zubiri writes: "The animal senses, but it does not sense itself. . . ."

In fact, the reflective self is exclusive and proper to man. Animals sense heat, cold, pleasure, pain, and even the care or rejection of their master, but they do not experience it reflectively, but only instinctively. Thus, the animal acts automatically and always flies from the unpleasant, mechanically acting out what it desires at the moment.

b. **Rational discernment.**

The capacity to reflect and to acquire conscience is not exhausted by man's sensations, rather, it is raised to a higher intellectual level. Thus, when someone acts hastily, they are warned of the need to reflect so that they can be conscious of what they should know or do. The term *intellectual conscience* is often used to describe this faculty.

c. **Moral conscience.**

The reflection of man does not end in sensation nor in thought, rather it accompanies him in all his actions, so that before acting, man reflects on what he ought to do or whether or not it is advantageous to bring about a given effect. Moreover, he is conscious at the very moment of his actions and, once he has acted, later reflects on the good and evil of his actions. That is, he realizes or becomes conscious of the good and evil involved in his acts.

Consequently, the moral conscience in ethical behavior is as real as the sensual conscience or the rational conscience. Then, if an attempt is made to abolish it, the other two expressions of conscience will also have to be denied. Thus, the denial of moral conscience is impossible, absurd and dehumanizing, for it would destroy that which makes a man human.

In fact, any man can experience, for himself, that his actions are not indifferent but are always valued. In this regard, it is confirmed that conscience does not keep silent, for it praises and reprimands; it exhorts and corrects; it incites and represses (cf. *VS*, 57-58).

This fact shows that conscience exists and that it is never a mute witness; rather, it is present in all our actions. Occasionally, especially before grave acts, it presents itself in a strong fashion, for it is said to "bite-back", almost as if the evil conduct would turn back aggressively on the agent.

9. The relationship between conscience and law

Both in theory and in life, there can be confrontations between conscience and the moral law. These conflicts have occurred throughout time, but appear at the present time to be more numerous. This can occur because both elements are involved in morality, and a synthesis of both is needed. In our own time there is noticeable conflict because the previous age was characterized by a sometimes excessive stress on law while the current age overemphasizes personal conscience, which is often confused with feelings. When these two positions are taken to the extreme, they give rise to two opposing positions that are not easy to harmonize (cf. *VS*, 55).

If moral value is found solely in law, then we are confronted with a normative ethics, an excessive rule of laws and imperatives, where little room is left for conscience to value and judge. On the other hand, if conscience is overemphasized without regard for the precepts of law, then there is the risk of falling into moral subjectivism, where the conscience of the individual becomes the only moral judge.

In certain circumstances, this contrast of opinions reaches its extreme, thus creating two moral paths: an *autonomous* morality and a *heteronomous* morality. The first treats conscience as the only moral authority which professes an autonomy of man before any law. The latter enslaves conscience to an absolute dependence on norms. In fact, conscience and norm ought to assist one another.

Conscience serves as an *immediate norm of moral action*, so that the judgment of conscience is the immediate criterion for moral actions. But, at the same time, conscience does not create law; rather, it finds it and takes it as a guide. Conscience is not an autonomous guide nor an exclusive one in determining good and evil; on the contrary, in conscience there is a deeply inscribed *principle of obedience*. Thus, conscience has traditionally been called a *normed norm*, that is, the rule for acting, but whose measure is prescribed by the law (cf. *CCC*, 1786; *VS*, 60).

Consequently, a continual confrontation between conscience and law is not the best way to understand the morality of our actions. Furthermore, divine laws are so intimately united to the proper being of man that they are found very near to conscience. The conflict may arise in relation to certain unjust positive laws, especially civil law (abortion, sodomy etc.), but in such cases the value of right conscience prevails over an unjust law.

The ultimate reason for this conflict is frequently rooted in a change in the concept of law in modern society; instead of defining law as an ordinance of reason—which never is in conflict with conscience—law is often seen as the arbitrary will of government or authority. Obedience to the law then becomes slavery.

10. Distortion and degradation of personal conscience

"Conscience, as the judgment of an act, is not exempt from the possibility of error" (*VS*, 62). A person can also corrupt and distort his conscience in many ways and for many reasons. Although a substantial portion of errors stem from bad formation received at an early stage, a right conscience can still corrupt itself at a later stage by many other causes. The most common causes are those mentioned in the *Catechism of the Catholic Church:*

a. **Ignorance of Christ and his Gospel,**

b. **Bad example given by others,**

c. **Enslavement to one's passions,**

d. **Assertion of a mistaken notion of autonomy of conscience,**

e. **Rejection of the Church's authority and her teaching,**

f. **Lack of conversion and of charity.**

These can be at the source of errors of judgment in moral conduct (*CCC*, 1792).

The risks of distortion of conscience—along with the degradation of personal conduct—demand from each man, especially the Christian, a concern for individual conduct. At the same time, it stresses the need to attend to the proper means of forming the conscience.

In practice, a decisive way for the Christian to form his conscience is to follow the moral teachings of the Magisterium:

> Christians have a great help for the formation of conscience in the Church and her Magisterium. As the Council affirms: "In forming their consciences the Christian faithful must give careful attention to the sacred and certain teaching of the Church. . . . It follows that the authority of the Church, when she pronounces on moral questions, in no way undermines the freedom of conscience of Christians.
>
> This is so not only because freedom of conscience is never freedom "from" the truth but always and only freedom "in"

the truth, but also because the Magisterium does not bring to the Christian conscience truths which are extraneous to it; rather it brings to light the truths which it ought already to possess, developing them from the starting point of the primordial act of faith.

The Church puts herself always and only at the service of conscience, helping it to avoid being tossed to and fro by every wind of doctrine proposed by human deceit (cf. Eph. 4, 14), and helping it not to swerve from the truth about the good of man, but rather, especially in more difficult questions, to attain the truth with certainty and to abide in it (*VS*, 64).

Conclusion

Conscience is the practical judgment of reason which leads a person to perform or refrain from performing an action. As a faculty of reason, conscience must humbly seek the truth that is prior to it. Every person has the obligation to form his conscience according to the objective standards of good and evil that have been determined by God.

Man's highest ideal is to be faithful to right conscience since this equals being faithful to God and to himself. In a properly formed conscience lies a person's dignity and the means necessary to reach happiness. The pagan author and poet, Horace, states, "our inviolable rule ought to be never to do anything that wounds our conscience or that makes us ashamed of ourselves." The Magisterium of the Church is the most certain guide to the will of God, and must be consulted in educating one's conscience.

As a way of life, the words of St. Paul are worth noting: "Brethren, I have lived before God in all good conscience up to this day" (Acts 23, 1). The greatest happiness, according to popular thought, is to have a "clear conscience."

OUTLINE

I. Glossary

ANTECEDENT JUDGMENT OF CONSCIENCE:

Thought proceeds action; before acting, one deliberates whether it is good or evil.

AUTONOMOUS MORALITY:

Conscience as the only moral authority—self-government without any law.

CERTAIN CONSCIENCE:

Conscience that issues a judgment in certainty.

CONCOMITANT JUDGMENT OF CONSCIENCE:

The judgment that accompanies an action as it is taking place.

CONSCIENCE:

"Conscience is a judgment of reason whereby the human person recognizes the moral quality of a concrete act that he is going to perform, is in the process of performing, or has already completed" (CCC, 1778).

CONSEQUENT JUDGMENT OF CONSCIENCE:

The moral judgment done after the act.

DOUBTFUL CONSCIENCE:

Conscience that issues a judgment when there is doubt about a fact related to the act done or omitted, whether there is a law which prescribes or prohibits a certain action, or when the doubt is on the existence of such a law.

ERRONEOUS CONSCIENCE:

A judgment of conscience that does not correspond with what the law or norm requires. There are two types of erroneous conscience. The error may be *vincible* or *invincible* when the content of the law is unknown. He who acts with *invincible ignorance* does not sin, if he has taken the necessary steps to learn what is permitted and prohibited.

HETERONOMOUS MORALITY:

Absolute dependence of conscience on laws.

MORAL RECTITUDE:

Correctness of method of judgment.

II. Summary of Principles

1. One must always strive to act with a right conscience.

2. It is never permitted to act with a doubtful conscience. One must use reasonable means to resolve doubt about the morality of an act.

3. Negative doubt should not be considered when attempting an action.

4. An erroneous invincible conscience, when it permits what is objectively prohibited, does not sin.

5. An erroneous invincible conscience ought to be followed, lest one act against one's conscience.

6. Acting with a vincible, erroneous conscience is a sin.

7. Conscience is free, and it ought not be violated: God himself respects the freedom of the human person. But man is obligated to form a right conscience. He cannot neglect this responsibility without committing sin.

SUPPLEMENTARY READINGS

1. Conscience must be informed and moral judgment enlightened. A well-formed conscience is upright and truthful. It formulates its judgments according to reason, in conformity with the true good willed by the wisdom of the Creator. The education of conscience is indispensable for human beings who are subjected to negative influences and tempted by sin to prefer their own judgment and to reject authoritative teachings.

(CCC, 1783)

2. Conscience is a precious but delicate guide. Its voice is easily distorted or obscured. To dictate to conscience is to silence and, eventually, to destroy it. Conscience must be listened to and listened to sensitively. It needs to be interrogated, even to be cross-examined. And only those who habitually interrogate their conscience and are ready to pay heed even to its awkward answers, will not cheat their conscience or be cheated by it.

(Cormac Burke, *Conscience and Freedom*, 25)

3. First of all, an indispensable condition is the rectitude and clarity of the penitent's conscience. People cannot come to true and genuine repentance until they recognize that sin is contrary to the ethical norm written in their innermost being; until they admit that they have a personal and responsible experience of this contrast; until they say not only that "sin exists" but also "I have sinned", until they admit that sin has introduced a division into their conscience which then pervades their whole being and separates them from God and from their brothers and sisters. The sacramental sign of this clarity of conscience is the act traditionally called the examination of conscience, an act that must never be one of anxious psychological introspection, but a sincere and calm comparison with the interior moral law, with the evangelical moral norms proposed by the Church, with Jesus Christ himself who is our Teacher and Model of life, and with the heavenly Father, who calls us to goodness and perfection.

(*RP*, 31)

APPENDIX

Additional proofs for the existence of conscience

Besides the proof in section four of this chapter, there are other arguments which show that man is gifted with a moral conscience. They are the following:

a. **Profound personal experience.**

An argument can be made for the existence of conscience from the experience of each individual. Each man, in himself, experiences the voice of his conscience: conscience is the only witness. What occurs in the interior of the soul is hidden to those outside. Conscience directs its testimony only toward its owner. At the same time, only the person knows the proper response to the voice of conscience. Is anyone not aware of this invisible witness accompanying man? This fact, so intimately known, shows that conscience exists as a never silent witness present in all our activity.

b. Universal testimony.

The universal agreement of all times, cultures, and religious expressions is that conscience is the precondition needed to judge human acts as good or evil.

The most diverse ethical trends speak of conscience as a type of radar that detects good and evil, what man should do and avoid.

Present culture reflects the conviction noted above. The juridical acknowledgment of conscientious objection shows that conscience holds a high place in the modern notion of man's essence. It is seen as a fundamental right. In the end, those who pretend to deny conscience or imply that it is only a cultural prejudice of religion, expose their own hypocrisy and a true lack of sincerity.

QUESTIONS

1. What is conscience?
2. What are the means to forming a right conscience?
3. Why must conscience submit to truth and the natural law?
4. According to the Catechism, what are three functions of conscience?
5. What is a lax conscience?
6. What is a true, or correct, conscience?
7. What is an erroneous conscience?
8. What is a scrupulous conscience?
9. What are antecedent, concomitant and consequent judgments of conscience?
10. What are vincible and invincible ignorance?
11. What is right conscience?
12. In cases where one is obligated to act immediately, what are three rules must be followed?
13. List three proofs for the existence of conscience in man.

14. What is the relationship between conscience and law?

15. List five factors contributing to the degradation of conscience.

16. Why does one have the serious obligation to form conscience according to the teachings of the Magisterium of the Roman Catholic Church?

PRACTICAL EXERCISES

1. The word *conscience* appears thirty times in the New Testament. Explain the exact meaning of the sacred writers when they speak of conscience in three or four of the following instances:

   — Rm 2, 15; 13, 5;

   — 1 Cor 8, 12; 10, 27-29;

   — 2 Cor 1, 12; 5, 11;

   — 1 Tim 1, 19;

   — Heb 10, 22;

   — 1 P 3, 16; 3, 21.

2. What are some situations that might create problems for one's conscience?

3. Some of the causes of the moral crisis facing the Christian in the modern world are problems such as *materialism, hedonism, "the culture of death," pornography and sexual promiscuity.* What do each of these terms mean? How should a Christian conduct himself when confronted with some of these problems? Give specific examples to illustrate your answer.

4. Review Practical Exercise 1 from Chapter II. If one does not take care to form one's conscience according to true moral principles, is there not a danger that one will become like Adolf Hitler in his own life? Since conscience has the final word in moral judgments, couldn't one commit horrible crimes if he had not properly informed his conscience?

5. Reflect on instances in your own life in which conscience played a role in determining your response to a particular situation or problem, and describe how you responded in each situation. Include examples of both successes and failures.

CHAPTER V
ETHICAL NORMS, LAW

When in the course of human events, it becomes necessary for one people to dissolve the political bands which have connected them with another, and to assume among the Powers of the earth, the separate and equal station to which the Laws of Nature and of Nature's God entitle them, a decent respect to the opinions of mankind requires that they should declare the causes which impel them to the separation.

We hold these truths to be self-evident, that all men are created equal, that they are endowed by their Creator with certain unalienable Rights, that among these are Life, Liberty and the pursuit of Happiness;

That to secure these rights, Governments are instituted among Men, deriving their just powers from the consent of the governed;

That whenever any Form of Government becomes destructive of these ends, it is the Right of the People to alter or to abolish it, and to institute new Government, laying its foundation on such principles and organizing its powers in such form, as to them shall seem most likely to effect their Safety and Happiness.

(The Declaration of Independence)

Regarding our understanding of law, let us ask ourselves:

- What is the definition of law?

- What is the purpose of human laws in relation to the objective standards of the moral law as set forth by God?

- Are there different kinds of law, and do they make conflicting demands upon man's behavior?

- How are conflicts between conscience and law to be resolved?

Introduction

A common feature of life today is the claim that there are too many laws. Those who argue for more laws claim that the government is simply attempting to protect those who have no protection of law. On the other hand, those who argue for less law claim they are protecting the citizenry from too many laws which are taking away fundamental rights.

The purpose of law is to allow men in society a proper measure of freedom to protect their rights, and to remind them of their responsibilities to others. When the general populace is morally upright, there is a tendency not to enact laws, and when there is a tendency toward vice, the inclination is to enact many laws.

It should be obvious that if society is to function properly, there have to be laws to regulate man's social and personal conduct. Without laws, personal and social life would be reduced to mob rule, the law of the jungle.

1. Definition of law

Law is an ordinance of reason for the common good, promulgated by those who are in charge of the community. This definition illustrates the following properties of law:

a. Laws are an ordinance of reason.

Laws must always require something reasonable; they are supposed to protect objective values and are not something capricious stemming from the arbitrary will of authority. Laws seek to end any inconsistency on the part of either the legislator or subject.

b. Laws exist for the common good.

Laws seek a just society for all citizens, so they try to secure those conditions that promote the common good.

c. Laws are passed by those responsible for the care of the community.

Laws are executed by the one who has power to do so: that is, by legitimate authority. Only legitimate authority can make and pass laws.

d. Laws must be officially promulgated.

Laws need to be promulgated or communicated in an official manner to all subjects, for, before they are publicly known, they hold no legitimate power.

2. Division and kinds of law

There are different expressions of the moral law, all of them interrelated (cf. CCC, 1952):

a. **Eternal law.**

Eternal law "is nothing other than the plan of divine wisdom as directing all acts and movements" (St. Thomas Aquinas, *Summa theologiae*, II-I, q. 93, a. 1).

Briefly, eternal law is the cosmic order established by God. It is easy to recognize the existence of this law. The Greeks differentiated between chaos or confusion and cosmos or order. They called the universe cosmos, that is, an ordered thing.

In fact, all can acknowledge the harmony found in the world. Both the great planets and the minuscule atoms of matter reflect an admirable order. As the scientist who acknowledges that harmony calls it a law of nature, so the believer acknowledges its origin in God. The believer calls it eternal law; that is, he recognizes such order is not a product of chance or contingency, but was established by God.

> ... The supreme rule of life is the divine law, itself, the eternal objective and universal law by which God out of his wisdom and love, arranges, directs and governs the whole world and the paths of the human community. God has enabled man to share in this divine law, and hence man is able under the gentle guidance of God's providence increasingly to recognize the unchanging truth (*VS*, 43).

Eternal law has certain properties: it is the *first* law and it ought to be the starting point for all laws. It is the *foundation* of all law. It is *intrinsic*, since it orders interiorly by means of providence through which God governs the universe. It is *universal*, for it reaches out to each and every creature. Its purpose is to facilitate order and to establish harmony in the person and in the social order. Society, therefore, should see the order and harmony of the universe as a model of reference to God himself:

> The moral law presupposes the rational order, established among creatures for their good and to serve their final end, by the power, wisdom, and goodness of the Creator. All law finds its first and ultimate truth in the eternal law. Law is declared and established by reason as a participation in the providence of the living God, Creator and Redeemer of all (*CCC*, 1951).

b. **Natural law.**

Natural law "is nothing other than the rational creature's participation in the eternal law" (St. Thomas Aquinas, *Summa theologiae*, II-I, q. 91 a. 2).

Natural law is the eternal law, written in the heart of every human being, as it applies to the life of man. Since man is unique in his human nature (i.e., in his character, his intelligence and his freedom) it appears convenient to call this law the natural law. This helps to emphasize the fact that man surpasses both the cosmic world and the animal realm in his unique existence. So this law, which corresponds to his peculiar nature, is given the name natural law.

> But God provides for man differently from the way in which he provides for beings which are not persons. He cares for man not "from without", through the laws of physical nature, but "from within", through reason, which by its natural knowledge of God's eternal law is consequently able to show man the right direction to take in his free actions. . . . The natural law enters here as the human expression of God's eternal law (*VS*, 43).

In fact, man is not a chaotic being; rather harmony is reflected throughout his being. His bodily reality rests on the functioning order of all his organs and physical elements which constitute his body, so that if some disorder appears, illness will result. Thus, health means organic order, and death the rupture of that physical human order.

Also, in man there is a rich harmony reflected in his spiritual life. Intelligence and will contribute to man's spiritual character. But if there is any imbalance in the soul, then psychological abnormalities result. Sanity is harmony, while madness reflects inner disorder found in the soul of the person.

Man, besides being a living reality, is also an acting being: he not only exists, but he also acts. It should be obvious that man cannot be chaotic in his activity but is ruled by an order proper to his actions. The good man follows the norms governing his existence, while the morally evil man follows a morally disordered path (cf. *VS*, 50).

Consequently, the existence of natural law becomes self-evident; a knowledge of theology is not necessary to understand that murder, theft and adultery are wrong. Everyone just knows it (cf. Supplementary Readings 1-3). Everyone recognizes naturally that it would be contradictory to praise cosmic order and not to take into consideration the internal order of the human being. Also, it does not make sense to argue that all of man is ordered toward life and growth, but he is free to live a disordered life (cf. Supplementary Reading 4).

It is true that, while his body and soul are ruled by laws that are higher than himself, his conduct depends on his free will. And this is precisely what ethics demands: since man can direct his future, it is extremely important that he not act chaotically; rather, he ought to submit himself to those norms that will direct him to harmony and order, that is, to freedom.

> We will never fully understand Jesus' freedom. It is immense, infinite, as is his love. . . . Thus, we come to appreciate that freedom is used properly when it is directed toward the good. . . .
>
> Reject the deception of those who appease themselves with the pathetic cry of "Freedom! Freedom!" Their cry often masks a tragic enslavement, because choices that prefer error do not liberate. Christ alone sets us free, for he alone is the Way, the Truth, and the Life. . . .
>
> . . .Throughout my years as a priest, whenever I have spoken, or rather shouted, about my love for personal freedom, I have noticed some people reacting with distrust, as if they suspected that my defense of freedom could endanger the faith. Such fainthearted people can rest assured. The only freedom that can assail the faith is a misinterpreted freedom, an aimless freedom, one without objective principles, one that is lawless and irresponsible. In a word, license (Blessed Josemaría Escrivá, *Friends of God*, 26, 32).

Natural law has two basic characteristics:

- *universality*, which means it applies to everyone, and

- *immutability*, which means it cannot be changed. Its interpreter is the Magisterium, the pope and the bishops in communion with him.

To act against natural law is to oppose happiness, since such action damages human nature. On the other hand, to abide by natural law constitutes a foundation for a personal morality, and offers a channel to order social life, since it reveals the dignity of man. At the same time, it offers governments a base to formulate just laws that can regulate the common good of society:

> The natural law, the Creator's very good work, provides the solid foundation on which man can build the structure of moral rules to guide his choices. It also provides the indispensable moral foundation for building the human community. Finally, it provides the necessary basis for the civil law with which it is connected, whether by a reflection that draws conclusions from its principles, or by additions of a positive and juridical nature (CCC, 1959).

With all this in mind, it is important to state that there is no opposition between freedom and natural law:

> The natural law, thus understood, does not allow for any division between freedom and nature. Indeed, these two realities are harmoniously bound together, and each is intimately linked to the other (VS, 50).

It is important to distinguish between natural law and so-called *laws of nature*, such as the law of gravity. Laws of nature are not laws in the most precise meaning of the term, rather they are descriptions of the behavior of the material universe. A law is an ordinance of reason. A rock has no intellect and cannot know if to fall is according to its nature or not. A rock simply falls. Every human person, on the other hand, can come to know what is or isn't in accord with human nature. Natural law, then, is the command that human reason gives regarding what actions should be done (because they are in accord with human nature), and what actions should be avoided (because they are contrary to human nature).

c. **Positive law.**

Positive law is promulgated by those who have authority to do so. In moral theology, that proper authority can be either God or man, and in this case, it could be the hierarchy of the Church or the civil authority which is legitimately placed. These circumstances give rise to three kinds of positive laws:

- *Divine positive law* is legislated by God. For example, the precept of charity established by Jesus Christ. The Ten Commandments are another example of divine positive law, but they are also expressions of natural law.

- *Ecclesiastical positive law* emanates from the legislative power of the Church. For example, the fast in Lent or those laws that regulate a canonical marriage. The principal laws of the Church are found in its *Code of Canon Law.*

- *Civil positive law* is legislated by a legitimate government. For example, traffic laws or tax law. They can be found in the laws of each locality.

d. Evangelical or New Law.

This law is specifically Christian. As was stated in Chapter I, supernatural anthropology shows that the baptized is a "new man", a "new creature", since by Baptism man acquires a special likeness to God; St. Peter says, "[We] become partakers of the divine nature" (2 P 1, 4).

> The New Law is called a *law of love* because it makes us act out of the love infused by the Holy Spirit, rather than from fear; a *law of grace*, because it confers the strength of grace to act, by means of faith and the sacraments; a *law of freedom*, because it sets us free from the ritual and juridical observances of the Old Law, inclines us to act spontaneously by the prompting of charity and, finally, lets us pass from the condition of a servant who "does not know what his master is doing" to that of a friend of Christ—"For all that I have heard from my Father I have made known to you"— or even to the status of son and heir[1] (*CCC*, 1972).

It seems logical for the Christian to have a new law, since the new man also needs to maintain an order and harmony in his actions, based on the new way. So, the Christian, in keeping with this way of looking at life, should live a life ordered according to what he really is. The harmony and blend between act and the whole person can only be reached in this way.

This goal can be reached because the New Law is an interior law—law of the Spirit—and also an exterior one, since it is found in the Sermon on the Mount (cf. *CCC*, 1716-1717). This law guides the believer to his duty and also gives him the strength through grace to do it. Similarly, this "law of grace" confirms the ethical foundations of natural law and adds new precepts and teachings, as Jesus Christ explained in the Beatitudes (Mt 5, 17-48; 6, 1-24). Lastly, the New Law is the law of love which perfects freedom and culminates in eternal glorification, where love culminates.

The content of this new law responds to the obligation of the Christian to shape his life according to Jesus Christ. For this the Christian, with the aid of the Holy Spirit and the sacraments, needs to develop his life in grace, communicated in Baptism. Hence the different names: Law of grace or Law of the Spirit. And, since it attempts to dictate a life lived according to the Gospel, it is also called evangelical law.

3. Meaning and purpose of law

The morally good and evil proceed from the nature of things, and the effects of Original Sin in our human nature. Things do not become good or evil because we would like them to be, or because society says that something is acceptable or unacceptable. Understanding this will help man in his efforts to require and respect the rights and duties of each person.

In the final analysis, laws should correspond to God's will, who is the creator and knower of all that aids our human life. God is not arbitrary, but knows and indicates what is permitted or prohibited, because he knows what aids or harms man.

> The supreme rule of life is the divine law itself, the eternal, objective and universal law by which God out of his wisdom and love arranges, directs and governs the whole world and the paths of the human community. God has enabled man to share in this divine law, and hence man is able under the gentle guidance of God's providence increasingly to recognize the unchanging truth (DH, 3).

Consequently, good and evil have a foundation based on the truth. It is an evil to kill another person, not just because it is prohibited by law but because every man has the right to live. Similarly, it is an evil to blaspheme against God, because it offends the divine goodness and power, and not just because it is prohibited by the first commandment. It is also an evil to slander, because reputation belongs to the person, and not because society prohibits such actions.

The same could be said of the good. For example, to help return a criminal to society is a good, because it restores human dignity and not because society seeks to include marginal people. To give alms to one who needs them is a good, because by it charity is practiced and not because some organization requires it. To demand the fulfillment of a penalty is a good because it brings about justice, and not because society seeks to take revenge on criminals.

Law is a reasonable requirement of the legitimate authority to protect the dignity of man and the social order. In the case of divine precepts, its origin is in the fact that God knows what is good or evil for man and he warns him by a precept or law.

It should be clear from this chapter that a just law is a great good. It is a support which man uses to protect his own existence, for it offers him an extraordinary means to protect his personal and social being. Similarly, Christian moral life represents a light that points to the ethical values of the New Testament, so that the Christian is able to live a life worthy of a true follower of Jesus Christ.

4. Just law

St. Thomas Aquinas teaches that a law is just if it corresponds to the divine law. If it does, then it has the power to bind us in conscience, and to disobey such a law would be a sin. St. Thomas outlines the following conditions which must be met for a law to be just:

a. **It must promote the common good.**

A just law must seek the good of all the members of a society, and not just some of its members. By contrast, a law which seeks only the good of a certain segment of society while neglecting the needs of others would be unjust, as in the case of a law which required military service only of the poorer members of society while exempting the wealthy. A just law also must defend rights and promote the fulfilment of social duties without demanding what is impossible or extremely difficult to do.

b. **The burdens which the law imposes on society must reflect an "equality of proportion."**

This means that the burden of the law's fulfillment must be shared by all the members of society and not just some. A law which taxes the citizens of a society for social programs is just, but all members of that society must be taxed, and they should bear the burden of the tax in proportion to their ability to pay. To demand payment from someone who is incapable of paying is unjust.

c. **It must not exceed the power of its human authors.**

The law which is promulgated must correspond to the divine law. No human authority can declare what is morally evil to be morally good. For this reason, laws permitting slavery, abortion, euthanasia, divorce and "marriages" between persons of the same gender are immoral, and therefore unjust (St. Thomas Aquinas, *Summa theologiae*, I-II, q. 96, a. 5).

If any of these conditions are violated, the law is unjust. In such a case the old dictum, "An unjust law is no law at all," applies.

St. Augustine said that *every just law is transcribed and transferred to the heart of the man who works justice, not by wandering but by being, as it were, impressed upon it, just as the image from the ring passes over to the wax, and yet does not leave the ring* (De Trinitate, XIV, 15, 21: CCL 50/A, 451) .

5. Conflicts between conscience and law

Although conscience can be seen as a light to moral values, it does not fabricate such values, but takes them from objective reality. Thus, law offers conscience an extraordinary means to detect the morally good and evil. Hence, natural law, divine positive law, the norms of the Church, and civil legislation offer to conscience avenues of light to what is good and evil, just or unjust. Conscience gratefully accepts all that it is offered by law. And, if sincere, it listens to those teachers who instruct on what is to be done.

Obedience to law does not enslave conscience nor takes away from its autonomy, since truth never enslaves, rather it liberates: "The truth will set you free" (Jn 8, 32). Nor does it reduce its freedom, since laws are not foreign to man, but are part of his essential being. In regards to the precepts of natural law, St. Paul sees them as "written on their hearts" (Rm 2, 15). Above all, the New Law, by which Christianity governs, is also called, the law of the Spirit, insofar as it is found in the very soul of man and elevates him by virtue of the same grace; that is, the "new law is the same grace of the Holy Spirit that gives itself to the faithful of Christ" (St. Thomas Aquinas, *Summa theologiae*, I-II, q. 106, a. 1).

It is ordinary for an informed conscience to find with clarity what it ought to do and not do, so that there should be no need for conflicts between conscience and the law. It is unfortunately true, however, that unjust laws exist. How is the Christian to respond to the existence of such laws? Given that Christians have an obligation to bear witness to the truth, one is not bound in conscience to cooperate with an unjust law. In fact, there may be times when he is called upon by his conscience to actively oppose such a law.

Such actions should never be undertaken easily. Even among unjust laws, not all bear the same degree of moral evil (A law condoning slavery and unfair parking regulations do not have equally evil consequences.). At times, it may be necessary to permit a lesser evil or to yield one's rights for the sake of a greater good, namely, the avoidance of scandal or the prevention of public disturbances (cf. Matt 5, 38-41; St. Thomas Aquinas, *Summa theologiae*, I-II, q. 96, a. 5). The question which should be asked in such a case is "in what would the greater evil consist, submission to the law or the scandal and disturbance which would follow resistance to it?"

Laws which contravene the divine law and inflict serious injury upon the lives or dignity of the members of a society, however, cannot be cooperated with; they must be opposed and lawful means to overturn them must be sought. It is always important to remember that a concern for justice and resistance to evil must be balanced by Christian love for all people and a genuine respect for authority of civil government.

It is also true that, at times, a conflict arises not over the truth of a judgment of conscience or the justice of the precepts of the law, but over the difficulty of accepting and fulfilling what the law commands. Those who find constant conflicts in fulfilling various laws need to ask themselves if they are not lacking in consistency in regards to their faith and their Christian practice, for there can be no real conflict between divine laws and the conscience of man. What is required is responsibility and the desire to come to God for assistance, so that the person will sacrifice his unruly desires to the law of God.

Conclusion

Man ought to be always open to what has been given by law, since it is given in good faith and it will help him act rightly in life. The prudent man always acts in this way:

> The truth about the moral good, stated in the law of reason, is recognized practically and concretely by the *prudent judgment* of conscience. We call that man prudent who chooses in conformity with this judgment (CCC, 1780).

And, in regard to Christian precepts, the Christian is guided by St. John's words:

> Little children, let us not love in word or speech but in deed and in truth. By this we shall know that we are of the truth, and reassure our hearts before him whenever our hearts condemn us; for God is greater than our hearts, and he knows everything. Beloved, if our hearts do not condemn us, we have confidence before God; and we receive from him whatever we ask, because we keep his commandments and do what pleases him (1 Jn 3, 18-22).

On the other hand, it is never permitted to follow a law which is contrary to morality as given by Christ or his Church. Unjust laws give rise to the obligation to do what is possible to overturn them or minimally to attempt to reduce their force.

OUTLINE

I. Glossary

CIVIL LAW:

The law promulgated by legitimately constituted civil authority.

ECCLESIASTICAL LAW:

The law which directs the life and worship of the Church.

ETERNAL LAW:

The plan flowing from God's wisdom directing all acts and movements.

HUMAN LAW:

Law promulgated by human authority, either civil or ecclesiastical. In order to be legitimate, human law must be consistent with divine law, conform to the natural law and promote the good of society.

LAW (JUST LAW):

An ordinance of reason for the common good, corresponding to divine law and promulgated by one who has care of the community.

MORAL LAW:

The ethical norm revealed by God which imposes obligations on the conscience of man.

NATURAL LAW:

The rational creature's participation in eternal law.

POSITIVE LAW:

Laws created by human beings which enjoin specific obligations upon individuals (i.e., the ecclesiastical law requiring abstinence from meat on the Fridays of Lent, or a civil law mandating the payment of taxes) and bind in conscience insofar as they conform to the dictates of the divine and natural laws.

UNJUST LAW:

Human laws which contradict or fail to conform to divine and natural law. Such laws are never binding on a person's conscience, and must be opposed by conscientious objection.

II. Summary of Principles

1. Divine positive law and the natural law cannot be opposed.

2. Every man is born and remains subject to natural law.

3. "[The natural law] expresses the dignity of the human person and forms the basis of his fundamental rights and duties" (CCC, 1978).

4. "The natural law is immutable, permanent throughout history. The rules that express it remain substantially valid. It is a necessary foundation for the erection of moral rules and civil law (CCC, 1979)."

5. All who are subject to their jurisdiction must observe just human laws.

6. All and only the baptized, after their seventh birthday and with use of reason, are subject to Church law.

7. All law, by virtue of its legitimate origin-ecclesiastical or civil-imposes some obligation in conscience.

8. Only acts, whose action or omission contribute to the common good, can be subject to law.

9. The hierarchy of the Church, by virtue of power received from Christ Jesus and because of the social and public condition of the Church, can make laws that bind in conscience.

SUPPLEMENTARY READINGS

1. Nor did I think your orders were so strong
   that you, a mortal man, could overrun
   the gods' unwritten and unfailing laws.
   Not now, nor yesterday's, they always live,
   and no one knows their origin in time.
   So not through fear of any man's proud spirit
   would I be likely to neglect these laws,
   draw on myself the gods' sure punishment.

   (Sophocles, *Antigone*, ln. 452-460)

2. True law is right reason in agreement with nature; it is of universal application, unchanging and everlasting. . . . It is a sin to try to alter this law, nor is it allowable to attempt to repeal any part of it, and it is impossible to abolish it entirely. We cannot be freed from its obligations by senate or people, and we need not look outside ourselves for an expounder or interpreter of it.

   And there will not be different laws at Rome and at Athens, or different laws now and in the future, but one eternal and unchangeable law will be valid for all nations and at all times, and there will be one master and ruler, that is, God, over us all, for he is the author of his law, its promulgator, and its enforcing judge. Whoever is disobedient is fleeing from himself and denying his human nature, and by reason of this very fact he will suffer the worst penalties, even if he escapes what is commonly considered punishment.

   (Cicero, *De Republica*, III, 22)

3. Two things fill the mind with ever new and increasing admiration and awe, the more often and the more steadily we reflect

on them: the starry heavens above and the moral law within. I have not to search for them and conjecture them. . . . I see them before me and connect them directly with the consciousness of my existence. The former begins from the place I occupy in the external world of sense. . . . The second begins from my invisible self, my personality, and exhibits me in a world which has true infinity, but which is traceable only by the understanding.

(I. Kant, *Critique of Practical Reason*, Part II, Conclusion [312-313] p. 260)

4. . . . Rather was it intended that man alone might have something to glory of, in that he alone had been worthy to receive from God a law: and that, as a rational animal, capable of understanding and knowledge, he might be held in restraint by that rational liberty besides, being subject to God who had to him made all things subject.

(Tertullian, *Against Marcion*, II, 4)

5. Deep within his conscience man discovers a law which he has not laid upon himself but which he must obey. Its voice, ever calling him to love and to do what is good and to avoid evil, tells him inwardly at the right moment: do this, shun that. For man has in his heart a law inscribed by God. His dignity lies in observing this law, and by it he will be judged.

(*GS*, 16)

6. This becomes even clearer if one considers that the highest norm of human life is the divine law itself—eternal, objective and universal, by which God orders, directs and governs the whole world and the ways of the human community according to a plan conceived in his wisdom and love. God has enabled man to participate in this law of his so that, under the gentle disposition of divine providence, many may be able to arrive at a deeper and deeper knowledge of unchangeable truth. . . .

. . . It is through his conscience that man sees and recognizes the demands of the divine law.

(*DH*, 3)

7. No believer will wish to deny that the teaching authority of the Church is competent to interpret even the natural moral law. It is, in fact, indisputable, as our predecessors have many times de-

clared, that Jesus Christ, when communicating to Peter and to the apostles his divine authority and sending them to teach all nations his commandments, constituted them as guardians and authentic interpreters of all the moral law, not only, that is, of the law of the Gospel, but also of the natural law, which is also an expression of the will of God, the faithful fulfillment of which is equally necessary for salvation.

(HV, 4)

APPENDICES

1. Legal positivism

Legal (or juridical) positivism is a concept of law that looks exclusively to existing laws or to those that have existed previously for evaluating a situation. Within the concept is an explicit desire to exclude any supernatural or metaphysical basis for law, replacing it with the study of laws already enacted in a particular time and place. The authority of law, therefore, exists within the power of the existing State which promulgates them.

The question that positivism raises is whether these laws or norms are legitimate by the mere fact that they have been issued by a secular authority. Christianity, and more exactly, Catholicism, says no. Since the State has the power to command according to reason, the obligatory source of law must emanate from the natural order, which has God as its source and ultimate end (cf. Pope John XXIII. *PT,* n. 47).

Positivists deify the State by reducing moral compulsion to the will of the lawmaker. This theory attributes a gross majesty to the enactment of purely human laws, eventually separating law from morality. Without a guiding natural law the will of the legislator must find its principles in the collective vote of the majority. As such, positive law may deviate from right reason and end up doing violence to the natural order because it has placed moral compulsion in the hands of legislators, who may or may not be virtuous (cf. St. Thomas Aquinas, *Summa theologiae,* q. 93, a. 3, ad 2).

Catholicism responds by affirming that all legitimate human authority derives from the natural law. The natural law originates from God and guides man to right action. How do we know this law? St.

Paul tells us that it is the law "written in our hearts" (cf. Rm 2, 15) and discernible by the use of reason. Human beings, created in the image and likeness of God, have this knowledge as part of their nature. We are, so to speak, "wired for the truth". Enactments by the State, then, must pattern their legal commands upon the divine plan (cf. Edward J. Murphy, "The Sign of the Cross and Jurisprudence," *Notre Dame Law Review*, May/June 1996, 581).

If one recognizes that God is the author of all life and the only one with true authority to ordain how it should be lived then this will indeed influence one's views on abortion, euthanasia, capital punishment, homosexuality, *in vitro* fertilization, and many other issues (cf. Ibid., 582). The Church is a sure guide in resolving these issues through its divine mandate as teacher and in its reflection on God's "positive" law found in the Bible. As such, one must critique human law in light of what is known of the law of God (Ibid.).

2. Freedom and the Law of God

Man, as the living image of God, is willed by his Creator to be ruler and lord. Saint Gregory of Nyssa writes that "God made man capable of carrying out his role as king of the earth. . . . Man was created in the image of the One who governs the universe. Everything demonstrates that from the beginning man's nature was marked by royalty. . . . Man is a king. Created to exercise dominion over the world, he was given a likeness to the king of the universe; he is the living image who participates by his dignity in the perfection of the divine archetype."

Called to be fruitful and multiply, to subdue the earth and to exercise dominion over other lesser creatures (cf. Gn 1, 28), man is ruler and lord not only over things but especially over himself, and in a certain sense, over the life which he has received and which he is able to transmit through procreation, carried out with love and respect for God's plan. Man's *lordship* however is not absolute, but *ministerial:* it is a real reflection of the unique and infinite lordship of God. Hence man must exercise it with *wisdom and love,* sharing in the boundless wisdom and love of God. And this comes about through obedience to God's holy Law: a free and joyful obedience (cf. Ps 119) born of and fostered by an awareness that the precepts of the LORD are a gift of grace entrusted to man always and solely for his good, for the preservation of his personal dignity and the pursuit of his happiness.

(EV, 52.3)

3. More on freedom and the Law of God

Consequently, there is a need to recover the *basic elements of a vision of the relationship between civil law and moral law,* which are put forward by the Church, but which are also part of the patrimony of the great juridical traditions of humanity.

Certainly *the purpose of civil law* is different and more limited in scope than that of the moral law. But "in no sphere of life can the civil law take the place of conscience or dictate norms concerning things which are outside its competence," which is that of ensuring the common good of people through the recognition and defense of their fundamental rights, and the promotion of peace and of public morality. The real purpose of civil law is to guarantee an ordered social coexistence in true justice, so that all may "lead a quiet and peaceable life, godly and respectful in every way" (1 Tim 2, 2).

Precisely for this reason, civil law must ensure that all members of society enjoy respect for certain fundamental rights which innately belong to the person, rights which every positive law must recognize and guarantee. First and fundamental among these is the inviolable right to life of every innocent human being. While public authority can sometimes choose not to put a stop to something which – were it prohibited – would cause more serious harm, it can never presume to legitimize as a right of individuals – even if they are the majority of the members of society – an offense against other persons caused by the disregard of so fundamental a right as the right to life.

The legal toleration of abortion or of euthanasia can in no way claim to be based on respect for the conscience of others, precisely because society has the right and the duty to protect itself against the abuses which can occur in the name of conscience and under the pretext of freedom.(*EV,* 71)

QUESTIONS

1. What is the purpose of law?

2. What are the four properties of law?

3. What are the conditions for a just law?

4. What is eternal law? What are the properties of eternal law?

6. What is natural law? What are the two basic characteristics of natural law?

7. What is the difference between natural law and laws of nature?

8. What is positive law?

9. Why could there be no objective morality, valid for all, if that morality were not founded in the law of God?

PRACTICAL EXERCISES

1. Upon what does Antigone base her argument to disobey the king (whom she is addressing) in Supplementary Reading 1? Now compare Supplementary Readings 1 and 6. What truth, identified in this chapter, are both Antigone and the bishops of the Second Vatican Council defending in their statements?

2. Summarize and explain the characteristics of natural law, according to Cicero.

3. List the characteristic qualities of natural law as described by the *Catechism of the Catholic Church* (CCC 1954-1960).

4. What are some civil and ecclesiastical laws that oblige one in conscience? Why are they obligatory?

5. Why does the Magisterium have the authority and duty to interpret natural law?

6. Some people claim that law and freedom are mutually exclusive. How would you persuade them that law and freedom complement each other?

7. In 1854, the United States Supreme Court decided that Dred Scott, an African-American and a slave, was not a human being, but the property of his "owner". What arguments would you use to refute this decision? Would you appeal to a positivist understanding of law? Would you appeal to natural law? What other decisions of the Supreme Court neglect to consider natural law?

CHAPTER VI
MORALITY AND ACTION

On August 6, 1945, an American B-29 dropped the first atomic bomb on Hiroshima, Japan. Three days later another American plane dropped a second bomb on Nagasaki. It is estimated that more than 120,000 civilians were killed in these attacks. The Japanese government soon surrendered, and World War II was brought to a close.

This first use of nuclear weapons is often justified by arguing that to otherwise end the war the United States would have had to invade the home Islands of Japan. In such an invasion, American casualties were expected to near one million, and Japanese casualties would have certainly been two to three times as high. It is claimed that the destruction of the two cities was the right thing to do, because in the end the total number of lives lost was lower.

This case reflects the sources from which the morally good and evil flow or spring forth. These principal elements determine from the moral perspective whether an act is good or evil. And so we can ask ourselves to consider the following:

Consider the following questions:

• Was the use of atomic bombs on Hiroshima and Nagasaki morally justifiable?

• Could there have been an alternate solution?

• What factors must be taken into account when determining the morality of a course of action?

Introduction

In a sense, human lives can be compared to a canvas on which a picture is to be painted. On the day a person is born he is presented with a blank canvas on which others, parents and relations will paint for the first year or so. Sometime during the second year of life, the person begins to add some paint himself. From two to age six, more or less, he is adding the paint of personal responses to different situations. For the most part the colors are bright ones indicating the joys of growing up. Around age six, there is a definite change, for the child begins to make choices between good and evil. With the beginning of school he becomes more formally aware of the rules of right and wrong which guide life. From this point forward the painting will be mainly the work of the individual person, so it can be said that at the end of life, each person has a painting which reflects the choices, both good and bad, which have been made during life: reds, whites, yellows, and blues for the good choices, and grays, blacks, and purples for the evil choices which made up his or her life. Since the colors of the paint represent his choices, it can truly be said that in reality, the choices he makes to a large extent determine the portrait he has painted.

1. Human acts

Since human acts are involved in making choices regarding right and wrong, it is best to review a human act. A human act is one done with knowledge and consent. Man chooses to do or not to do, while animals respond to instinct. Since human actions involve the use of the intellect and will, those acts which do not do so can be called nonhuman actions: breathing, sneezing, etc. It should be obvious that a human act is one which is preceded by knowledge, for to be able to choose there must be a choice between one thing and another. A human act may be good or evil. Intrinsically evil acts are those which are always wrong in all circumstances such as abortion, divorce, sodomy, etc.

2. Components of the moral choice

A moral choice involves three elements: the act, the circumstances, and what a person intends by the act. This doctrine is captured in the Catechism of the Catholic Church in the following words:

> A *morally good* act requires the goodness of the object, of the end, and of the circumstances. . . . The object, the intention, and the circumstances make up the three "sources" of the morality of human acts (*CCC*, 1755, 1757; cf. *VS*, 74).

The sources or principles of a moral act are the object, the end or intention, and the circumstances. All three elements need to be considered in order to determine whether an act is morally good or evil.

To evaluate the goodness or malice of an act, it is necessary to consider the act being done (object), the intention in mind (end), and the different conditions surrounding the act (circumstances). But these three elements do not have the same importance. The roles played by the object and the end, which are the primary moral elements, are different from each other and from the circumstances, which only shape the prior elements in a lesser manner. As we begin the study of the morality of individual acts, remember that Christian morality aims at being the best that a person can be in all situations. For a Christian, doing the moral minimum is never enough.

> "Will any one of you, who has a servant plowing or keeping sheep, say to him when he has come in from the field, 'Come at once and sit down at table'? Will he not rather say to him, 'Prepare supper for me, and gird yourself and serve me, till I eat and drink; and afterward you shall eat and drink'? Does he thank the servant because he did what was commanded? So you also, when you have done all that is commanded you, say, 'We are unworthy servants; we have only done what was our duty'" (Lk 17, 7-10).

A key element in doing good and avoiding evil, therefore, is being disposed to do the best that can be done in all situations.

After the discussion of the moral act, some other ethical systems which are based on false premises and have been rejected as false by the Church will be discussed.

3. The object

The *object* is the act or action done. The object determines the morality of an act; thus, it is not moral to steal, lie, blaspheme, etc. On the contrary it is good to tell the truth, be just, and respect God's name. The human act receives its goodness or malice primarily from the object and the nature of the act itself, not from the intention. For example, adultery is always an evil by its object, independently of the purpose of the one who does it. So, when the moral object is in itself an absolute evil, the action in question is an intrinsically evil act (cf. Supplementary Reading 2).

By their objects acts can be either good or evil. As the encyclical *Veritatis splendor* teaches:

> The morality of the human act depends primarily and fundamentally on the "object" rationally chosen by the deliberate will, as is borne out by the insightful analysis, still valid today, made by Saint Thomas (*VS*, 78).

4. The intention or end

While the object is the matter of the human act, the *end* refers to the subject or person: the end is the motive or intention for which a person commits a good or evil act. Thus, for example, a thousand dollars can be given to aid someone, but it can also be given out of vanity in order to be praised, which would change the act to an evil act because of its evil end or intention.

It is common to find different ends: one can be the determining factor while the others concur with the action, without being decisive. Such can be the case of the gift of a thousand dollars, which reduces poverty, while at the same time raising the status of the donor in the eyes of society (Mt 6, 2-4). In this case, the person donating the money wishes to aid the poor and merely accepts the honor without seeking it by intention.

If the object of an act is evil, and, at the same time, has an evil end, then the malice of the act increases. This is reflected in the case of slander where the end is to deny someone a significant post: to slander is added an injustice of causing him to lose an important position.

On the other hand, an intrinsically evil act cannot be made good simply by the end sought. For example, a poor man may not rob a bank to secure funds to save his mother from cancer "And why not do evil that good may come?" (Rm 3, 8). The Magisterium also addresses this issues (cf. *VS*, 79).

5. Circumstances

The word *circumstance* comes from the Latin *circum-stare*, that is, what stands around; in other words, those situations that concur with the act and that contribute to the morality of the act.

Six have traditionally been cited:

a. Who?

The subject acting; a lie said by a child and one said by a governor carry different moral weight.

b. What?

The thing done; it is more serious to steal a sacred object than it is to steal an ordinary one, although they may have the same monetary value.

c. Where?

The circumstance of the place; a sin in public is different from a sin in private.

d. Why?

Considers either the immediate reasons for performing a particular action, e.g. I stole the film because my boss was out of town, or some additional purpose that a sinner may have for committing this sin, e.g. I lied because she had previously hurt me in some other way.

e. How?

Refers to the manner in which the act is done; for example, a crime done with premeditation and treachery.

f. When?

Time affects the morality of an act; for example, abstinence in Lent; also the duration of an act: it is not the same to get angry for a moment and plan to be angry for a long time.

Although the repeated commission of venial sins in itself does not make mortal sin, venial sin does weaken a person's resistance to mortal sin. For example, the habit of pilfering small items from the workplace diminishes the person's love of justice, and readies the pilferer to commit more serious injustices. Or, stealing items that are dedicated for Church use, such as a chalice or other sacred vessel, is a circumstance that aggravates the theft by adding the sin of sacrilege, or the profanation of something dedicated to the service of God. Sometimes the circumstances of a venial sin produce the more serious sin of scandal, as when a person who holds authority commits a transgression in a circumstance that leads others to imitate his bad example.

Not all circumstances influence the morality of an act in the same manner. Some circumstances actually lessen the gravity of a sin. Obviously, to steal a bottle of water from a well-stocked canteen is not the same offence as to steal the last supply of water from a person stranded in the desert. Or, to lie so as to protect an innocent person from serious harm, even death, is not the same thing as to lie so as to inflict harm on an innocent person. But no circumstance can alter the intrinsic evil of a bad action, and so every lie compromises the good of human communication and the truth speaking that makes it possible:

> Circumstances of themselves cannot change the moral
> quality of acts themselves; they can make neither good nor
> right an action that is in itself evil (*CCC*, 1754).

Or, as *Veritatis splendor* teaches, "particular circumstances can
diminish their evil, but they cannot remove it" (*VS*, 81).

For an act to be morally good, the object of the act, the intention
behind it, and the circumstances surrounding it must all be good.
"A morally good act requires the goodness of its object, of its end,
and of its circumstances together" (*CCC*, 1760). Once again it must
be emphasized that care has to be taken that the study of the components of the moral act does not lead to a mind-set which seeks
to do the moral minimum in a given situation. For instance, a discussion of how to help the poor should not lead to determining the
least a person has to give. The best way to approach moral choices
is by having a determination to always do the best possible that can
be done in a given situation.

These sources must always be on our minds when we confront
an action. We must analyze every act in all the points: the act itself
(*object*), the ends sought (*intention*), and the different conditions surrounding the act (*circumstances*). In this regard, the teachings of the
encyclical *Veritatis splendor* are very clear (cf. *VS* 74-78).

6. The moral categories of good and evil are objective

Unfortunately, after an era in which morality was actively involved in evaluating all acts, ethical doctrine has undergone a historical period in which the reality of the morally good and evil has been
denied. It is common to find many who acknowledge the existence of
good and evil, but few see these divisions as objective. They see them
instead as corresponding to the different circumstances of an individual, and thus susceptible to change.

It is said that an action is good or evil in a particular circumstance
and for a particular person. So it is said, "What is evil for you, may
be good for me," or "What is good today, can be evil tomorrow,"
and vice versa. With this attitude, the moral categories of good and
evil lose their objectivity and are turned into variables.

This train of thought leads to a moral relativism (morality
changes with each new situation) that destroys any true ethical system, since it denies any moral divisions of acts into good and evil.

This ethics is called *moral relativism,* where good and evil are relative terms (cf. *VS,* 33).

The causes behind this ethical relativism are many and complex. They relate to cultural influences and to different philosophical ideas.

7. History shows that certain moral goods and evils are always judged as either good or evil

Relativism is simply false. A basketball is a basketball. It cannot be changed into a baseball by giving it to a pitcher and telling him to throw it. Similarly, blasphemy is always blasphemy, and it can't be changed into something else by calling it something else. Blasphemy done by an unbeliever or a believer is still blasphemy, though the degree of guilt is different for the believer. The same is true with charity. Whether it is done by a Christian or by an unbeliever, it is always charity, though an action which is done out of supernatural motives is more praiseworthy than one which is done for purely human reasons.

The same issue of relativism is found in morality. In this, one must make a distinction: there is more objectivity in the case of moral values than there is with things in general because the moral value or worth of good and evil is founded on the word of God.

History can attest to this: there are acts that have transcended time and are seen as heroic by all; such is the case of the love of enemy exemplified by the saints. Also, there are acts that have been considered as evil from the beginning of time. Who could deny that an injustice done to an innocent person, slander done to an honorable person or homicide are not morally objective evils, independent of any personal opinion or historical circumstance?

As has been shown, circumstances can be a significant factor in judging the goodness or malice of an act, but never does the morally good or evil depend solely on the circumstances.

8. Some errors derived from ethical relativism

This error in moral theology has given rise to different erroneous and deficient theories. The most common are the following: situation ethics, consequentialism and proportionalism.

a. **Situation ethics.**

Situation ethics maintains that moral good and evil result from the situation in which the person finds himself. Hence, it is said that the act cannot be judged alone, but only in its circumstances. It is also called *circumstantial ethics*. For example: John decided not to get drunk on Friday night since he was driving, but on Saturday he got drunk because he was home and no one would be hurt by his action. Thinking that he acted morally in not driving drunk, he has ignored the question of the morality of drunkenness itself.

Situation ethics tries to respond to the life of each individual; thus it claims that moral conduct cannot be guided by universal principles. Rather, moral conduct must be guided by the concrete circumstances in which each person finds himself. This doctrine, in its origins, was described by Pope Pius XII in the following words:

> The characteristic of this morality is that it is not based, in any way, in universal moral laws—as are, for example, the Ten Commandments— but in the conditions or circumstances, real and concrete, in which the action takes place and according to which each individual conscience judges and chooses. A particular state of things is unique and valid for each human action. The particular decision of the conscience—state the defenders of this ethic—cannot be directed by universal ideas, principles and laws (Pius XII, *Discourse,* June 18, 1952, n. 4).

The Pope also explains the objection which had motivated the error: How is it possible to apply a universal law to each person when they are all in different circumstances?

> It will be asked in what way can the moral law, which is universal, apply to and even be obligatory for a particular case, which in its concrete situation is always unique and happens only once. It can and it does because, precisely as a result of its universality, the moral law comprehends necessarily and intentionally all of the particular cases, in which its concepts are verified. And in these innumerable cases it acts with such conclusive logic that even the conscience of simple faith perceives immediately and with full certainty the decision that must be made (Pius XII, *Discourse,* June 18, 1952, n. 9).

What has to be realized is that God has given us moral principles which anticipate every moral act.

b. Consequentialism.

Situation ethics practically disappeared from Catholic morality after the condemnation of Pius XII. But, a new theory followed, which is also held by some moral theologians. Those theologians derive the moral concepts of good and evil from the consequences that follow an act, and not from the objectivity of the law which determines them. For consequentialism an act is good if goodness results from the act; and if evil results from the action, then the act is evil.

This theory was originally applied in the social realm when Max Weber, its inventor, distinguished between ethics of responsibility and social ethics. The latter is exercised by a man who is guided by conscience, while the former ought to be followed by one who keeps the consequences of his actions in mind. The error was to argue there were situations in which consequences could justify acts evil in themselves.

For example, suppose that a young man pressured his girlfriend into procuring an abortion because they are both young and have very little money with which to support a child, and have discovered through pre-natal tests that the child will be born severely handicapped. He argues that it is better to abort the child because, in this way, the child will not suffer a life of pain, their families will not be burdened by the child's handicap, and they will not have to face the huge financial burden of caring for a handicapped child. For the consequentialist, this action is morally justified because he judges the consequences which will result from his actions to be good.

Slowly this doctrine spread to other levels until it reached all the dimensions of human activity. According to its advocates, the purpose is to create a moral responsibility so that man always keeps in mind the consequences of his actions. If the consequences will be evil, then the action ought to be avoided; but if there are good effects, the act can be done even if the act itself is evil.

There are at least three errors in consequentialism:

- The effects are overvalued, so that it ignores the principle set by St. Paul: never do the evil to bring about a good (cf. Rm 3, 8).

- It justifies the morality of means, regardless of their nature, and violates the basic moral principle, "the end does not justify the means."

- The question can be raised: good follows for whom? It could happen that the advocate of consequentialism may consider those consequences that are good for him, but not good for another person or for society. Thus, the advocates of this ethical system can use immoral means, or seek immediate personal gain, and, in the end, become egotistical. The fact that it is also known as ethics of intention makes even clearer its fundamental flaw, since good intentions do not justify immoral acts. Besides, who can measure the intention of an individual?

c. **Proportionalism.**

Proportionalism is a variation of consequentialism. It seeks to justify the morality of an act by the proportion of the effects that follow it. If the evil that follows is less in proportion to the good, then the act is good. And if the evils are greater in proportion to the goods, then the act is evil and, therefore, to be avoided.

Returning to the earlier example of abortion, suppose that the young man in question pressured his girlfriend into procuring an abortion with the argument that the scandal of unmarried pregnancy would be avoided, their reputations would not be destroyed and she would not be forced to drop out of school or to give up her plans to go to college or to pursue a chosen career path. Pope John Paul II has addressed this proportionalist approach to the morality of abortion in the following words:

> It is often claimed that the life of an unborn child or a seriously disabled person is only a relative good: according to a proportionalist approach or one of sheer calculation, this good should be compared with and balanced against other

goods. It is even maintained that only someone present and
personally involved in a concrete situation can correctly judge
the goods at stake: consequently, only that person would be
able to decide on the morality of his choice. The State, therefore, in the interest of civil coexistence and social harmony,
should respect this choice, even to the point of permitting
abortion and euthanasia (*EV,* 68.2).

The same negative judgment given to consequentialism is applied to this system, since it is derived from it. Furthermore,
the judgment is stronger, since good and evil are valued "pro-
portionally," as if they could simply be measured in a balance. This method trivializes the importance of morality and
many rights can be undermined. For example: Edward
burned down his business to get money to buy better, faster
equipment with the argument that insurance companies are
not persons so no one was hurt, and the fire had saved his
employees' jobs.

It is important to know that neither the circumstances nor the
good results are the criteria for morality. If this were the case, there
would always be a circumstance not to forgive; or an end that would
justify stealing; or an innumerable list of goods that follow an unjust act. A morality based on such criteria would be vulnerable to
profound changes that would destroy the moral concepts of good
and evil.

These risks, in themselves, show that the ethical criteria defended
by these systems are not valid. Thus, these errors are rejected by the
Catechism of the Catholic Church:

> It is therefore an error to judge the morality of human acts
> by considering only the intention that inspires them or the
> circumstances (environment, social pressure, duress or
> emergency, etc.) which supply their context. There are acts
> which, in and of themselves, independently of circum-
> stances and intentions, are always gravely illicit by reason
> of their object; such as blasphemy and perjury, murder and
> adultery. One may not do evil so that good may result from
> it (*CCC,* 1756).

This same teaching is stressed by *Veritatis splendor:*

> One must therefore reject the thesis, characteristic of teleologi-
> cal and proportionalist theories, which holds that it is impos-
> sible to qualify as morally evil according to its species—its

"object"—the deliberate choice of certain kinds of behavior or specific acts, apart from a consideration of the intention for which the choice is made or the totality of the foreseeable consequences of that act for all persons concerned (*VS*, 79).

Conclusion

It is important to be aware that the errors discussed in this chapter are fashionable because they contain an element of truth. It is true that circumstances are important, but the crucial fact which must be remembered is that man has a final end, which is eternal life with God. If every choice was made with this end in mind, moral choices would be easier. Likewise, one cannot reduce morality to a kind of mathematical formula in which actions are justified because "the proportion of good outweighs the amount of evil."

A society that guides itself by efficiency or utility is tempted to reduce the freedom of man, as the arguments used to justify abortion demonstrate, for they are a mix of these three false ethical positions of situation ethics, consequentialism and proportionalism.

Man has the opportunity to serve God or serve himself. It is in the specific moral choices which he makes that man directs himself to his final end, paradise with God. An evil act cannot be made good by a good intention. The rule to keep in mind is that no good, however great, may be sought by committing an evil act.

OUTLINE

I. Glossary

CONSEQUENTIALISM:

An ethical system that determines good and evil from the consequences that follow an act.

CIRCUMSTANCES:

The moral conditions which are added to and modify the moral nature of an action. Circumstances can increase or lessen the seriousness of morally evil actions, but they cannot make them morally good.

END (OF AN ACTION):

The good or evil which results naturally from an action (See Object below).

FUNDAMENTAL OPTION:

The free and responsible choice a person makes to orient, in a radical manner, his whole existence in a moral direction toward good or evil.

HUMAN ACTS:

Actions which are performed with deliberation and free choice. Actions which are involuntary, or which are performed without the use of reason or under compulsion are not human actions. Only properly human actions can be moral or immoral.

MORAL RELATIVISM:

There are no absolute truths. Morality changes with each new situation.

OBJECT (OF AN ACTION):

The moral nature of the action which one performs. The object of an action should not be confused with the *intention* which a person has when performing the act.

PROPORTIONALISM:

An ethical system that deduces the moral value of an act from the proportion of good and evil effects.

RATIONALISM:

The doctrine that rejects supernatural revelation and makes reason the sole source of knowledge.

SITUATION ETHICS:

An ethical theory that derives good and evil from the circumstances that accompany the acting agent.

II. Summary of Principles

1. The morality of human acts depends upon the object, the intention, and the circumstances.

2. An act is morally good when the object, intention, and circumstances are good.

3. An act is evil when one of the three elements is evil.

4. An act evil in itself is not justified by a good intention.

5. Moral good and evil never depend solely upon the circumstances.

6. Evil may never be done to obtain a good result.

7. The end does not justify the means, even if the end is good.

8. Some concrete acts are always wrong because their choice entails a disorder of the will, that is, a moral evil. One may not do evil so that good may result from it.

SUPPLEMENTARY READINGS

1. The problem of truth to which I have briefly alluded is only a single example. The same situation arises in the case of the moral and juristic standard which is supposed to regulate our wills, as truth regulates our thought. Goodness and justice, if they are what they claim to be, must necessarily be unique. Justice which is only just for a certain time, or for a certain race, cancels its own meaning. In ethics and law, then, too, the principles of relativism and rationalism arise, as they do also in art and religion. This is as much as to say that the problem of truth is dispersed throughout all the spiritual orders which we imply when we use the word, "culture."

(Jose Ortega y Gasset, *The Modern Theme*, p.37)

2. Reason attests that there are objects of the human act which are by their nature "incapable of being ordered" to God, because they radically contradict the good of the person made in his image. These are the acts which, in the Church's moral tradition, have been termed "intrinsically evil" (intrinsece malum): they are such always and per se, in other words, on account of their very object, and quite apart form the ulterior intentions of the one acting and the circumstances. Consequently, without in the least denying the influence on morality exercised by circumstances and especially by intentions, the Church teaches that "there exist acts

which per se and in themselves, independently of circumstances, are always seriously wrong by reason of their object. . . .

In teaching the existence of intrinsically evil acts, the Church accepts the teaching of Sacred Scripture. The Apostle Paul emphatically states: "Do not be deceived: neither the immoral, nor idolaters, nor adulterers, nor sexual perverts, nor thieves, nor the greedy, nor drunkards, nor revilers, nor robbers will inherit the Kingdom of God" (1 Cor 6, 9-10).

(VS, 80-81)

3. In reality, it is precisely the fundamental option which in the last resort defines a person's moral disposition. But it can be completely changed by particular acts, especially when, as often happens, these have been prepared for by previous more superficial acts. Whatever the case, it is wrong to say that particular acts are not enough to constitute mortal sin.

(PH, 10)

4. In any case, in the democratic culture of our time it is commonly held that the legal system of any society should limit itself to taking account of and accepting the convictions of the majority. It should therefore be based solely upon what the majority itself considers moral and actually practices. Furthermore, if it is believed that an objective truth shared by all is *de facto* unattainable, then respect for the freedom of the citizens – who in a democratic system are considered the true rulers – would require that on the legislative level the autonomy of individual consciences be acknowledged. Consequently, when establishing those norms which are absolutely necessary for social coexistence, the only determining factor should be the will of the majority, whatever this may be. Hence every politician, in his or her activity, should clearly separate the realm of private conscience from that of public conduct.

As a result we have what appear to be two diametrically opposed tendencies. On the one hand, individuals claim for themselves in the moral sphere the most complete freedom of choice and demand that the State should not adopt or impose any ethical position but limit itself to guaranteeing maximum space for the freedom of each individual, with the sole limitation of not infringing on the freedom and rights of any other citizen. On the other hand, it is held that, in the exercise of public and professional duties, respect for other people's freedom of choice requires that each one should set aside his or her own convictions in order to satisfy every demand of the citizens which is recognized and guaranteed by law; in carrying out one's duties, the only moral criterion should be what is laid down by the law itself. Individual responsibility is thus turned over to the civil law, with a renouncing of personal conscience, at least in the public sphere.

(EV, 69)

APPENDICES

1. The "fundamental option"

The basic commitment for or against God made by a human person—the basic orientation of his life in relation to God—either towards obedience and fidelity or to selfishness and disobedience of God could be called the fundamental option. This basic commitment gives unity to the moral and spiritual life of a man and, as St. Thomas Aquinas noted, is "not easily lost" (*De Veritate*, 27, 1 and 9).

> There is no doubt that Christian moral teaching, even in its biblical roots, acknowledges the specific importance of a fundamental choice which qualifies the moral life and engages freedom on a radical level before God (*VS*, 66).

Nevertheless, some contemporary theologians use the term *fundamental option* in a way that is contrary to revelation as presented by the Church's magisterium. According to them, the fundamental option is "brought about by that fundamental freedom whereby the person makes an overall self-determination, not through a specific and conscious decision on the level of reflection, but in a 'transcendental' and 'athematic' way" (*VS*, 65). But for them, particular moral acts which flow from this option only partially express a person's basic stance. The fundamental option itself remains untouched by specific moral choices.

They assert that the mortal sin which separates one from God is that which involves a direct and formal refusal to respond to the call of God or found in an egoism by which one completely and deliberately closes himself to love of God and neighbor. Only then—they say—will there be a change in the fundamental option, that is to say, one of those decisions which completely commits the person and which will be necessary in order to constitute mortal sin.

At the same time, according to these authors, a change in the *fundamental option* is very difficult, especially in the area of sexual activity. They say that a man generally does not destroy the moral order in a way that is entirely deliberate and responsible, when he acts under the influence of passion, weakness or immaturity, at those moments when he wants to demonstrate his love for another person. Besides, such actions are frequently the result of pressures in the social environment in which he lives.

They reduced serious sin to an act of *fundamental option* against God, which consists either in an explicit and formal rejection of God, as in the case of apostasy, or in an implicit and unconscious repudiation of charity, as in the case of lifelong debauchery.

> As we have just seen, reflection on the fundamental option has also led some theologians to undertake a basic revision of the traditional distinction between mortal sins and venial sins. They insist that the opposition to God's law which causes the loss of sanctifying grace – and eternal damnation, when one dies in such a state of sin – could only be the result of an act which engages the person in his totality: in other words, an act of fundamental option. According to these theologians, mortal sin, which separates man from God, only exists in the rejection of God, carried out at a level of freedom which is neither to be identified with an act of choice nor capable of becoming the object of conscious awareness. Consequently, they go on to say, it is difficult, at least psychologically, to accept the fact that a Christian, who wishes to remain united to Jesus Christ and to his Church, could so easily and repeatedly commit mortal sins, as the "matter" itself of his actions would sometimes indicate. Likewise, it would be hard to accept that man is able, in a brief lapse of time, to sever radically the bond of communion with God and afterwards be converted to him by sincere repentance. The gravity of sin, they maintain, ought to be measured by the degree of engagement of the freedom of the person performing an act, rather than by the matter of that act (*VS*, 69).

These contemporary theologians, rather than attend to the morality of particular actions, fix their attention on the habitual disposition of the man who has decided to do good, or, on the contrary, who has ordered his life decidedly for evil.

> The conclusion to which these erroneous doctrines eventually lead is that the properly moral assessment of the

person is reserved to his fundamental option, prescinding in whole or in part from his choice of particular actions, of concrete kinds of behavior (*VS*, 65).

In one sense, it is true that a man possesses a profound inclination toward or away from God, but this disposition is formed, confirmed or altered by each particular action. A person's *fundamental option* can be radically changed by particular acts (cf. VS, 67). The object chosen by the will in any individual action is either properly ordered toward man's true end or misdirected toward some other object. The moral determination of an action lies in the rectitude of the object chosen.

Therefore mortal sin which offends God does not consist only in a formal rejection of the law of charity: it also consists in that opposition to authentic love which is part of every deliberate transgression, in grave matters, of the moral law (cf. Supplementary Reading 3).

> For mortal sin exists also when a person knowingly and willingly, for whatever reason, chooses something gravely disordered. In fact, such a choice already includes contempt for the divine law, a rejection of God's love for humanity and the whole of creation: the person turns away from God and loses charity. Consequently, the fundamental orientation can be radically changed by particular acts. Clearly situations can occur which are very complex and obscure from a psychological viewpoint, and which influence the sinner's subjective imputability. But from a consideration of the psychological sphere one cannot proceed to create a theological category, which is precisely what the 'fundamental option' is, understanding it in such a way that it objectively changes or casts doubt upon the traditional concept of mortal sin (*RP*, 17).

In short, the ideal moral person is not only one who chooses a definitive and radical mode of conduct befitting a follower of Christ, but one who also believes that he ought to be careful of each and every one of his actions, because they manifest the coherency of his faith and his commitment to God.

2. Cooperation in evil actions: the Principle of the Double Effect

Not every human action has only good effects or bad effects. Moral theologians have offered the Principle of Double Effect to determine the permissibility of such actions that have a good and an evil effect.

The decision to carry out this kind of actions must be taken when the good effect cannot be reasonably brought about in any other way and under the following conditions:

a. The action must be good in itself.
   (An intrinsically evil action like abortion is never permissible, even if it has a good effect, because abortion is always evil in itself.)

b. The agent must have the right intention, that is the good effect must be directly intended, and the bad effect, although foreseen, must not be intended and can be only permitted.
   (One may never directly intend an evil; rather one allows the evil to occur because it cannot be separated from the good intended.)

c. The first effect must be good or at least equal first with the evil effect.
   (The good effect must be the direct result of the action taken since the end does not justify the means.)

d. There must be a proportionate grave reason to justify the action.
   (Thus, one cannot commit an action that the evil effect is greater than the good).

An action that meets all four of these conditions may be permissible. Applying this Principle to a specific situation will help to clarify the issue:

> A young woman is expecting her third child when she is diagnosed with uterine cancer. The cancer is advanced, and without an immediate hysterectomy (removal of the uterus) the expectant mother will die. Her unborn child, however, is unable to survive outside the womb at this stage of his development, and to await the viability of the child would, in the doctor's best judgment, likely cause the death of both the mother and the child, as the cancer is in an advanced stage. However, the proposed operation will also certainly cause the child's death, though it will save the mother's life.

Is the surgeon permitted to perform the operation?

Applying the first condition to this case, one first asks whether the action is good or indifferent. The removal of a diseased organ that threatens the life of a young woman is surely a good action. The first effect is good: the restored heath of the mother.

The second condition would be met if the physician intends to save the mother's life, and, although he foresees the death of the unborn child, he only permits it as an undesired and inseparable side-effect of his actions.

The third condition one needs to answer is whether the good effect comes about as a result of the evil effect. In this case the good effect, saving the life of the mother, is not a result of the death of the child. The mother's life is saved by the removal of the diseased uterus. Whether an unborn child is in that uterus or not does not change the fact that removing the organ saves the mother's life.

The fourth condition of proportionality must also be applied. In this situation, the life of the mother and the life of the child are proportional. The good of saving the mother's life is commensurate with the evil of the child's death.

In conclusion this action meets all five conditions of the Principle of Double Effect. The surgeon is therefore permitted to remove the cancerous uterus despite the fact that the death of the unborn child will result since there is not other way to do it.

QUESTIONS

1. What is a human act? What distinguishes a *human act* from an *action performed by a human being* (i.e., breathing)?

2. What is the object of an action?

3. What effect does the object have on the question of whether or not a particular action is moral or immoral?

4. What is the end or intention of an action?

5. What effect does the intention which lies behind an action have on the morality of the object? Can a bad intention make an action with a morally good object immoral? Likewise, can a good intention make an action whose object is morally bad a good action?

6. What are circumstances of an action? List six examples of circumstances which can affect the morality of an action.

7. What are three common errors in moral theology today? Explain the fallacies in each of these errors.

PRACTICAL EXERCISES

1. In the case that begins this chapter, determine the object, the end, and the circumstances which surround the case.

2. Explain behavior occurring today which is excused by some because "the ends justify the means".

3. Determine the object, the end, and the circumstances of the actions in Lk 21, 1-4.

4. Write a brief essay in which the similarities, differences and connections between situation ethics, proportionalism, and consequentialism are discussed.

5. Read the Appendix about the Fundamental Option, and explain the errors in this theory.

6. Do the ends ever justify the means?

CHAPTER VII
SIN AND CONVERSION

I had performed many thousands of abortions on innocent children, and I had failed those whom I loved. . . .

The following is the true story of Bernard Nathanson, M.D. Dr. Nathanson was a leading abortionist who came to realize the sanctity of unborn human life. His belief in the pro-life cause led him to the recognition of his own need and desire for God. This story was taken with permission from Dr. Bernard Nathanson's book entitled, *The Hand of God*, published by Regnery Publishing, Inc.

It was not supposed to work this way. The whole unimaginable sequence has moved in reverse, like water flowing uphill. The usual and customary progression is: belief in God and his splendid gift of life leads the believer to defend it, and to become pro-life. With me, it was just the opposite. Perversely, I journeyed from being anti-life to belief in God. I was not seeking anything spiritual; my desires have always been, for the most part, earthly and of the flesh, my goals concrete and tangible—and readily liquefiable into cash. To make matters worse, I was openly contemptuous of all this, as a stiff-backed Jewish atheist, or as Richard Gilman would have taxonomized, "a perfunctory Jew."

Getting from there to here wasn't easy. I went through a ten year "transitional time"—perhaps 1978-1988—when I felt the burden of sin growing heavier and more insistent. It was as if the contents of the baggage of my life were mysteriously absorbed in some metaphysical moisture, making them bulkier, heavier, more weighty and more impossible to bear. I found myself longing for a magical phlogiston, a substance that would contribute a negative weight to my heavy burden.

During this decade, it was the hour of the wolf that was the most trying time. I would awaken each morning at four or five o'clock, staring into the darkness and hoping (but not praying, yet) for a message to flare forth acquitting me before some invisible jury. After a suitable period of thwarted anticipation, I would once again turn on my bedside lamp, pick up the literature of sin (by this time I had accumulated a substantial store of it), and reread passages from St. Augustine's Confessions (a staple), Dostoyevski, Paul Tillich, Kierkegaard, Niebuhr, and even Lewis Mumford and Waldo Frank. St. Augustine spoke most starkly of my existential torment but, with no St. Monica to show me the way, I was seized by an unremitting black despair. . . .

Like the diagnostician I was trained to be, I commenced to analyze the patient's humors, the patient being myself. I determined that I was suffering from an affliction of the spirit; the disorder had arisen, at least in part, from an excess of existential freedom, and this had created penumbral despair. I had been cast adrift in a limitless sea of sensual freedom—no sextant, no compass, no charts, simply the dimly apprehended stars of the prevailing penal code, an imitative grasp of the manners and mores of society (a chimpanzee could be trained to do so well), a minimalist concept of justice, and a stultified sense of decency. I required not a cure but healing.

I had performed many thousands of abortions on innocent children, and I had failed those whom I loved....

The keenest of human tortures is to be judged without law, and mine had been a lawless universe. Santayana once wrote that the only true dignity of man is his capacity to despise himself. I despised myself. Perhaps I had at least arrived at the beginning of the quest for human dignity. I had begun a serious self-examination (the unexamined life is barely worth living) and had begun to face the twisted moral homunculus reflected in the mirror of self-examination.

I knew now that the primary illness is the severing of the links between sin and fault, between ethically corrupt action and cost. There had been no concrete cost to my corrupt actions, only behavioral exegesis, and that would not do. I needed to be disciplined and educated. I had become as Hannah Arendt had described Eichmann: a collection of functions rather than an accountable human being.

Now I had not been immune to the religious fervor of the pro-life movement. I had been aware in the early and mid-1980s that a great many of the Catholics and Protestants in the ranks had prayed for me—were praying for me—and I was not unmoved as time wore on. But it was not until I saw the spirit put to the test on those bitterly cold demonstration mornings, with pro-choicers hurling the most fulsome epithets at them, the police surrounding them, the media openly unsympathetic to their cause, the federal judiciary fining and jailing them, and the municipal officers threatening them—through it all they sat smiling, quietly praying, singing, confident and righteous of their cause, and ineradicably persuaded of their ultimate triumph—that I began seriously to question what indescribable Force led them to this activity. Why, too, was I there? What had led me to this time and place? Was it the same Force that allowed them to sit serene and unafraid at the epicenter of legal, physical, ethical, and moral chaos?

And for the first time in my entire adult life, I began to entertain seriously the notion of God—a god who problematically had led me through the proverbial circles of hell, only to show me the way to redemption and mercy through his grace. The thought violated every eighteenth century certainty I had cherished; it instantly converted my past into a vile bog of sin and evil; it indicted me and convicted me of high crimes against those who had loved me, and against those whom I did not even know; and simultaneously—miraculously—it held out a shimmering sliver of hope to me, in the growing belief that Someone had died for my sins and my evil two millennia ago.

This dramatic story of Dr. Nathanson's personal moral conversion can help us to reflect on the following questions about the nature of sin and conversion:

- What is sin?

- Where did sin originate, and in what does it consist?

- What personal responsibility does man bear for sin?

- What are the means to conversion and the forgiveness of sin?

Introduction

Before the Original Sin of Adam, there was no evil in the world, no moral evil nor physical evil. Once Adam and Eve had sinned, both moral and physical evils became ever-present facts in the lives of every living person. Physical evils can cause scandal, for the premature death of an infant, traffic accidents, floods, and earthquakes obviously have the power to touch all of us, negatively.

Yet, next to these physical evils, there are many moral evils—sins—committed, such as slander, infidelity, the murder of unborn children, abandonment of the elderly, and blasphemy which do not appear to touch us in the same way.

There is a noticeable difference in the reaction given to physical evil and moral evil. In the former case there is much sadness and sympathy, and the cry is often heard, "Why did God let this happen?" Some even wish to place the blame on God, directly, as if he planned the disaster. In the case of moral evil—sin—there is much indifference, if not happiness over a sinful life. People today who are guilty of acts which once were seen to be sins are now celebrated. Watching people on talk shows who brag about their sinful lives has become a national pastime. Some of them will admit to having made mistakes and say they are sorry, but there is rarely an admission of guilt for sin. This difference in reaction ought to be seriously evaluated. If the culture celebrates sin, how is one to determine what sin is?

To understand the problem better, distinctions should be made:

a. **All physical evils are the result of Adam's sin.**

   If there are famines, it is because hunger in the world has its origin in the sin of Adam, "Because you have listened to the voice of your wife, and have eaten of the tree of which I commanded you not to eat, cursed is the ground because of you" (Gn 3, 17).

b. There are physical evils that are not dependent on the will of the one who suffers them, and which are unavoidable.

Moral evil, on the other hand, is always freely committed and can always be avoided. A man is therefore guilty of sin in the case of moral evil.

c. Moral evil hurts both the agent and recipient, but it engenders worse consequences in the agent than in the victim.

Every sin causes an immeasurable evil for the sinner. Human passions may have an initially pleasant effect, but they can leave an emptiness and a restlessness. For example, sexual satisfaction, except for conjugal love between married persons, degrades the person. The result is an internal battle in the sinner, who is enslaved by appetites.

Socrates constantly repeated this maxim which applies to all evil: "The one who commits an injustice merits more compassion than the one receiving the injustice, even if the one receiving it is myself." Bertolt Brecht wrote: "It takes work to do evil!" This is so because moral evil denigrates the person and it ends up leading man to disgrace and unhappiness.

Sin is not unique to Catholic morality; rather all religions have a list of sins that are condemned, for they offend God and injure the dignity of man. But sin is not only a human evil because it carries with it disgrace and restlessness. What is decisive about sin is that it consists in an offense against God. Thus, it is the only absolute evil, and it is the cause of many other evils.

1. Definition of sin

Sin has many definitions. The following three are the classical definitions of two of the Church's greatest theologians, St. Augustine and St. Thomas Aquinas:

a. Sin is any deed, word, or desire against eternal law. (St. Augustine)

Eternal law is the divine wisdom directing creatures to their proper end. Thus, to act against eternal law is to transgress moral law, offending God.

This Augustinian definition considers both eternal law, which refers to the cosmos, and *natural law*, which is the application of eternal law to human creatures. With respect to natural law, all that violates the nature of man is considered sinful. This definition takes into consideration the fact that sin can occur in thought, word, or deed.

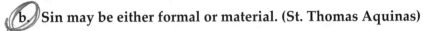 **b. Sin may be either formal or material. (St. Thomas Aquinas)**

A *formal sin* is a voluntary and freely chosen action contrary to the law of God; a *material sin* is an involuntary transgression committed without full deliberation.

c. Sin is the voluntary transgression of the law of God. (St. Thomas Aquinas)

According to this definition, a sin occurs when God's law is broken. Thus, those acts are sinful that break the Ten Commandments. And, since the hierarchy of the Church has the power to impose laws on Christians, one sins by ignoring ecclesiastical laws, for example, the Precepts of the Church. It is also sinful to disobey just civil laws—though a distinction regarding their gravity must be made between laws which involve seriously binding obligations (i.e., the payment of taxes and service in the military) and those which function as civil directives (such as laws prohibiting smoking in public places).

d. Sin is a turning away from God, to creatures, in a disordered way. (St. Thomas Aquinas)

This definition is common in moral theology. It graphically expresses the actual makeup of sin. In fact, man, in his freedom, is constantly choosing. For example, he can fulfill his will by doing as he pleases or God's will which calls for the love of neighbor; he can say the truth or simply lie; he can follow God's plan for sexuality or act sexually according to his own plan. In summary, man sins when he chooses out of his own egotism and out of disdain for God's will (cf. *VS*, 70).

In fact, consciously or unconsciously, man at times prefers himself before God. When choosing between his will or God's will, man will often favor his own desire, and so he sins.

These three definitions are implicitly stated in the teaching of the *Catechism of the Catholic Church*:

Sin is an offense against reason, truth, and right conscience; it is failure in genuine love for God and neighbor caused by a perverse attachment to certain goods. It wounds the nature of man and injures human solidarity. It has been defined as "an utterance, a deed, or a desire contrary to the eternal law" [St. Augustine, *Contra Faustum*, 22; PL 42,18; St. Thomas Aquinas, *Summa theologiae*, I-II, 71,6].

Sin is an offense against God. . . . Sin sets itself against God's love for us and turns our hearts away from it. Like the first sin, it is disobedience, a revolt against God through the will to become "like gods,"[1] knowing and determining good and evil. Sin is thus "love of oneself even to contempt of God."[2] In this proud self-exaltation, sin is diametrically opposed to the obedience of Jesus, which achieves our salvation[3] (CCC, 1849-1850).

2. The real meaning of sin in the Bible

In order to express the negative significance of sin, it is helpful to recall some of the common names given to sin in the Bible. The sacred writers, by divine inspiration, tried to convey the evils involved in sin through different terms. In the original Hebrew of the Old Testament, sin is signified as a *deviance* or *fall*. Another term used is *rebelliousness*. Other terms are *error, disgrace, madness, crime, impiety*, an *evil act, treachery, malice* and *foolishness*. The New Testament writers also used a number of terms to designate the reality of sin. The most frequent are *deviance* or *"to lose the path," iniquity, injustice* and *impiety*.

The Bible is in fact a history of the evil effects of sin. There is no lower form of existence than to be permanently in serious sin.

3. Sin is a personal act

Since sin is an act of human freedom which proceeds from our knowledge and freedom, a person is always responsible for his sins.

Sin, in the proper sense, is always a *personal act*, since it is an act of freedom on the part of an individual person, and not properly of a group or community. This individual may be conditioned, incited and influenced by numerous and powerful external factors. He may also be subjected to tendencies, defects and habits linked with his personal condition. In not a few cases such external and internal factors may attenuate, to a greater or lesser degree, the person's freedom and therefore his responsibility and guilt.

But it is a truth of faith, also confirmed by our experience and reason, that the human person is free. This truth cannot be disregarded, in order to place the blame for individual's sins on external factors such as structures, systems or other people. Above all, this would be to deny the person's dignity and freedom, which are manifested—even though in a negative and disastrous way—also in this responsibility for sin committed. Hence there is nothing so personal and untransferable in each individual as merit for virtue or responsibility for sin.

As a personal act, sin has its first and most important consequences in the *sinner himself*: that is, in his relationship with God, who is the very foundation of human life; and also in his spirit, weakening his will and clouding his intellect.... (*RP,* 16).

4. The loss of the meaning of sin

The judgment of sin found in the Bible contrasts radically with the view of sin today. In fact, some societies which were once Christian have lost the understanding of what sin is. For example, assisted suicide is gaining increasing acceptance in many of the countries of Western Europe and the United States, and societies which previously did not permit civil divorce now freely grant it.

The first warning was made by Pope Pius XII in 1946, when he stated that "the sin of the century is the loss of the meaning of sin" (Pius XII, *Radio message to the United States National Catechetical Congress*, 26 October, 1946).

This warning is repeated in later documents of the Magisterium. The most recent and solemn of these is the following of Pope John Paul II:

> Nevertheless, it happens not infrequently in history, for more or less lengthy periods and under the influence of many different factors, that the moral conscience of many people becomes seriously clouded. . . . Too many signs indicate that such an eclipse exists in our time. This is all the more disturbing in that conscience . . . "the most secret core and sanctuary of a man" [cf. *GS,* 16] is "strictly related to human *freedom.* . . . For this reason conscience, to a great

extent, constitutes the basis of man's interior dignity and, at the same time, of his relationship to God" [John Paul II, *Angelus* of 14 March, 1982]. It is inevitable therefore that in this situation there is an obscuring also of the sense of sin, which is closely connected with the moral conscience, the search for truth and the desire to make a responsible use of freedom (*RP*, 18).

The loss of the meaning of sin represents a great evil for the whole of humanity and not just for the Christian.

In fact, humanity is already suffering greatly because, to a certain extent, the notion of sin is being lost, and with it the notion of what is good and evil. A culture that becomes insensitive to such issues becomes impoverished and ignorant, since good and evil exist regardless of any denial or acceptance on the part of society. Here we recall St. John: "If we say we have no sin, we deceive ourselves, and the truth is not in us" (1 Jn 1, 8).

The moral evil of sin cannot disappear; what can diminish is the awareness of sin and the hate for sin. Some factors that contribute to the loss of the sense of sin are the following:

a. **Cultural and ethical relativism.**

The denial of sin as something real and permanent will increase to the degree that a given society professes a cultural and ethical relativism which permits the individual person to decide what is good for himself (cf. *VS*, 53).

Examples of this relativism abound on radio and television, today, where both music and conversation are used to promote all kinds of vices.

b. **Incorrect statements of modern psychology.**

Some psychologists today deny the existence of sin, based on the idea that it shocks the conscience. They propose a morality without sin to liberate man from a morose feeling of shame. They refuse to see that sin can permanently harm man only when shame and pardon are lacking. According to the Christian conception, an awareness of sin, far from harming, helps liberate, since in Christianity every sin has the possibility of forgiveness, in which God's love is seen (cf. *VS*, 61).

c. **The confusion between morality and legality.**

It is clear that a society ruled by laws will naturally judge as good those things permitted by the law, and will condemn as evil those things prohibited by law. Divorce and abortion are two sins which have come to be accepted as moral because they are legal.

d. **Secularism/Humanism.**

Secularism sees the world as having no place for God or permanent ideas of good and evil. A religious view of existence will facilitate the acceptance of sin as a reality, and a lack of religious sense will diminish that acceptance. Perhaps this is the reason today for the loss of the meaning of sin; after all, where the sense of God is obscured, so will the sense of sin be blurred.

As Pope John Paul II has noted:

> The attempt to set freedom in opposition to truth, and indeed to separate them radically, is the consequence, manifestation and consummation of another more serious and destructive dichotomy that separates faith from morality.

> This separation represents one of the most acute pastoral concerns of the church amid today's growing secularism, wherein indeed, too many people think and live "as if God did not exist" (*VS*, 88).

The very life of the Church is affected by this trend. John Paul II states this fact in the following words:

> Even in the field of the thought and life of the church certain trends inevitably favor the decline of the sense of sin. For example, some are inclined to replace exaggerated attitudes of the past with other exaggerations: From seeing sin everywhere they pass to not recognizing it anywhere; from too much emphasis on the fear of eternal punishment they pass to preaching a love of God that excludes any punishment deserved by sin; from severity in trying to correct erroneous consciences they pass to a kind of respect for conscience which excludes the duty of telling the truth (*RP*, 18).

Briefly, then, we could say that the shift has been from a misconception of seeing sin everywhere to not seeing sin anywhere. A clear case of going from one extreme to the other.

Thus, there is a need for a rediscovery of the existence of sin, that is, of the meaning of good and evil as an offense against God. But man must first return to God before this can truly happen (cf. *VS*, 88).

5. Division of sin

The reading of Sacred Scripture shows that sins are not all of the same kind nor are all equally sinful. As a result, there are many classifications; here, we mention only four:

a. By its origin: original or actual.

- *Original sin* finds it origins in the disobedience of the first parents at the beginning of human history and every person is born with its effect on his soul.

- *Actual sin* is the sin committed by each one of us.

b. By its gravity: mortal or venial.

- *Mortal sin* is a grave offense against God that destroys our relationship with him by severing us from his divine love. Mortal sin is "something grave and disordered" (*VS*, 70). This relationship can be restored through reconciliation.

   Moral theology lists three conditions for mortal sin:

   — Grave matter "is specified by the Ten Commandments" (*CCC*, 1858), that is, it must be something serious;

   — Full knowledge "presupposes knowledge of the sinful character of the act, of its opposition to God's law" (*CCC*, 1859);

   — Complete consent "implies a consent sufficiently deliberate to be a personal choice" (*CCC*, 1859). It is enough that one has done a prohibited thing, and he has done it deliberately.

   If these three conditions are not met, no mortal sin is committed (cf. *VS*, 70). Consequently, there is no such thing as committing a sin "by surprise;" however, sin can occur even though one does not want to offend God.

- *Venial sin* offends the love of God. While it does not separate man from God, it weakens our relationship with him.

Venial sins should be confessed as a way of avoiding mortal sin.

> One commits *venial sin* when, in a less serious matter, he does not observe the standard prescribed by the moral law, or when he disobeys the moral law in a grave matter, but without full knowledge or without complete consent (CCC, 1862).

c. Numerical distinction.

Numerical distinction refers to the number of times that a particular sin has been committed. Some actions involve more than one sin, usually due to the interruption of the act.

It is necessary to reveal this number in confession when the sin involves a serious matter. On those occasions when it is impossible to remember the number of times that the sin has been committed, it is enough to make a prudent estimation.

d. Whether it is a sin of commission or omission.

- A *sin of commission* is the positive act against a precept. A prohibited act is "committed." Stealing would be an example.

- A *sin of omission* occurs when a required act is omitted, for example, choosing to miss Mass on Sunday.

> In Jesus' preaching, all sins are condemned, but in the Gospel of Matthew the punishment for sins of omission is stressed (Mt 25, 1-46). The reason may be that it is easier to be sorry for those sins committed than it is for those omitted, since it requires more sensitivity to see sin in omission.

Both sins of commission and omission create a corrupt atmosphere in which evil is sought. This state can lead to *social* or *institutional sins*.

> . . . To speak of *social sin* means in the first place to recognize that, by virtue of a human solidarity which is as mysterious and intangible as it is real and concrete, each individual's sin in some way affects others. This is the other aspect of that solidarity which on the religious level is developed in the profound and magnificent mystery of the *Communion of Saints*, thanks to which it has been possible to say that "every soul

that rises above itself, raises up the world" (cf. Elisabeth Leseur, *Journal et pensées de chaque jour*, p. 31).

To this *law of ascent* there unfortunately corresponds the *law of descent*. Consequently one can speak of a *communion of sin*, whereby a soul that lowers itself through sin drags down with itself the Church and, in some way, the whole world. In other words, there is no sin, not even the most intimate and secret one, the most strictly individual one, that exclusively concerns the person committing it. With greater or lesser violence, with greater of lesser harm, every sin has repercussions on the entire ecclesial body and the whole human family. According to this first meaning of the term, every sin can undoubtedly be considered as *social* sin. . . .

. . . Hence if one speaks of *social sin* here, the expression obviously has an analogical meaning. However, to speak even analogically of *social sins* must not cause us to underestimate the responsibility of the individuals involved. It is meant to be an appeal to the consciences of all, so that each may shoulder his or her responsibility seriously and courageously in order to change those disastrous conditions and intolerable situations (*RP*, 16).

These two realities are often mentioned in recent Church documents and in the *Catechism of the Catholic Church*:

Sins give rise to social situations and institutions that are contrary to the divine goodness. "Structures of sin" are the expression and effect of personal sins. They lead their victims to do evil in their turn. In an analogous sense, they constitute a "social sin"[4] (*CCC*, 1869).

Refusing to pay just wages because of a person's color or religion would be examples of social sins.

e. **By its manifestation: external or internal.**

- *External sin* is committed with words or actions.

- *Internal sin* is found in thought or desire. Hence, evil thoughts, daydreaming, desires, and memories could be mortal sins which need to be confessed. Such sins are found in every matter, and not just in sexual matters.

Some find it hard to admit that man can sin in thought or desire, without sinning in action (cf. Chapter II). Internal sins are clearly condemned by Jesus (Mt 15, 10-20; Mk 7, 14-23).

6. Effects of sin

The Bible constantly shows that sin is an offence against God. Thus it considers sin an absolute moral evil. Furthermore, every sin spawns endless evils for the sinner and society.

In regards to the effects of sin, the *Catechism of the Catholic Church* has this to say:

> "*Mortal sin* destroys charity in the heart of man . . . it turns man away from God, who is his ultimate end and his beatitude. . . .
>
> *Venial sin* allows charity to subsist, even though it offends and wounds it "(*CCC*, 1855).

Habitual, deliberate venial sin can lead to mortal sin through a gradual weakening of the love of God.

7. The forgiveness of sins. Conversion

Attitudes toward sin can vary. The sinner can be indifferent, remorseful or repentant, that is, seeking forgiveness.

These attitudes exhibit themselves when a man offends another man. The offender either becomes insolent and indifferent or admits his fault and asks for forgiveness.

These same dispositions may be reflected in regards to God. The Bible and the teachings of Jesus make this clear. They ask man to repent for his sins and to turn back to God whom he has offended.

The call to conversion is the central theme of the preaching of John the Baptist, who sees repentance as the preparation for the coming of the Messiah: Only those who repent will be able to enter the Kingdom of God which will be instituted by the Messiah (Mt 3, 1-12; Mk 1, 2-4; Lk 3, 3-18). "Prepare the way of the LORD, make his paths straight" (Mk 1, 3).

The public ministry of Jesus also begins with the call to conversion: "The time is fulfilled, and the kingdom of God is at hand; repent, and believe in the Gospel" (Mk 1, 15). "Repent, for the kingdom of heaven is at hand" (Mt 4, 17). This call to repentance is repeated throughout his public life. That attitude finds forgiveness in Christ Jesus; every time the sinner repents, the Bible indicates that God forgives him endlessly.

If there is a quality that shines in the public life of Jesus it is his willingness to forgive sinners. Forgiveness is exemplified by narratives of the adulterous woman (Jn 8, 1-11); the Samaritan woman (Jn 4, 4-42); the public sinner who is forgiven because "she loves greatly" (Lk 7, 36-50), and the case of the thief and criminal who seeks forgiveness at the end of his life (Lk 23, 43). "There are, then, no lost cases, and furthermore, the Son of man came to seek and to save the lost" (Lk 19, 10; Mt 18, 11).

St. Luke narrates the three great parables of sin that speak of God's attitude towards the repentant sinner (cf. Lk 15). And Jesus still points out that his mission is to "seek and to save the lost" (Lk 19, 10). Thus he accomplishes the meaning of his own name, "Jesus", "for he will save his people from their sin" (Mt 1, 21).

The call to conversion is one of the objectives of moral doctrine:

> It is the Gospel which reveals the full truth about man and his moral journey, and thus enlightens and admonishes sinners; it proclaims to them God's mercy, which is constantly at work to preserve them both from despair at their inability fully to know and keep God's law and from the presumption that they can be saved without merit. God also reminds sinners of the joy of forgiveness, which alone grants the strength to see in the moral law a liberating truth, a grace-filled source of hope, a path of life (VS, 112).

8. The Sacrament of Reconciliation

Here the institution of the sacrament of Reconciliation plays a central role, since it gives peace to the one who receives it. Sacramental reconciliation is, by Jesus' designation, the ordinary path to forgiveness of sins for those who believe in him:

> And when he had said this, he breathed on them, and said to them, "Receive the Holy Spirit. If you forgive the sins of any, they are forgiven; if you retain the sins of any, they are retained" (Jn 20, 22-23).

According to St. Luke, this was Jesus' last recommendation before the Ascension:

> Then he opened their minds to understand the scriptures, and said to them, "Thus it is written, that the Christ should suffer and on the third day rise from the dead, and that repentance and forgiveness of sins should be preached in his name to all nations, beginning from Jerusalem. . . ." (Lk 24, 45-47).

Like Jesus, the Church, faced with a world that has lost an awareness of sin, responds with a call to conversion. Such is the content of *Reconciliation and Penance*. The *Catechism of the Catholic Church* also teaches:

> The Lord Jesus Christ, physician of our souls and bodies, who forgave the sins of the paralytic and restored him to bodily health (cf. Mk 2, 1-12), has willed that his Church continue, in the power of the Holy Spirit, his work of healing and salvation, even among her own members. This is the purpose of the two sacraments of healing: the sacrament of Penance and the sacrament of Anointing of the Sick (CCC, 1421).

The Sacrament of Reconciliation should be received regularly (monthly confession is a good practice in keeping with sound Christian piety) to enable a program to be followed which would make overcoming sinful habits a real possibility.

Conclusion

In a period of history in which the reality of sin is being denied, and there is general indifference to moral evil, the Christian is called to be Christ to others by his conduct. Men will attempt to invent other theories or explanations of the way to live life, but in regard to any attempt to justify evil, the revelation of God will speak out, as it has done in the Bible. Nevertheless, the Christian cannot renounce his era, even though sin may abound because Christians are given life to be martyrs, witnesses to the truth. Sin has always existed, and Christ will always be there to forgive man and to bring him back.

I. Glossary

ACTUAL SIN:

As opposed to Original Sin, actual sins are those sins against God committed by the deliberate will of the individual.

EXTERNAL SIN:

Sin committed by word or deed.

FORMAL SIN:

A sin which is freely and deliberately committed. A formal sin always involves knowledge of the evil of the action that is being committed, and freedom to do or to avoid the action.

HABITUAL SIN:

The permanent state of culpability, caused by the frequent commission of actual sins.

INTERNAL SIN:

Sin committed in thought or desire.

MATERIAL SIN:

An action which is sinful but does not admit culpability because of ignorance. A conscious and voluntary act against God.

MORTAL SIN:

A grave offense against God which destroys sanctifying grace and causes the death of the soul.

NUMERICAL DISTINCTION:

It refers to the concrete number of acts that are committed contrary to a virtue or precept.

ORIGINAL SIN:

The condition into which all human beings are born, lacking God's grace and inclined by concupiscence toward sin.

SECULARISM (SECULAR HUMANISM):

A philosophy which rejects any reference to God or religion and seeks the improvement of human society through purely human means, i.e., science, social organization, and human reason.

SIN:

An offense against God, because his will is not done.

SIN OF COMMISSION:

An act contrary to a negative precept, i.e., stealing.

SIN OF OMISSION:

A failure to perform some act required by a positive precept, i.e., missing Mass on Sunday.

SPECIFIC DISTINCTION:

It refers to sins that are differentiated because they offend different virtues or precepts.

VENIAL SIN:

An offense against God which does not deprive the soul of sanctifying grace, but which weakens a person's love for God and neighbor.

II. Summary of Principles

1. "[Sin] is an offense against God. It rises up against God in a disobedience contrary to the obedience of Christ" (*CCC*, 1871).

2. "Sin is an act contrary to reason. It wounds man's nature and injures human solidarity" (*CCC*, 1872).

3. "The root of all sins lies in man's heart. The kinds and the gravity of sins are determined principally by their objects" (*CCC*, 1873).

4. Material sins do not require repentance or pardon. Only formal sins require repentance and pardon

5. One may sin gravely both internally (in thought or intention) and externally (in deed).

6. Sins of omission, unless committed in ignorance, are of the same theological species and have the same gravity as sins of commission.

7. Habitual sins (rooted in vice), can diminish the gravity of a sinful act. But the obligation to remove the habit still holds. The repetition of a sin does not in itself diminish guilt.

8. The Sacrament of Reconciliation is the ordinary means by which Christ willed to forgive sins.

9. For confessional integrity, it is necessary to confess the kind and number of all mortal sinsof which one is conscious that have not previously been forgiven.

SUPPLEMENTARY READINGS

1. It is not difficult to see how certain sins—idolatry, for example— offend God. But all immoral acts offend God. Treating one's neighbor unfairly is an offense against God. But why? How is it that every kind of immorality concerns God?

   In considering this question, it is necessary to put aside anthropomorphic notions. God is not offended as we are. He does not get angry in the way we do, his feelings are not hurt, he does not suffer wounded pride. Yet our sins do offend him. How?

   We begin by considering our relationship with God in the context of the covenant. God offers us the covenant for our good, for the sake of our human well-being. When we do moral evil, we act against God's love, contrary to his will. Even apart from the covenant, moreover, one who sins sets aside reason and so implicitly sets aside God, the source and meaning and value in creation. Sinners, as it were, declare their independence of anything beyond themselves, including God. In that sense, too, sin is an offense against God.

   (Germain Grisez and Russell Shaw,
   Fulfillment in Christ, p. 154)

2. Verbally there is very general agreement; for both the general run of men and people of superior refinement say that it is happiness, and identify living well and faring well with being happy; but with regard to what happiness is they differ, and the many

do not give the same account as the wise. For the former think it is some plain and obvious thing, like pleasure, wealth, or honor; they differ, however, from one another—and often even the same man identifies it with different things, with health when he is ill, with wealth when his is poor; but, conscious of their ignorance, they admire those who proclaim some great thing that is above their comprehension . . . men of this kind are evidently quite slavish in their tastes, preferring a life suitable to beasts. . . . A consideration of the prominent types of life shows that . . . according to them, at any rate, virtue is better.

(Aristotle, *The Nichomachean Ethics*, I, 4-5)

3. Sin has become almost everywhere today one of those subjects that is not spoken about. Religious education of whatever kind does its best to evade it. Theater and films use the word ironically or in order to entertain. Sociology and psychology attempt to unmask it as an illusion or a complex. Even the law is trying to get by more and more without the concept of guilt. It prefers to make use of sociological language, which turns the concept of good and evil into statistics and in its place distinguishes between normative and non-normative behavior. Implicit here is the possibility that the statistical proportions will themselves charge: what is presently non-normative could one day become the rule; indeed, perhaps one should even strive to make the non-normative normal.

In such an atmosphere of quantification, the whole idea of the moral has accordingly been generally abandoned. This is a logical development if it is true that there is no standard for human beings to use as a model—something not discovered by us but coming from the inner goodness of creation.

(Joseph Cardinal Ratzinger, *In The Beginning*, pp. 78-79)

APPENDICES

1. Mortal, grave or venial?

Certain authors have recently introduced a threefold division of sin: *mortal*, *grave*, and *venial*.

- *Mortal sins* are those actions done in express and direct rebellion against God. Such sins, according to these authors, are very rare and only these sinful actions can separate man from God.

- *"Grave" sins*, on the other hand, are a lesser species of serious sin, closer to venial sins, still somewhat distinct because the matter is more serious or the subject more malicious. These sins are committed only out of weakness.

- *Venial sins* are sins which, like grave sins, are committed primarily out of weakness or habit, but which neither involve a direct rebellion against God nor matter which is serious or a subject that is malicious.

The Magisterium of the Church has condemned this triple distinction, saying it has no foundation in Scripture, which specifies only two classes of sin. Consequently, mortal and "grave" sins are identical. Serious sins do admit of a difference in degree (for example, blasphemy against God is more serious than sins against charity toward one's neighbor); nonetheless, all separate a man from God, and are, therefore, serious sins.

> This threefold distinction might illustrate the fact that there is a scale of seriousness among grave sins. But it still remains true that the essential and decisive distinction is between sin which destroys charity and sin which does not kill the supernatural life: there is no middle way between life and death (*RP*, 17).

2. Democracy and the dangers of moral relativism

In any case, in the democratic culture of our time, it is commonly held that the legal system of any society should limit itself to taking account of and accepting the convictions of the majority. It should therefore be based solely upon what the majority itself considers moral and actually practices. Furthermore, if it is believed that an objective truth shared by all is *de facto* unattainable, then respect for the freedom of the citizens – who in a democratic system are considered the true rulers – would require that on the legislative level the autonomy of individual consciences be acknowledged. Consequently, when establishing those norms which are absolutely necessary for social coexistence, the only determining factor should be the will of the majority, whatever this may be. Hence every politician, in his or her activity, should clearly separate the realm of private conscience from that of public conduct.

As a result we have what appear to be two diametrically opposed tendencies. On the one hand, individuals claim for themselves in the moral sphere the most complete freedom of choice and demand that the State should not adopt or impose any ethical position but limit itself to guaranteeing maximum space for the freedom of each individual, with the sole limitation of not infringing on the freedom and rights of any other citizen. On the other hand, it is held that, in the exercise of public and professional duties, respect for other people's freedom of choice requires that each one should set aside his or her own convictions in order to satisfy every demand of the citizens which is recognized and guaranteed by law; in carrying out one's duties, the only moral criterion should be what is laid down by the law itself. Individual responsibility is thus turned over to the civil law, with a renouncing of personal conscience, at least in the public sphere.

At the basis of all these tendencies lies the *ethical relativism* which characterizes much of present-day culture. There are those who consider such relativism an essential condition of democracy, inasmuch as it alone is held to guarantee tolerance, mutual respect between people and acceptance of the decisions of the majority, whereas moral norms considered to be objective and binding are held to lead to authoritarianism and intolerance.

But it is precisely the issue of respect for life which shows what misunderstandings and contradictions, accompanied by terrible practical consequences, are concealed in this position.

It is true that history has known cases where crimes have been committed in the name of "truth." But equally grave crimes and radical denials of freedom have also been committed and are still being committed in the name of "ethical relativism." When a parliamentary or social majority decrees that it is legal, at least under certain conditions, to kill unborn human life, is it not really making a "tyrannical" decision with regard to the weakest and most defenseless of human beings? Everyone's conscience rightly rejects those crimes against humanity of which our century has had such sad experience. But would these crimes cease to be crimes if, instead of being committed by unscrupulous tyrants, they were legitimated by popular consensus?

Democracy cannot be idolized to the point of making it a substitute for morality or a panacea for immorality. Fundamentally, democracy is a "system" and as such is a means and not an end. Its "moral" value is not automatic, but depends on conformity to the moral law to which it, like every other form of human behavior, must be subject: in other words, its morality depends on the morality of the ends which it pursues and of the means which it employs. If today we see an almost universal consensus with regard to the value of democracy, this is to be considered a positive "sign of the times," as the Church's Magisterium has frequently noted. But the value of democracy stands or falls with the values which it embodies and promotes. Of course, values such as the dignity of every human person, respect for inviolable and inalienable human rights, and the adoption of the "common good" as the end and criterion regulating political life are certainly fundamental and not to be ignored.

The basis of these values cannot be provisional and changeable "majority" opinions, but only the acknowledgment of an objective moral law which, as the "natural law" written in the human heart, is the obligatory point of reference for civil law itself. If, as a result of a tragic obscuring of the collective conscience, an attitude of skepticism were to succeed in bringing into question even the fundamental principles of the moral law, the democratic system itself would be shaken in its foundations and would be reduced to a mere mechanism for regulating different and opposing interests on a purely empirical basis.

Some might think that even this function, in the absence of anything better, should be valued for the sake of peace in society. While one acknowledges some element of truth in this point of view, it is easy to see that without an objective moral grounding not even democracy is capable of ensuring a stable peace, especially since peace which is not built upon the values of the dignity of every individual and of solidarity between all people frequently proves to be illusory. Even in participatory systems of government, the regulation of interests often occurs to the advantage of the most powerful, since they are the ones most capable of maneuvering not only the levers of power but also of shaping the formation of consensus. In such a situation, democracy easily becomes an empty word (*EV*, 69-70).

QUESTIONS

1. What is sin?

2.. List some examples of how modern society denies the reality of sin. Use a newspaper, if you like, to find your examples.

3. List and briefly explain the four factors presented in this chapter which contribute to the loss of a sense of sin.

4. What is a mortal sin?

5. List and explain the three conditions which must be met before a man can be guilty of mortal sin. Give an example of an action which is a mortal sin, *being careful to show how each of the conditions is met by the situation in your example.*

6. What is a venial sin? How does venial sin differ from mortal sin?

7. Are there any circumstances under which something which is ordinarily a venial sin could become a mortal sin? If so, describe such circumstances.

8. What is original sin?

9. Define the difference between sins of omission and commission.

10. What is actual sin?

11. What is meant by "social sin?"

12. What is the usual means of forgiveness that God has established through his Church?

PRACTICAL EXERCISES

1. List the sins which can be found in the following texts of St. Paul:

   — Rm 1, 29-31;13,13

   — 1 Cor 5, 10-11; 6, 9-10

   — 2 Cor 12, 20-21

— Gal 5, 19-21

— Eph 4, 31; 5, 3-5

— Col 3, 5-8

— 1 Tim 1, 9-10; 4, 12; 6, 9-11

— 2 Tim 3, 2-5

— Tt 3, 3

Compare the seriousness of sins against justice and chastity.

2. Comment on the following words of Socrates:

> But if it were necessary for me either to do or to suffer injustice, I'd elect to suffer injustice rather than do it (Plato, *Gorgias*, 469 c).

> Then we ought not to retaliate or render evil for evil to any one, whatever evil we may have suffered from him (Plato, *Crito*, 49 c-d).

3. Comment on the excerpt of Pope John Paul II's writing on the Sacrament of Reconciliation contained in the reading in the Appendix. Why does the Church reject the distinction between *mortal sin* and *grave sin*? Why is it impossible for a person to commit a sinful action, involving *grave matter*, without this action involving a concrete rebellion against God?

4. Resolve the following case: John and his friend Patrick are discussing the human sins of passion, namely the sexual sins, sins of anger, and gluttony. John holds that actions such as blasphemy against God and grave social injustices that destroy the dignity of man are sins, but he denies that premarital sex is a sin. "How can you call it a sin if a man and a woman of mutual consent decide to have sexual relations, when children are starving in Africa and being murdered in wars all over the globe?" he asks. Patrick argues that any evil consists in an offense against God, and since extramarital relations are serious disorders of the human passions and contrary to the express purpose for which God created human sexuality, they offend the dignity of man, who is made in the image of God (cf. Gn 1, 27).

Explain why, according to the text, people like John tend to reduce sin to blasphemy and social crimes? According to Scripture, why are the most serious sins those that offend the dignity of man? What criteria can be given to determine both what is sinful and the gravity of the sin?

Part II

Commandments and Beatitudes

Chapter VIII
The Ten Commandments
and the Beatitudes

And behold, one came up to Jesus, saying, "Teacher, what good deed must I do, to have eternal life?"

Jesus said to him, "Why do you ask me about what is good? One there is who is good. If you would enter life, keep the commandments."

He said to him, "Which?"

And Jesus said, "You shall not kill, You shall not commit adultery, You shall not steal, You shall not bear false witness, honor your father and mother, and, You shall love your neighbor as yourself."

The young man said to him, "All these I have observed; what do I still lack?"

Jesus said to him, "If you would be perfect, go, sell what you possess and give to the poor, and you will have treasure in heaven; and come, follow me." (Mt 19, 16-21)

The question which the rich young man puts to Jesus of Nazareth is one which rises from the depths of his heart. It is an essential and unavoidable question for the life of every man, for it is about the moral good which must be done, and about eternal life. The young man senses that there is a connection between moral good and the fulfillment of his own destiny. He is a devout Israelite, raised as it were in the shadow of the Law of the LORD (*VS*, 8.1).

In his reply to the young man, Jesus expresses the nucleus and spirit of Christian morality. Through this dialogue Christ reveals "the essential elements of revelation in the Old and New Testament with regard to moral action." The answer to the question about moral goodness and its connection to eternal life can be found only in God. One cannot know what is good without knowing goodness itself. For the believer, God is "the One who 'alone is good'; the One who despite man's sin remains the 'model' for moral action." To become good is to become like God.

People need to turn to Christ; they receive from him "the answer to their question about what is good and what is evil." Essential to all morality is the recognition of God's sovereignty over the moral order: "acknowledging the LORD as God is the very core, the heart of the Law" (J. Michael Miller, C.S.B., *The Encyclicals of Pope John Paul II*, p. 654).

The specific obligations which guide the Christian life are enumerated in the Ten Commandments and the Beatitudes. It is therefore appropriate to ask ourselves the following:

- What are the Ten Commandments and the Beatitudes?

- Are these ancient codes of moral conduct still relevant guides for life in the modern world?

- How do the Ten Commandments, the Beatitudes and the natural law guide man in forming and fulfilling the dictates of his conscience?

Introduction

As treated in the section *Principles of Morality,* Christian morality has new elements— *foundations* and *principles* —which are not founded on human reason alone, but are given by revelation.

In fact, Christian ethics is rooted in the new condition of the baptized. Baptism communicates a singular participation in divine nature, by which the Christian is a son of God in Christ and is expected to conduct his life in a Christ-like manner. Consequently, Christian morality demands of the baptized a life appropriate to a son of God.

For this end, God has given man some norms of conduct which are new. These are the Ten Commandments of the Old Testament and the ethical commands of the New Law, proposed by Christ Jesus. By fulfilling these precepts, man discovers the will of God, the Father.

1. The Ten Commandments

The Ten Commandments were given by God to Moses on Mount Sinai (ca. 1200 BC). Around the time of the Egyptian exile, the Israelites were a nation of common ancestry whose sufferings had united them closely, but they were also stubborn and unorganized. Nonetheless, God had a plan for them.

This plan is fulfilled by God in the desert, in the foothills of Mount Sinai:

> On the third new moon after the people of Israel had gone forth out of the land of Egypt, on that day they came into the wilderness of Sinai. And when they set out from Rephidim and came into the wilderness of Sinai, they encamped in the wilderness; and there Israel encamped before the mountain (Ex 19, 1-2).

Then Moses went up the mountain to pray and God manifested himself and asked him to prepare his people, for he was going to make a pact, by virtue of which they would be his "people" and he would be their God. This pact is called the Covenant. In this pact, God gives Israel some norms of behavior, a code of conduct, which is the Ten Commandments:

I. The LORD . . . said: "I am the LORD your God, who brought you out of the land of Egypt, out of the house of bondage. You shall have no other gods before me. You shall not make for yourself a graven image, or any likeness of anything that is in heaven above, or that is on the earth beneath, or that is in the water under the earth; you shall not bow down to them or serve them; for I the LORD your God am a jealous God, visiting the iniquity of the fathers upon the children to the third and fourth generation of those who hate me, but showing steadfast love to thousands of those who love me and keep my commandments.

II. "You shall not take the name of the LORD your God in vain: for the LORD will not hold him guiltless who takes his name in vain.

III. "Observe the sabbath day, to keep it holy, as the LORD your God commanded you. Six days you shall labor, and do all your work; but the seventh day is a sabbath to the LORD your God; in it you shall not do any work, you, or your son, or your daughter, or your manservant, or your maidservant, or your ox, or your ass, or any of your cattle, or the sojourner who is within your gates, that your manservant and your maidservant may rest as well as you. You shall remember that you were a servant in the land of Egypt, and the LORD your God brought you out thence with a mighty hand and an outstretched arm; therefore the LORD your God commanded you to keep the sabbath day.

IV. "Honor your father and your mother, as the LORD your God commanded, that your days may be prolonged, and that it may go well with you, in the land which the LORD your God gives you.

V. "You shall not kill.

VI. "Neither shall you commit adultery.

VII. "Neither shall you steal.

VIII. "Neither shall you bear false witness against your neighbor.

IX. "Neither shall you covet your neighbor's wife;

X.   and you shall not desire your neighbor's house, his field, or
his manservant, or his maidservant, his ox, or his ass, or anything that is your neighbor's." (Dt 5, 6-21).

The book of Deuteronomy later reiterates and synthesizes these
commandments (Dt 5, 6-21), which are also known in Judaism as
"the ten words" (cf. Ex 34, 28; Dt 4, 13; 10, 4). They constitute the
Decalogue or Ten Commandments which God gave to his people.
Fidelity to these precepts carries with it God's aid and assistance.
Their duty was to transmit those precepts to the future generations;
Deuteronomy explicitly states:

> When your son asks you in time to come, "What is the
> meaning of the testimonies and the statutes and the ordi-
> nances which the LORD our God has commanded you?"
> then you shall say to your son, "We were Pharaoh's slaves
> in Egypt; and the LORD brought us out of Egypt with a
> mighty hand; and the LORD showed signs and wonders,
> great and grievous, against Egypt and against Pharaoh and
> all his household, before our eyes; and he brought us out
> from there, that he might bring us in and give us the land
> which he swore to give to our fathers.
>
> And the LORD commanded us to do all these statutes, to
> fear the LORD our God, for our good always, that he might
> preserve us alive, as at this day. And it will be righteous-
> ness for us, if we are careful to do all this commandment
> before the LORD our God, as he has commanded us" (Dt
> 6, 20-25).

The Israelites remained grateful to God for his revelation of the
code of conduct, and they knew that their destiny—for better or
worse—was tied to the fulfillment of the precepts. This was their
history: the glorious years of Israel coincide with their fidelity to the
Ten Commandments. On the other hand, the times of struggle and
defeat correspond to their infidelity.

2. The code of the Covenant

The Ten Commandments are part of the revelation given to Moses
and ought to be understood within the context of the Covenant of
God with his people and, ultimately, humanity. Because God loved
the world, he gave it a code of conduct. To fulfill these general precepts represents man's fidelity to and acceptance of the plan of God
in his life:

> The "ten words" are pronounced by God in the midst of a theophany ("The LORD spoke with you face to face at the mountain, out of the midst of the fire" [Dt 5,4]). They belong to God's revelation of himself and his glory. The gift of the Commandments is the gift of God himself and his holy will. In making his will known, God reveals himself to his people (*CCC*, 2059).

The fulfillment of these general precepts represent man's fidelity to the salvation offered by God. If God is faithful, man ought to also be loyal. The guarantee of such fidelity is the fulfillment of these precepts:

> The Commandments take on their full meaning within the covenant. According to Scripture, man's moral life has all its meaning in and through the covenant. . . .
>
> The Commandments properly so-called come in the second place: they express the implications of belonging to God through the establishment of the covenant. Moral existence is a *response* to the Lord's loving initiative. It is the acknowledgement and homage given to God and a worship of thanksgiving. It is cooperation with the plan God pursues in history (*CCC*, 2061-2062).

Consequently, when man keeps these precepts, he gives an affirmative response to God. He tells God that he accepts his will in his human life; by this man remains directly related to and grateful to God and also praises and acknowledges His power. As the fruits of this fidelity, man will reach his goal, which is happiness.

3. Ethical content of the Ten Commandments

The reading of the Decalogue (Ex 20, 2-17; Dt 5, 6-21) confirms that we have a basic code of conduct. In fact, in the Ten Commandments God does not offer a complete ethical program, but general and primitive principles of conduct.

The reason is clear: God could not demand from the Israelites great ethical requirements because Israel, at that time, was a primitive culture.

A quick analysis of these ethical contents confirms this thesis. The first three refer to the relationship of the people to God: Israel ought not to adore other gods, it ought to respect his name and offer worship on the sabbath. They try to defend monotheism against the polytheism of other cultures. In fact, the fulfillment of man demands the existence of a being in whom he can find his fulfillment. In this sense, both atheism and polytheism degrade the dignity of the person for one deny's God's existence while the other denies him the honor due him as the only God.

The remaining commandments outline other fundamental ethical requirements:

- Love for your parents: "Honor your father and mother" (fourth).

- Respect for life; man cannot capriciously disposes of another's life: "You shall not kill" (fifth).

- Make right use of sexuality according to the purpose for which God created it. By sexual intercourse, human life is generated, so any misuse of sexuality is to be avoided: "You shall not commit adultery" (sixth).

- Respect private property and the common good. Social life is impossible if there is no respect for private property: "You shall not steal" (seventh).

- The dignity of another person ought to be respected, so there can be no room for slander or lies: "You shall not give false testimony against your brother" (eighth).

- Finally, there is also the need to attend to internal desires, so that they may not lead the person on the wrong path: "You shall not covet your neighbor's wife" (ninth), and "You shall not covet your neighbor's goods" (tenth).

4. The Ten Commandments and natural law

The ethical content of the Decalogue corresponds to what later is called natural law. God made man with an interior code of conduct which, if he fulfills it, will aid him in living a life in the dignity worthy of man. On the other hand, if man does not keep it, he destroys himself. The Decalogue points to the fundamental nature of man:

> The Ten Commandments belong to God's revelation. At the same time they teach us the true humanity of man. They bring to light the essential duties, and therefore, indirectly,

the fundamental rights inherent in the nature of the human person. The Decalogue contains a privileged expression of the natural law (*CCC*, 2070).

The Fathers constantly teach that the Decalogue is a primitive statement of natural law. The sins of humanity had obscured it, and God reveals it to help us remember and fulfill it. Thus, spoke St. Irenaeus:

> From the beginning of time, God had placed in the hearts of men the precepts of natural law. Firstly, he was pleased to call their attention to them (St. Irenaeus, *Against Heretics*, IV, 15, 1).

5. The code of the New Covenant: the Beatitudes

To the precepts set forth by God's revelation of the Decalogue to the People of Israel, Jesus added the Beatitudes. The Beatitudes do not replace or contradict the demands of the New Testament; quite the contrary, they fulfill those demands in a remarkable way, emphasizing their interior spirit and challenging the Christian to aspire to a life of heroic virtue that transcends an external observance of the letter of the law.

> Seeing the crowds, he went up on the mountain, and when he sat down his disciples came to him. And he opened his mouth and taught them, saying:

I. "Blessed are the poor in spirit, for theirs is the kingdom of heaven.

II. Blessed are those who mourn, for they shall be comforted.

III. Blessed are the meek, for they shall inherit the earth.

IV. Blessed are those who hunger and thirst for righteousness, for they shall be satisfied.

V. Blessed are the merciful, for they shall obtain mercy.

VI. Blessed are the pure of heart, for they shall see God.

VII. Blessed are the peacemakers, for they shall be called sons of God.

VIII. Blessed are those who are persecuted for righteousness' sake, for theirs is the kingdom of heaven.

IX. Blessed are you when men revile you and persecute you and utter all kinds of evil against you falsely on my account. Rejoice and be glad, for your reward is great in heaven, for so men persecuted the prophets who were before you" (Mt 5, 1-12).

In this passage we can see that the moral behavior required of the Christian is something more than merely avoiding behavior forbidden by a set of precepts. Rather, the Christian should aspire to a life in which he actively seeks the good of others and does not merely strive to avoid harming them.

6. The present moral value of the Decalogue and its relation to the Beatitudes

Since it formulates the fundamental duties of man, the value of the Decalogue is not limited to a particular time; it is still valid today. In addition, the Ten Commandments are not abolished by the moral message of the New Testament.

Jesus emphatically states "Think not that I have come to abolish the law and the prophets; I have come not to abolish them but to fulfill them" (Mt 5, 17). Neither the new commandment of love nor the Sermon on the Beatitudes diminish the value of the Decalogue.

> Since they express man's fundamental duties towards God and towards his neighbor, the Ten Commandments reveal, in their primordial content, *grave* obligations. They are fundamentally immutable, and they oblige always and everywhere. No one can dispense from them. The Ten Commandments are engraved by God in the human heart (*CCC*, 2072).

And John Paul II relates the Decalogue to the Beatitudes:

> The Beatitudes are not specifically concerned with certain particular rules of behavior. Rather, they speak of basic attitudes and dispositions in life and therefore they do not coincide exactly with the commandments.

> On the other hand, there is no separation or opposition between the Beatitudes and the commandments: both refer to the good, to eternal life. The Sermon on the Mount begins with the proclamation of the Beatitudes, but also refers to the commandments (cf. Mt 5, 20-48).

> At the same time, the Sermon on the Mount demonstrates the openness of the commandments and their orientation toward the horizon of the perfection proper to the Beatitudes.

These latter are above all promises, from which there also indirectly flow normative indications for the moral life. In their originality and profundity they are a sort of self-portrait of Christ, and for this very reason are invitations to discipleship and communion of life with Christ (*VS*, 16).

7. Development of Christian morality in view of the Ten Commandments

Despite the novel message preached by Jesus, Christians have had difficulty with the precepts found in the Decalogue. Already, in the second century, St. Irenaeus of Lyons states:

> The LORD prescribed the love of God and taught justice towards our neighbor so that man might not be unjust, or unworthy of God. Thus, with the Decalogue, God was preparing man to be his friend and to have the same heart for his friend. . . . The words of the Decalogue persist also among us. Far from being abolished, they have received an amplification and development in the Incarnation of the LORD (St. Irenaeus, *Against Heretics*, IV, 16, 3-4).

The Ten Commandments are enriched by the life and teachings of Jesus Christ. For example, the acceptance and worship of one God is enhanced by the love of God as Father, and the transcendence of God as triune is acknowledged. The respect for life is enriched by the new commandment to love all men, including the enemy. Sexuality no longer just prohibits adultery, but now seeks internal chastity of thoughts and desires (Mt 5, 17-48). Likewise, they no longer merely forbid injuring another through malicious acts, but now seek internal charity and an active love of neighbor manifested in word and deed.

Consequently, when in moral theology the Decalogue is proposed and an attempt is made to articulate its moral content, the Ten Commandments then become the framework upon which the rich moral teachings of Jesus can be understood.

Conclusion

A Christian knows that when he obeys the Ten Commandments and lives according to Christ's teaching in the Beatitudes, besides fulfilling the moral content that fortifies him, he also fulfills the teachings of Jesus. And the Church, in presenting the Decalogue and the Beatitudes to every culture, gives a great service to all of humanity, since, at times, man loses his orientation in life and thus obscures fundamental elements of his moral life. According to some theologians, this was precisely the moral situation of humanity at the time of God's revelation to Moses:

> In the state of sin, a full explanation of the commandments of the Decalogue was necessary because of the obscurity of the light of reason and the deviation of the will (St. Bonaventure, *Commentary on the Sentences*, IV, 37, 1-3).

Additionally, there is need for the Church to remind men of every age that simply avoiding evil and satisfying our duties to our neighbors in a minimalistic way can never be acceptable if we wish to have a truly just society. Hence the importance of the Beatitudes, which point the way to a truly free and human existence.

Today, as Christians, we know the ethical contents of natural law by our conscience and by revelation, as understood by the Magisterium of the Church (cf. *CCC*, 2071; *VS*, 13-15).

CHAPTER IX
THE FIRST COMMANDMENT:
TO LOVE GOD ABOVE ALL ELSE

Peter was raised a Catholic, and had attended a Catholic grade school. He received a good education in general, but never gained a meaningful understanding of his faith. When he went to college, he began to date Rebecca, a non-practicing Jewish girl. As Peter began spending more and more time with Rebecca, he became less diligent in the practice of his faith. He often neglected to attend Sunday Mass in order to go to the beach or to do other social activities with Rebecca.

After several years, Peter and Rebecca realized that they had fallen in love, and began to consider marriage seriously. Peter recalled that as a Catholic, he had to insist that the children whom he and Rebecca might have would be baptized and raised Catholics.

Rebecca was very skeptical about the Catholic faith and refused to agree to raise her future children as Catholics. As Peter tried to persuade Rebecca to accept his opinion, he began to realize how important his faith was to him. He regretted his recent laxity in religious matters. He reevaluated his relationship with God, realizing that he owed everything to his Creator. He had a serious duty to carry out his obligations as a Christian, and so he returned to the active practice of his Catholic faith.

With these realizations, Peter faced more of a dilemma than ever. He truly loved Rebecca, but he also knew his love of God prevented him from marrying a woman who would not agree to raise their children in the Faith. Although he did his utmost to persuade Rebecca, she remained adamant in her opposition to Catholicism. After much careful thought and prayer, Peter came to the conclusion that he must break up with Rebecca and pursue their relationship no further.

- Why does the Catholic Church teach that human beings have an obligation to worship God?

- How does the Christian's relationship with God differ from that of the followers of other religions?

- What is the relationship between love of God and love of neighbor?

- What other obligations does knowledge of the truth place on the Christian?

Introduction

The theologian, from the start, tries to unite God and man in religion, for he knows that the obligation to worship God is unquestionable, since it is clearly stated in the Bible and flows out of the revelation that there is but one God. The original formulation of biblical monotheism is forceful: "You shall have no other gods before me" (Ex 20, 3; Dt 5,7). This precept demands a proper monotheism [belief in one god], in the midst of the cultural polytheism [belief in many gods], so firmly rooted in the regions surrounding Israel.

The book of Deuteronomy is more explicit and rich. Man ought to love and worship God. "Hear, O Israel: The LORD our God is one LORD, and you shall love the LORD your God with all your heart, and with all your soul, and with all your might" (Dt 6, 4-5; 10, 12).

The love of neighbor immediately follows the love of God. This double precept is found throughout the Jewish tradition, just as it is in Jesus' response to the scribes:

> And one of them, a lawyer, asked him a question, to test him. "Teacher, which is the great commandment of the law?" And he said to him, "You shall love the LORD your God with all your heart, and with all your soul, and with all your mind. This is the great and first commandment. And the second is like it: You shall love your neighbor as yourself. On these two commandments depend all the law and the prophets" (Mt 22, 35-40).

This great commandment summarizes the first three commandments of the Decalogue—*the first tablet*. The second is the remaining seven—*the second tablet*. This is why Jesus presents these two precepts to be a summary of the law and the teachings of the prophets (cf. Mt 22, 40).

It is important to bear in mind that the commandments, above all else, reflect God's love for man. Therefore, man is expected to return the love of God by fulfilling the commandments.

> God has loved us first. The love of the One God is recalled in the first of the "ten words." The commandments then make explicit the response of love that man is called to give to his God (CCC, 2083).

This chapter is devoted to the first commandment, which makes clear the obligation to love God and the need to condemn all hostile or profane (irreverent) actions in relation to God.

1. God, the foundation of human existence: the virtue of religion

The first commandment states the fundamental obligation of man to acknowledge the existence of God and, furthermore, to worship him, because without God man would not exist. Without an awareness of God, man's existence lacks meaning.

Moral theology is that part of theology which makes use of a series of practical judgments to direct human acts toward God, under the guidance of revelation. Moral theology seeks only to determine what man must do to maintain his relationship with God. Since man owes his existence to God, he ought to acknowledge him within the context of worship.

What distinguishes Christian revelation is not the existence of God, but his relation to man, for the God revealed in the Bible is not a "solitary god", but one who continuously acts in favor of man, as a father for his children. Questioned by Moses, Yahweh responds: "I am who am. . . . The God of your fathers, the God of Abraham, of Isaac, and of Jacob" (Ex 3, 13-15). And before giving the Decalogue, God speaks of himself, thus: "I am the LORD your God, who brought you out of the land of Egypt, out of the house of bondage" (Ex 20, 2).

This intervention of God on behalf of man is the theme of all scripture. The Incarnation of the Son is nothing less than God's will to save the whole of humanity: "For God so loved the world that he gave his only Son" (Jn 3, 16). Briefly stated, Christianity is the history of salvation, God's plan concerning humanity. The Christian God is not, then, a distant and impassive god but an intimate and active one. The very name of *Jesus* means *God saves* (Lk 1, 31; Mt 1, 21).

If such is God's intent, then man cannot remain passive before him and must respond accordingly. The response must be to believe in him, to trust in his aid, and to love him (cf. *CCC*, 2086). When that threefold intention is maintained before God, the Christian is in fact exercising the three theological virtues: faith, hope and love.

2. Worship of God as a practical exercise of the theological virtues

The exercise of believing, trusting and loving someone belongs to those three basic attitudes of human existence in interpersonal relationships. To foster and practice them furthers personal maturity. For this reason, we could consider them to be human virtues.

For a Christian and in reference to God, that threefold attitude finds new meaning in the grace infused by God, which springs forth from the new life in Baptism.

As a matter of fact, sanctifying grace makes it possible for the baptized to believe in, hope in, and love God by the infusion of the three theological virtues (supernatural virtues which originate with God and which place man in direct contact with him). These theological virtues are:

a. Faith.

> Faith is the theological virtue by which we believe in God and believe all that he has said and revealed to us, and that the Holy Church proposes for our belief, because he is truth itself (*CCC*, 1814).

Faith is the acceptance of the truths revealed by God without proof. In this sense, faith widens the capacity of human knowledge, since the human person will not only have a collection of truths given by reason, but will add those truths revealed by God. In this sense, to believe is to accept truths guaranteed by the authority of God.

Faith does not contradict reason. Therefore, once the truths revealed by God are accepted, human reason attempts to understand and defend those truths. Faith seeks and questions, rigorously attempting to understand those revealed truths, for it desires to understand both what God has revealed and the consequences of those truths for human life. Faith may be understood as "faith seeking understanding" (cf. *CCC*, 154-159).

Therefore, two fundamental attitudes of man are required in response to God's revelation:

- *To receive it with humility.* If human truth, according to the Greeks, manifests itself only to those who seek it humbly, then Divine revelation can only be accepted by those who are humble. Thus, the biblical passage: "God opposes the proud, but gives grace to the humble" (Jas 4, 6).

- *To intellectually cultivate it.* Once revelation is received, the Christian has the duty to nourish his faith. Faith, by its very nature, requires that it be strengthened through efforts to understand its content more clearly. A faith that one refuses to understand, as intended by God, is no faith at all.

Once faith is known and its content understood, the Christian has two additional duties:

- *To safeguard the faith.* Man has the serious obligation of protecting his faith and avoiding any risks. Faith can be lost, either by false theories planting doubt in the truth of revelation or by the habit of error obscuring it.

  A person—young or old, cultured or uncultured—can be deceived over simple matters. Or a man, confronted by a truth that he does wish to accept, may choose to dismiss it out of sheer discomfort.

It is important to mention the prudence which needs to be exercised in the reading of books that attack faith or distort it. It can never be stressed enough that the most profound convictions can be obscured when attacked by contradictory ideologies that are often presented in clever and appealing ways. When there is a question regarding a particular subject or book, it is imperative that the matter be discussed with one's confessor.

- *To communicate the faith received.* Since God reveals to man certain realities, he should share them with others. From this stems the obligation to "transmit the faith which has been received." Jesus advised this with severe words:

  > So everyone who acknowledges me before men I also will acknowledge before my Father who is in heaven; but whoever denies me before men, I also will deny before my Father who is in heaven (Mt 10, 32-33).

This warning, while it primarily refers to acknowledging the Person of Jesus, can also be seen to include his teachings:

> The disciple of Christ must not only keep the faith and live on it, but also profess it, confidently bear witness to it, and spread it (CCC, 1816).

But the meaning of faith is not exclusively something of the mind. Faith in its original Aramaic language is expressed by the word *emet* which denotes *to sustain*. With this meaning, to have faith is to "sustain oneself in God," to trust in him.

The greatness of faith contrasts with the sins against this virtue. Chief among them are:

- *Voluntary doubt* disregards or refuses to hold what God has revealed as true.

- *Involuntary doubt* hesitates in believing or in overcoming difficulties connected with the faith and fails to attempt to dispel the difficulties

- *Atheism* is the refusal to accept God's existence.

- *Heresy* is the obstinate denial by a baptized person of some truth which must be believed with divine and Catholic faith.

- *Apostasy* is the total repudiation of the Christian faith.

- *Schism* is the refusal to submit to the pope or to be united with the Church subject to him (cf. *CCC*, 2087-2089, 2123).

b. **Hope.**

> Hope is the theological virtue by which we desire the kingdom of heaven and eternal life as our happiness, placing our trust in Christ's promises and relying not on our own strength, but on the help of the grace of the Holy Spirit (*CCC*, 1817).

The theological virtue of hope builds upon the basic human attitude that allows for hope and trusts in the present and future life, since this attitude is a natural desire for happiness.

> The virtue of hope responds to the aspiration to happiness which God has placed in the heart of every man; it takes up the hopes that inspire men's activities and purifies them so as to order them to the Kingdom of heaven; it keeps man from discouragement; it sustains him during times of abandonment; it opens up his heart in expectation of eternal beatitude. Buoyed up by hope, he is preserved from selfishness and led to the happiness that flows from charity (*CCC*, 1818).

All these aspirations find their fulfillment in the divine plans. Thus, in the Old Testament God continually fosters the hope of his people. He sustains it while chastising their infidelity (Ezk 36, 6-38), but he also fosters hope when they are faithful. Moreover, that hope also includes the hope of salvation for all (Is 49, 6). The Bible praises the hope found in Abraham: "In hope he believed against hope, that he should become the father of many nations" (Rom 4, 18).

The first commandment requires that the Christian have trust in God and that he foster hope in eternal life. A sin against this commandment can occur either by defect or excess:

- *Despair*, that is, the loss of trust in God because of doubt in his fidelity or his interest in man.

   By *despair*, man ceases to hope for his personal salvation from God, for help in attaining it or for the forgiveness of his sins. Despair is contrary to God's goodness, to his justice—for the Lord is faithful to his promises—and to his mercy (*CCC*, 2091).

- *Presumption* can occur in two ways: when man expects salvation without personal effort, or when he trusts solely in his effort without God's aid:

   There are two kinds of *presumption*. Either man presumes upon his own capacities, (hoping to be able to save himself without help from on high), or he presumes upon God's almighty power or his mercy (hoping to obtain his forgiveness without conversion and glory without merit) (*CCC*, 2092).

Close to the certainty that God is faithful to his word, hope includes fear of punishment if man should offend God: A son's trust does not negate a father's justice.

c. **Love (Charity).**

   Charity is the theological virtue by which we love God above all things for his own sake, and our neighbor as ourselves for the love of God (*CCC*, 1822).

Christian love has three objects: God, neighbor, and self.

- *Love of God.* First, man ought to love God because he is his Creator and Father. The love of man for God should reflect the love of God for man. As St. John states, we ought to love

God "because he first loved us" (1 Jn 4, 19). He had also previously noted the real motive behind the love of God for man and vice versa:

> See what love the Father has given us, that we should be called children of God; and so we are. The reason why the world does not know us is that it did not know him (1 Jn 3,1).

One can sin against God's love in various ways:

— *Indifference* refuses to reflect on the prior goodness and power of divine charity.

— *Ingratitude* does not acknowledge divine charity and does not return his love.

— *Lukewarmness* is failure or hesitation in responding to divine love, and can imply refusal to obey the promptings of charity.

— *Acedia* refuses the joy God gives and causes one to be repelled by divine goodness. It is a form of depression stemming from lax ascetical practices that leads to discouragement.

— *Hatred of God* opposes the love of God, denies his goodness, and curses him as the one who forbids sin and inflicts punishment. It is a result of pride (cf. CCC 2094).

• *Love of neighbor.* All human beings are children of God and thereby brothers and sisters to one another. This requirement often appears strange and impossible to achieve to human sensibilities, for how is a victim to love the person who robs him, or what can lead the family of a murder victim to love the person who committed the crime? As individuals, nothing or next to nothing unites them, but as persons, much. All men are persons and thereby have their dignity. Moreover, as Christians, all differences and enmities ought to end because the first pages of the Bible state that man has been created in God's "image and likeness" (Gn 1, 26-27), and the words of St. Paul affirm that Christians "become partakers of the divine nature" (2 P 1, 4).

St. John adds many reasons encouraging the love of neighbor. Among them:

— Since "God is Love," charity flows from God; whoever does not love, does not know God:

Beloved, let us love one another; for love is of God, and he who loves is born of God and knows God. He who does not love does not know God; for God is love (1 Jn 4, 7-8).

— The path of Jesus and his commandment of love continue to be stressed in the teachings of the New Testament:

Jesus makes charity the *new commandment*.[1] By loving his own "to the end,"[2] he makes manifest the Father's love which he receives. By loving one another, the disciples imitate the love of Jesus which they themselves receive. Whence Jesus says: "As the Father has loved me, so have I loved you; abide in my love." And again: "This is my commandment, that you love one another as I have loved you"[3] (*CCC*, 1823).

• *Love of self.* Man is commanded to love others as he loves himself because they are created in the image and likeness of God. That he is obliged to have a genuine love for himself is presupposed by the command that he love his neighbor "as himself." Because our bodies , as well as our souls, were created for eternal glory, this commandment obliges us to care for both.

3. The relationship between the love of God and of neighbor

The question is often asked in an argumentative fashion: which of the two loves comes first and is more significant? Should the Christian love God first or his neighbor?

In reality, it is impossible to separate both loves, because the source of them both is God himself, who "is Love" (1 Jn 4, 8). There is, then, no Christian love that does not flow from God as love.

Which love is first ? It is obvious that the love of God ought to be prior, since the Decalogue calls it the first love. At the same time, a genuine love of God necessarily leads to the love of neighbor. St. John clearly states this: "If any one says, 'I love God,' and hates his brother, he is a liar" (1 Jn 4, 20). Hence, if the love of God comes first then the proof of its validity is found in the love of neighbor.

The encyclical *Veritatis splendor* addresses the relationship between the two great commandments:

> This certainly does not mean that Christ wishes to put the love of neighbor higher than, or even to set it apart from, the love of God. This is evident from his conversation with the teacher of the Law. . . . These two commandments, on which "depend all the Law and the Prophets" (Mt 22, 40), are profoundly connected and mutually related. *Their inseparable unity* is attested to by Christ in his words and by his very life: his mission culminates in the Cross of our Redemption (*VS*, 14; cf. Jn 3, 14-15).

4. Worship of God: the virtue of religion

The first commandment requires the acknowledgment of God and the worship due to him; in other words, living out the requirements of the virtue of religion which leads one to give to God the honor and worship due him as a requirement of justice. This virtue regulates the relationship between man and God.

The fulfillment of this virtue is fundamentally accomplished in the sacrifice of the Mass (cf. *CCC*, 2099-2100).

In the Mass, a summary of the acts belonging to the virtue of religion is commonly found They are adoration, atonement, petition, and thanksgiving.

The logic of these four acts is self-evident. First, God's greatness is poured out, which then requires acknowledgment by an act of worship (adoration). Then, man realizes that he falls short, that is, he sees his actions as not measuring up to what God desires of him, so he becomes aware of the need to ask for forgiveness (atonement). At the same time, man recognizes his finiteness and his need for God's aid, so he asks for it (petition). Finally, both the greatness of God and his forgiveness create a stance of constant thanksgiving.

The virtue of religion is essential to the life of the Christian. Practicing this virtue sometimes requires heroic effort today, for secular society can be a hindrance to religious expression, both in the personal and social sphere. As a consequence, a Christian is required to be ever more vigilant in the protection of his faith.

Other ways of worshiping God are promises and vows, covered in Chapter X (cf. *CCC*, 2101-2103).

5. Sins against the virtue of religion

In worshipping God, man often defiles the very act of worship by corrupt and false forms of religiosity. There are many reasons, but it is primarily due to a false concept of God. It seems normal for man —once he loses the transcendent understanding of God — to treat God according to some false notion. These false forms of religiosity can be reduced to five:

a. Idolatry.

Idolatry is the elevation of other realities to the state of gods, thereby making them take the place of the real God:

> Idolatry not only refers to false pagan worship. It remains a constant temptation to faith. Idolatry consists in divinizing what is not God. Man commits idolatry whenever he honors and reveres a creature in place of God, whether this be gods or demons (for example, satanism), power, pleasure, race, ancestors, the state, money, etc.... Idolatry rejects the unique Lordship of God; it is therefore incompatible with communion with God[4] (*CCC*, 2113).

b. Superstition.

Superstition takes many forms. Sometimes, it involves worshipping God in an improper manner or using legitimate religious devotions in a superstitious way. At other times, it involves a form of idolatry, because it attributes to created things powers which belong to God alone.

Practices of these sorts vary according to the times and culture of the individual or society. Consequently, it is not easy to list them, but a few examples may be provided:

- A Catholic who formally worships God in non-Christian or pagan religious ceremonies commits a sin of superstition, for the truth of Christ's divinity is denied.

- Legitimate religious devotions such as the rosary, novenas, medals of patron saints and the like are a manifestation of the virtue of religion. But even legitimate devotions can be distorted into superstitious practices when, for example, one insists that certain prayers be said a specific number of times for a specific number of days in order to obtain favors from God, or when one uses only candles of a specific color for specific prayers. Chain letters containing prayers which must be recited at certain times or in a particular number are also sins of superstition, because the results desired are attributed to the external rituals involved and not to God's goodness.

- A football player who believes that his team's loss to an opposing team was due to his failure to perform some pregame ritual or wear a particular article of clothing is guilty of a sin of superstition. Such actions attribute supernatural powers to created things.

- The businessman who refuses to schedule meetings or flights on the 13th day of the month also sins by superstition, for by so doing, he denies God's providence and refuses to trust him to direct and protect his life.

The fact that these and many other superstitious practices vary from one culture to another already reflects their falsity, since it is not common to find good customs changing dramatically from one culture to another.

Superstition has nothing to do with so-called "popular devotions," which are themselves religious expressions proper to a culture and its many generations (cf. Supplementary Reading 5).

c. **Divination.**

Divination is the prediction of the future or the revelation of the unknown through so-called paranormal means. The desire to know the future is second nature to man. While the religious person trusts in God for the future, divination and other magical means want to predict the future and wish to unveil the mystery of life.

The desire to predict the future by means that contradict a true religious faith cannot be seen as religious practice, and is false worship of God. The false means are many; the *Catechism of the Catholic Church* summarizes them in the following manner:

> All forms of *divination* are to be rejected: recourse to Satan or demons, conjuring up the dead or other practices falsely supposed to "unveil" the future.[5] Consulting horoscopes, astrology, palm reading, interpretation of omens and lots, the phenomena of clairvoyance, and recourse to mediums all conceal a desire for power over time, history, and, in the last analysis, other human beings, as well as a wish to conciliate hidden powers. They contradict the honor, respect, and loving fear that we owe to God alone (*CCC*, 2116).

In this broad summary, the practices of divination are diverse. Particularly serious is recourse to the devil or to the dead because it includes the possibility of fraud and presents an indirect avenue to demonic spirits. All of them deny freedom and man's ability, with God's aid, to reach his destiny.

d. Magic.

Magic is the desire to know and control the occult forces which supposedly influence man's life. This has always been an attractive temptation for human beings, and has existed in various forms in every human culture. Witchcraft is one of the most common and seriously sinful forms of this evil.

Characteristic of magic are the various practices in which an individual attempts, through rituals, formulas or items and natural forces believed to have power in themselves, to use occult forces, not only to avoid some evils but also to bring about other evils.

> All practices of *magic* or *sorcery*, by which one attempts to tame occult powers, so as to place them at one's service and have a supernatural power over others—even if this were for the sake of restoring their health—are gravely contrary to the virtue of religion. These practices are even more to be condemned when accompanied by the intention of harming someone, or when they have recourse to the intervention of demons. Wearing charms is also reprehensible (*CCC*, 2117).

Magic differs essentially from the veneration of images, which are religious representations of different Christian mysteries. They represent the LORD, the Virgin and the saints. The Christian veneration of images unfolds in a sacred environment, whose form is the Eucharistic Liturgy, which is the highest form of worship.

e. Irreligion.

Irreligion is also condemned by the first commandment. The sin of irreligion includes;

- *Tempting God* is testing, in word or deed, the goodness and power of God.

- *Sacrilege* is disrespect for sacred persons, places or things.

- *Simony* is the buying or selling of spiritual powers or gifts (cf. *CCC*, 2118-2132; cf. Acts 8, 9-24).

6. Biblical condemnation of all forms of superstition

The condemnation of superstitions is not a recent stance by the Magisterium; rather, it has been constant in the history of Christianity. The first biblical testimonies recall these condemnations. The Old Testament fought against superstitions commonly present at that time:

> "When you come into the land which the LORD your God gives you, you shall not learn to follow the abominable practices of those nations. There shall not be found among you anyone who burns his son or his daughter as an offering, anyone who practices divination, a soothsayer, or an augur, or a sorcerer, or a charmer, or a medium, or a wizard, or a necromancer. For whoever does these things is an abomination to the LORD; and because of these abominable practices the LORD your God is driving them out before you. You shall be blameless before the LORD your God.

> "For these nations, which you are about to dispossess, give heed to soothsayers and to diviners; but as for you, the LORD your God has not allowed you so to do. The LORD your God will raise up for you a prophet like me from among you, from your brethren—him you shall heed—just as you desired of the LORD your God at Horeb on the day of the assembly, when you said, 'Let me not hear again the voice of the LORD my God, or see this great fire any more, lest I die.' And the LORD said to me, 'They have rightly said all that they have spoken. I will raise up for them a prophet like you from among their brethren; and I will put my words in his mouth, and he shall speak to them all that I command him. . . .'" (Dt 18, 9-18).

This testimony makes it clear that superstitions are ridiculous, ancient as man, common in an era of religious decadence, and totally rejected by God.

Also, the New Testament condemns all forms of superstitions, as in the case of St. Paul, who encourages pagans to "turn to God from idols, to serve a living and true God" (1 Th 1, 9). The Apostle stresses the difference between "God and idols" (2 Cor 6, 16). In the list of sins found in the New Testament, there is mention of idolatry and witchcraft (Gal 5, 20; Rv 21, 8), and those who have accepted the Gospel and later turn to idols are rejected (1 Cor 10, 14; 2 Cor 6, 14-17).

However, in the New Testament the term idols refers not only to pagan gods, but also pagan values; accordingly, the "immoral or impure man, or one who is covetous" (Eph 5, 5) is like the "lover of idols."

The different forms of false religiosity have a twofold significance: that man has lost true piety and has supplied with false forms what otherwise should reflect a Christian spirit. Furthermore, it shows the lack of religious and human culture: Is it possible for man today to confide his destiny to amulets, the conjunction of stars, or to a deck of cards? Consequently, when Catholic morality condemns those practices, besides directing to true piety, it liberates man from absurd and vain myths.

Conclusion

Humanly speaking, there is no way to understand the love of God for man. Who among all humans would be willing to suffer and die as Jesus did for man's sake? At the same time, it should be obvious that there is a return owed to God for the love he has lavishly poured forth on all. It is a great insult when man turns from him to creatures and pleasures of limited value.

The Old Testament compares sin against God to the adulterous partner in a marital relationship. This metaphor offers a good way to begin to try to understand God's love, for it is universally recognized that the greatest tragedies are the result of the abuse of the marital relationship on the human level. How much greater is the tragedy of one who refuses the love of God.

OUTLINE

I. Glossary

ADORATION:

Worship, in which we acknowledge and respond to the revelation of the glory and power of God

CHARITY:

The theological virtue by which a person loves God above all things, and loves his neighbor as he loves himself for the sake of God.

DESPAIR:

The loss of trust in God because of doubt in his fidelity or his interest in man.

FAITH:

The theological virtue by which we believe in God and all that he has revealed.

HOPE:

The theological virtue by which a person waits for eternal life as promised by Jesus Christ, relying on God's grace.

IDOLATRY:

The religious worship of imaginary gods, the devil or other created things, such as forces of nature, the stars or the cosmos, animals etc.

MORAL THEOLOGY:

That part of theology which makes use of a series of practical judgments to direct human acts towards their supernatural end, God, under the guidance of revelation.

RELIGION:

The constant attitude of man manifesting to God the honor due to him, as the Creator, LORD and Father.

SACRILEGE:

Profaning or treating in an unworthy manner the sacraments or other liturgical actions, as well as things consecrated to God in a special way, such as priests, religious women and men, churches, shrines, convents or monasteries, icons, statues etc.

SUPERSTITION:

Beliefs or practices which render false worship to God, or which attribute supernatural or magical powers to certain objects or ritual actions. The most common and grave sins of superstition are divination and magic.

THEOLOGICAL VIRTUES:

The virtues of faith, hope, and love (charity), which enable the Christian to live in a close relationship with God. They are called *"theological"* because they originate with God, and help to lead the believer to perfect union with him by enabling him to love God for his own sake.

THEOPHANY:

A word meaning "the manifestation of God." A theophany can be an actual appearance of God in his glory (as Moses witnessed on Mt. Sinai), or a manifestation of God through some medium such as a storm, fire, and angelic apparitions.

WORSHIP:

The response of the person that acknowledges the greatness of God, and renders signs of submission, reverence and love to him.

II. Summary of Principles

1. The love of God and of one's fellow man is the source, the sustenance and the end of the moral life.

2. By exercising the three theological virtues, the Christian develops the divine life and formation in Christ conferred by Baptism.

3. Faith is not a vague religious sentiment. It assents to truths proposed by God and acts according to his moral norms.

4. Belief is an act of the will aided by grace, so that each person can affirm:"we believe what we love" (J. Pieper).

5. In matters of faith and morals the Christian must give intellectual assent to the teachings of the Magisterium, and must apply them to his own life

6. Some Christian truths (faith and morals) are strictly supernatural and known only by revelation; others are also knowable by natural understanding.

7. The Christian has a grave obligation to publically confess his faith and to avoid occasions that could endanger his faith.

8. The Christian is obliged to propagate his faith by public witness.

9. The virtue of religion requires acknowledgement and worship of God as a matter of justice.

10. False religiosity such as idolatry or superstition is a grave offense against God.

11. An act of sacrilege constitutes a very grave sin.

12. The virtue of hope enables a Christian to trust Christ's promises instead of relying on himself.

SUPPLEMENTARY READINGS

1. The first commandment embraces faith, hope, and charity. When we say 'God' we confess a constant, unchangeable being, always the same, faithful and just, without any evil. It follows that we must necessarily accept his words and have complete faith in him and acknowledge his authority. He is almighty, merciful, and infinitely beneficent. . . . Who could not place all hope in him? Who could not love him when contemplating the treasures of goodness and love he had poured out on us? Hence the formula God employs in the Scripture at the beginning and end of his commandments: 'I am the LORD.' [6]

(CCC, 2086)

2. ...What the Church has decided definitively on matters of faith and morals, all Catholics must accept. On what has not been decided definitively, you may follow what theologian seems most

reasonable to you. On matters of policy you may disagree, or on matters of opinion. You do not have to accept everything your particular pastor says unless it is something defined by the whole Church, i.e., defined or canon law. We are all bound by Friday abstinence. This does not mean that the sin is in eating meat but that the sin is in refusing the penance; the sin is in disobedience to Christ who speaks to us through the Church; the same with missing Mass on Sunday...

(Flannery O'Connor, *Collected Works: Letter to Cecil Dawkins, 23 December 1959*, p. 1117)

3. If I speak in the tongues of men and of angels, but have not love, I am a noisy gong or a clanging cymbal. And if I have prophetic powers, and understand all mysteries and all knowledge, and if I have all faith, so as to remove mountains, but have not love, I am nothing. If I give away all I have, and if I deliver my body to be burned, but have not love, I gain nothing.

Love is patient and kind; love is not jealous or boastful; it is not arrogant or rude. Love does not insist on its own way; it is not irritable or resentful; it does not rejoice at wrong, but rejoices in the right. Love bears all things, believes all things, hopes all things, endures all things.

Love never ends; as for prophecies, they will pass away; as for tongues, they will cease; as for knowledge, it will pass away. . . . Now I know in part; then I shall understand fully, even as I have been fully understood. So faith, hope, love abide, these three; but the greatest of these is love.

(1 Cor 13, 1-13)

4. Now the human mind, in order to be united to God, needs to be guided by the sensible world, since "invisible things . . . are clearly seen, being understood by the things that are made," as the Apostle says (Rm 1, 20). Wherefore in the Divine worship it is necessary to make use of corporeal things, that man's mind may be aroused thereby, as by signs, to the spiritual acts by means of which he is united to God. Therefore the internal acts of religion take precedence of the others and belong to religion essentially, while its external acts are secondary, and subordinate to the internal acts.

(St. Thomas Aquinas, *Summa theologiae*, II-II, q. 81, a. 7)

5. Here we touch upon an aspect of evangelization which cannot leave us insensitive. We wish to speak about what today is often called popular religiosity.

   One finds among the people particular expressions of the search for God and for faith, both in the regions where the Church has been established for centuries and where she is in the course of becoming established. These expressions were for a long time regarded as less pure and were sometimes despised, but today they are almost everywhere being rediscovered. During the last Synod the bishops studied their significance with remarkable pastoral realism and zeal.

   (EN, 48)

6. The practice of placing sacred images in churches so that they be venerated by the faithful is to be maintained. Nevertheless their number should be moderate and their relative positions should reflect right order. For otherwise the Christian people may find them incongruous and they may foster devotion of doubtful orthodoxy.

   (SC, 125)

7. I answer that, as stated above (81, 5; I-II, 101, 4), a thing is called "sacred" through being deputed to the divine worship. Now just as a thing acquires an aspect of good through being deputed to a good end, so does a thing assume a divine character through being deputed to the divine worship, and thus a certain reverence is due to it, which reverence is referred to God. Therefore whatever pertains to irreverence for sacred things is an injury to God, and comes under the head of sacrilege.

   (St. Thomas Aquinas, *Summa theologiae*, II-II, q. 99, a. 1)

8. The New Age is ... appropriated by its disciples and is presented to its proselytes as a salvific wisdom. In this, it approximates to the gnostic enthusiasm which have troubled the Church from her inception, and which in fact ground all heresy. Gnosticism consists, in all its varied presentations, in a reversion to paganism under pseudo-Christian auspices. This camouflaging of an absolute and comprehensive antagonism to Christianity has characterized Gnosticism from its origins, as it did in the flower children in the Age of Aquarius, and as it does in the New Age disciples today. The New Age movement is only the current

Western version of this perennial perversion of the Christian faith. . . .

. . . In the end, the New Age is no more than one more pagan soteriology: it looks to the extinction of the good creation that is in Christ, the Image of God, in order that one may image Nothing.

> (Archbishop Francis J. Stafford, *The "New Age" Movement: Analysis of a New Attempt to Find Salvation Apart from Christian Faith*, Catholic Position Papers, March 1993)

APPENDICES

1. Religious liberty

If man ought to worship God, society not only has to recognize this right, but also to facilitate and defend the exercise thereof. It must be treated as a fundamental right, as *Vatican II* proclaims:

> This Vatican Council declares that the human person has a right to religious freedom. This freedom means that all men are to be immune from coercion on the part of individuals or of social groups and of any human power, in such wise that no one is to be forced to act in a manner contrary to his own beliefs, whether privately or publicly, whether alone or in association with others, within due limits (*DH*, 2).

In virtue of this principle, civil authority has no power to limit the exercise of the right to worship God in private. The Tradition of the Church has always affirmed these truths, which were solemnly declared at Vatican II :

> The social nature of man, however, itself requires that he should give external expression to his internal acts of religion: that he should share with others in matters religious; that he should profess his religion in community. Injury therefore is done to the human person and to the very order established by God for human life, if the free exercise of religion is denied in society, provided just public order is observed (*DH*, 3).

Many nations have come to recognize this right by including it in their constitutions. The United Nation's *Universal Declaration on the Rights of Man* enumerates religious liberty with the rights to freedom of thought and conscience.

> Everyone has the right to freedom of thought, conscience and religion; this right includes freedom . . . either alone or in his community with others and in public or private, to manifest his religion or belief in teaching, practice, worship and observance (*Universal Declaration on the Rights of Man*, Art. 18).

And the First Amendment of the Constitution of the United States, likewise formulates this fundamental right of man: "Congress shall make no law respecting an establishment of religion, or prohibiting the free exercise thereof . . ."

2. The supernatural and human virtues

A virtue is a firm and habitual disposition to do the good. The virtuous person tends toward the good with all his powers, both sensory and intellectual, pursues the good and chooses it in concrete actions (cf. CCC, 1804). All the virtues which a man may acquire may be divided into two general categories: *human* and *supernatural virtues.*

Of the human virtues, four (which may also be called moral virtues) play the most crucial role. They are accordingly called *cardinal,* for they are the foundation upon which all the others depend. They are: prudence, justice, fortitude and temperance. "If anyone loves righteousness, [Wisdom's] labors are virtues; for she teaches temperance and prudence, justice, and courage, and nothing in life is more useful for man than these" (Wis 8, 7) (CCC, 1805).

The *human virtues* are firm dispositions and habitual perfections of intellect and will that govern our actions and order our passions according to reason and faith. They make possible ease, self-mastery, and joy in leading a morally good life. "The virtuous man is he who freely practices the good" (CCC, 1804; cf. CCC, 1803-1804).

> It is not easy for man, wounded by sin, to maintain moral balance. Christ's gift of salvation offers us the grace necessary to persevere in the pursuit of the virtues. Everyone should always ask for this grace of light and strength, frequent the sacraments, cooperate with the Holy Spirit, and follow his calls to love what is good and shun evil (CCC, 1811).

The human virtues, acquired by education, by deliberate acts and by a perseverance ever-renewed in repeated efforts, are purified and elevated by divine grace. They are the fruit and seed of good acts, and with God's help they dispose all the powers of the human being for communion with divine love (cf. CCC, 1804, 1810).

> The human virtues are rooted in the theological virtues, which adapt man's faculties for the participation in the divine nature:[7] for the theological virtues relate directly to God. They dispose Christians to live in a relationship with the Holy Trinity. They have the One and Triune God for their origin, motive, and object (CCC, 1812).

Supernatural virtues (also called *theological virtues*), on the other hand, are infused into a person's soul by God's grace. They are not acquired by habit, but they must be habitually acted upon in order for them to increase and perfect the life of man. These virtues dispose a person to function according to the dictates of reason, guided by a conscience enlightened by faith. Their purpose is theological, because they lead the soul directly and immediately to God. These supernatural virtues are:

- *Faith*, by which a person believes all that God has revealed because God is Truth, who cannot deceive or be deceived;

- *Hope*, by which a person has confidence that God will fulfill all his promises, because he is all-powerful and true to his Word, and

- *Charity*, by which a person, motivated by the love of God, loves God above all things and his neighbor as himself.

> The theological virtues are the foundation of Christian moral activity; they animate it and give it its special character. They inform and give life to all the moral virtues. They are infused by God into the soul of the faithful to make them capable of acting as his children and of meriting eternal life. They are the pledge of the presence and action of the Holy Spirit in the faculties of the human being (CCC, 1813).

3. The "New Age" movement

A growing phenomenon in Western culture during the past thirty years has been the New Age movement.

The New Age movement is not really new in one sense; followers of the various groups who classify themselves as New Age incorporate ideas from numerous sources. Ancient religious systems such as gnosticism, oriental religions such as Buddhism and Hinduism, occult practices from Western history, and even modern science and psychology are all sources from which the New Age religions have drawn their beliefs and philosophies. The result is a strange blend of eastern religion, humanistic psychology, occultism and superstition.

However, the New Age movement appears to have its specific historical inception, or perhaps it catalyst, in the theosophist and occultist speculations of Alice Anne Bailey (1880-1949), whose copious and repetitive publications have been in print over the past 70 years in numerous editions, many of them recent. The contemporary rediscovery of and fascination with her New Age doctrine owes a great deal to those millions of unchurched people in the Western world who, once anchored in the certitudes of the Christian faith, have lost that spiritual security under the pervasive and corrosive influence of a counter Catholic symbolism of modernity, and now, seeking another spiritual haven, find themselves in the position, succinctly described by G.K. Chesterton, of the apostate from Christianity who, instead of now believing nothing, believes anything....

It is important to understand that in order to borrow from so many varied, and sometimes contradictory, sources, the followers of the New Age movements must water-down and transform the beliefs of these systems in order to popularize them. (It is also important to stress here that Buddhism and Hinduism, for example, are major world religions; they *are not* part of the New Age movement. Some of their religious beliefs have been absorbed into the New Age movement, but these beliefs have often been drastically modified in order to make them acceptable to New Age believers. It would be wrong to mistake these ancient religious beliefs as being part of the New Age movement.)

In addition, it is sometimes difficult to understand the different groups which belong to the New Age movement, because these groups tend to be very loosely structured. There is no central organization of these groups into a single, unified movement as such.

Stated most simply, New Age philosophies and religious practices are contrary to the revelation which God has given to humanity and to the First Commandment. They are therefore incompatible with the Christian faith. This can be demonstrated clearly by examining some of the errors common to all New Age groups:

- *Monism*: In general, most New Age religions are characterized by a belief in *monism,* the belief that everything that exists (human beings, the universe, God etc.) is one. Christians, on the other hand, believe that God is unique and separate from the created universe. God is eternal, while the material universe had a beginning and will have an end. Similarly, God is infinite, while the created world is finite and limited in its nature.

- *Pantheism:* New Age believers also believe that the nature of this monistic universe is divine, that everything which exists is God. While New Age books tend to focus more on the divine nature of human beings rather than of plants and animals, it is nevertheless possible to find many which equate human life with animal life and plant life. After all, if everything is divine, then no part of the world can be inherently more valuable than any other part. This is a denial of man's unique position in the created order, as well as the unique nature of his relationship with God. Christianity teaches that man alone, because he is a spiritual as well as a physical being, is created in the image and likeness of God. Man alone can acknowledge and love his creator. Further, God clearly states in the Old Testament that there is nothing in physical creation which is like himself, and therefore the Jews are warned not to make images of God in the form of any living creature, nor to fall into the error of worshipping created things as divine (cf. Dt 4,15-19).

- *Syncretism:* Syncretism is a word which means an attempt to bring into harmony contrasting or conflicting ideas. In religion, syncretists try to eliminate conflicts between different religious faiths by eliminating those doctrines which contradict each other, while holding on to the doctrines which seem to agree or complement one another. Thus, a syncretistic approach to the differences between, say, Christianity and Hinduism, would be to accept Jesus' claim to be divine by claiming that Jesus is an *avatar.* Because a number of men in the history of Hinduism claimed to be avatars, or incarnations of the divine being, a syncretist equates their claims with Jesus' claim, while ignoring the fact that Jesus clearly stated that he alone is "the way, the truth and the life," apart from whom no one can come to salvation (cf. Jn 14,6).

- *Gnosticism:* The word "gnosticism" comes from the Greek word *gnosis,* meaning knowledge. Gnostics are people who believe that a person can achieve enlightenment, healing or transformation only through possession of secret knowledge given to a special few. In order to obtain this knowledge, one must turn to this select elite for "enlightenment." This contrasts sharply with the Christian message that salvation is intended for all people, and that it is our relationship with Jesus, not our knowledge, which brings salvation.

A final problem with the New Age movement which should be noted is its denial of man's need for salvation. For followers of the New Age movement, because all people are inherently divine, there is no need for salvation bestowed on us from the outside by a redeemer. All that is necessary is that each person becomes conscious of his or her own divine nature. Further, there is a denial of the reality of sin. There are no objective moral goods or evils—there is only ignorance and unenlightenment.

QUESTIONS

1. What is the moral message of the story that begins this chapter?

2. What is the role of a theologian?

3. What are the two great Commandments?

4. Why is God the basic principle of man's life and being?

5. What does moral theology seek to do?

6. What distinguishes Christian revelation from other religious faiths?

7. What are the three fundamental attitudes Christians should have in their relationship with Jesus?

8. Define the virtue of Faith.

9. What are the sins against faith?

10. What two fundamental attitudes are required in response to God's revelation?

11. What does it mean to propagate and safeguard the faith?

12. Define the virtue of Hope.

13. What are the sins against hope?

14. Define the virtue of Charity.

15. What are the sins against charity?

16. What do monotheism and polytheism mean?

17. What is the theme of all scripture?

18. What are the sins against the virtue of religion?

19. What does Jesus' name mean?

20. What four acts of religion are exemplified in the Mass?

PRACTICAL EXERCISES

1. Read Supplementary Reading 1 and answer this question: What treasury of goodness has God poured out upon man?

2. Comment on 1 Cor 13. Include an enumeration of the qualities of charity, and determine if any of the marks of Christian love show up in everyday life?

3. Examine and comment on this excerpt from the *Catechism of the Catholic Church*:

> All practices of *magic* or *sorcery*, by which one attempts to tame occult powers, so as to place them at one's service and have a supernatural power over others—even if this were for the sake of restoring their health—are gravely contrary to the virtue of religion. These practices are even more to be condemned when accompanied by the intention of harming someone, or when they have recourse to the intervention of demons. Wearing charms is also reprehensible. *Spiritism* often implies divination or magical practices; the Church for her part warns the faithful against it. Recourse to so-called traditional cures does not justify either the invocation of evil powers or the exploitation of another's credulity (CCC, 2117).

4. Read and take note of the principles found in the following Scriptural passages which condemn superstition:

   — Lv 19, 26; 19, 31; 20, 6; 20, 27;
   — Dt 13, 2-4.

5. Read Supplementary Reading 5 and describe the pros and cons of some popular devotions with which you are familiar. Do you think that even legitimate Christian devotions can be abused and become superstitious? Support your answer with an example.

6. Discuss and enumerate several classes of superstition. Analyze and assess their plausibility. Do these superstitions describe what is real in any way? Why would anyone believe them?

7. What is the difference between wearing amulets or good-luck charms and wearing devotional medals, such as the Miraculous Medal or a patron saint medal? Likewise, what is the difference between divination with the dead and prayers to saints?

CHAPTER X
THE SECOND COMMANDMENT:
YOU SHALL NOT TAKE THE NAME
OF THE LORD YOUR GOD IN VAIN

"What's in a name? That which we call a rose by any other name would smell as sweet." These famous words of Shakespeare are only half true. A name, whether it be of a person or a thing, gathers many emotional overtones by constant use. A name ceases to be just a group of letters taken from the alphabet; a name comes to represent the person or the thing which bears the name. The emotions aroused in us by the word "rose" are quite different from those evoked by the name "skunk cabbage." A young man in love only has to hear his sweetheart's name mentioned casually by a stranger, to make his pulse rate rise. A man who has suffered a great injury at the hands of someone named George will forever have a great distaste for the name "George." Men have killed—and have been killed—"in defense of their good name." Whole families have been grieved because some member of the family "brought disgrace on the family name." In short, a name stands for the one who bears the name—and our attitude toward a name reflects our attitude toward the person whose name it is.

All of this is obvious, of course. But it serves to recall to mind why it is a sin to misuse God's name—to use it carelessly or irreverently. If we love God we shall love his name and never speak it except with reverence and respect. We shall never use it as an expletive, as an expression of anger or impatience or surprise; we shall do nothing to bring infamy upon his name. Indeed, our love for God's name will extend to those of Mary, his mother, and to his friends the saints, and to all holy things which belong to God. Their names, too, will pass our lips only with thoughtful reverence. That we may never forget this aspect of our love for God, he has given us the second commandment (Leo J. Trese, The Faith Explained).

Let us ask ourselves:

- Under what circumstances may God's name be legitimately invoked?

- What are the obligations which the invocation of God's name places upon a person?

- How can sins against the Second Commandment be avoided?

Introduction

The expression, "He is a man of his word," indicates that the speaker is a person of high moral character. When he makes a promise or a statement, there is no need for him to sign his name, and this guarantee arises out of who he is, for his personhood guarantees that he will follow through and keep his word.

When a person takes an oath using God's name, it is a statement saying the personhood of God is standing behind the oath, so it would be seriously wrong to use the name of God to guarantee a lie.

1. The grandeur of God's Name

As the Supreme Being and man's creator, God is owed such reverence and devotion that his very name is sacred. As the *Catechism of the Catholic Church* states:

> Among all the words of revelation, there is one which is unique: the revealed name of God. God confides his name to those who believe in him; he reveals himself to them in his personal mystery (CCC, 2143).

In the New Testament, St. Paul emphasizes the importance and power of God's name in the person of Christ.

> Therefore God has highly exalted him and bestowed on him the name which is above every name, that at the name of Jesus every knee should bow, in heaven and on earth and under the earth, and every tongue confess that Jesus Christ is LORD, to the glory of God the Father (Phil 2, 9-11).

It is, therefore, the duty of every Christian to avoid the irreverent use of God's name, and, furthermore, to accord the name of God devotion and praise.

> Respect for his name is an expression of the respect owed to the mystery of God himself and to the whole sacred reality it evokes. The *sense of the sacred* is part of the virtue of religion. . . .
>
> The faithful should bear witness to the Lord's name by confessing the faith without giving way to fear.[1] Preaching and catechizing should be permeated with adoration and respect for the name of our Lord Jesus Christ (CCC, 2144-2145).

2. Oaths. Definition and division

> An oath is the invocation of the divine Name as witness to the truth. It cannot be taken except in truth, judgment and justice (*CIC*, 1199).

To take an oath is to call upon God as a witness. Expressions like "God is my witness," "I speak before God," and "As God is my Judge" are phrases often repeated in everyday conversation. On some occasions they come out spontaneously, but at other times they are used deliberately, and ordinarily such statements are not truly oaths, for the speaker has no intention to make an oath. Nevertheless, it is good to cultivate the habit of avoiding the use of phrases which call upon God's testimony in unimportant matters, for to call upon God as a witness to the truth of one's words demands the greatest possible discretion.

We can distinguish two kinds of oaths: *assertory* and *promissory*. In an assertory oath, God is called on as a witness to the truth of what is being said. An example of an assertory oath would be the oath taken by witnesses in court when giving testimony in a trial. One may take a promissory oath when he calls upon God as witness to what will happen, frequently if some conditions are met. An example of a promissory oath is the oath taken by an elected public official who solemnly swears before God to fulfill the duties of his office.

An oath can be public or private. A *public oath* is taken before a public authority or tribunal. A *private oath*, on the contrary, is taken before private citizens.

In order to take a true oath, God must be called upon as a witness. When one only calls on God, but without demanding his testimony, that is not considered to be an oath—and consequently, the virtue of religion is not being exercised. For this reason, formulas like "God knows everything!" or "God knows!" do not constitute oaths. When one says something on his own honor, he is not taking a real oath. Formulas like "on my word of honor" are used to guarantee a higher grade of veracity, but should not be considered oaths.

3. Old Testament doctrine concerning the custom of taking oaths

The recognition of only one God, transcendent and creator, besides requiring from man the worship due to him, demands that man also respect his very name. This respect may be seen in a special way in oaths.

When dealing with others and on solemn occasions, man has always called upon God as a witness. This custom was not unknown to nations at the time of Israel. For this reason, when Yahweh dictates the moral code to his people, he forbids them to use his name in vain. The two expressions of this commandment in the Old Testament fully agree on this point:

> You shall not take the name of the LORD your God in vain; for the LORD will not hold him guiltless who takes his name in vain (Ex 20, 7; Dt 5, 11).

It is worth noting that the Old Testament relates the promises of God which are accompanied by oaths. For example, God promises his blessings with this oath:

> "By myself I have sworn," says the LORD, "because you have done this, and have not withheld your son, your only son, I will indeed bless you, and I will multiply your descendants as the stars of heaven and as the sand which is on the seashore. And your descendants shall possess the gate of their enemies" (Gn 22, 16-17).

This oath is remembered by Moses (Dt 6, 3), is recorded in the *Magnificat* (Lk 1,73) and is mentioned in the letter to the Hebrews (Heb 6, 13-17). Through Nathan, God swears to David that he will have a successor (2 Sm 7, 11-13). The psalmist also recalls this oath (Ps 132, 11) and St. Peter mentions it in his first discourse in which he acknowledges Christ as God of all humanity (Acts 2, 30).

The book of Numbers regulates the use of oaths (Nb 30, 2). Later, the book of Sirach gives this advice:

> Listen, my children . . . do not accustom your mouth to oaths, and do not habitually utter the name of the Holy One; for as a servant who is continually examined under torture will not lack bruises, so also the man who always swears and utters the name will not be cleansed from sin.

> A man who swears many oaths will be filled with iniquity, and the scourge will not leave his house; if he offends, his sin will remain on him (Sir 23, 7-11).

Jesus Christ explained this second commandment and strongly urged its observance (Mt 5, 33-37). As a whole, the second commandment is a practical application of the virtue of religion which guides man's conversations with God, demands respect for his name and person and refinement in holy things related to him.

4. New Testament doctrine concerning the custom of taking oaths

The New Testament also permits the use of oaths. Jesus Christ explained this second commandment and strongly urged its observance (Mt 5, 33-37). As a whole, the second commandment is a practical application of the virtue of religion which guides man's conversations with God, demands respect for his name and person and refinement in holy things related to him.

But the words of Jesus are restrictive:

> Again you have heard that it was said to the men of old, 'You shall not swear falsely, but shall perform to the LORD what you have sworn. But I say to you, do not swear at all, either by heaven, for it is the throne of God, or by the earth, for it is his footstool, or by Jerusalem, for it is the city of the great King. And do not swear by your head, for you cannot make one hair white or black. Let what you say be simply 'Yes' or 'No'; anything more than this comes from evil (Mt 5, 33-37).

From a brief look at this reading, one might deduce that Jesus revises the teaching of the Old Testament and condemns every kind of oath. This is not true, however. For example, in the Gospel of Matthew Jesus does not rebuke the High Priest who demanded a response under oath (Mt 26, 63-64). Therefore, Jesus' words do not contain an absolute no. They intend to purify this practice which was perhaps corrupt in his time:

> Following St. Paul,[2] the tradition of the Church has understood Jesus' words as not excluding oaths made for grave and right reasons (for example, in court) (CCC, 2154).

Nevertheless, Jesus' words regarding certain conditions to be met for the legitimate use of an oath guide us. The *Catechism* indicates some of these limitations:

> The holiness of the divine name demands that we neither use it for trivial matters, nor take an oath which on the basis of the circumstances could be interpreted as approval of an authority unjustly requiring it. When an oath is required by illegitimate civil authorities, it may be refused. It must be refused when it is required for purposes contrary to the dignity of persons or to ecclesial communion (*CCC*, 2155).

5. Necessary conditions for the lawful use of oaths

Because taking an oath, by its very nature, is an action of the most solemn and serious nature, an oath cannot be taken except in truth, necessity and justice (cf. *CIC*, 1199). To do otherwise is a sin. Let us examine these three conditions under which an oath may be legitimately made:

a. Truth.

An oath may not be taken to support a lie. This condition is decisive. Moral certainty is required in order to take an oath. Probability is not sufficient. When one takes an oath about falsehood, he commits the very grave sin of perjury.

b. Necessity.

An oath should be taken with discretion, out of necessity and not for superficial things, when one's word would suffice. God should never be called as witness to an unimportant affair.

c. Justice.

An oath can only be taken for something morally good. To take an oath about something illicit is unjust. For example, something like the following would have absolutely no validity: "I swear I'll get revenge," when revenge is in itself a condemnable act.

Regarding a promissory oath, or committing oneself by oath to carry out something in the future, one must have the following:

- Intention of taking an oath, or committing oneself before God.

- Deliberation before taking an oath.

- Full knowledge of what is being promised and of the difficulties that go with its accomplishment.

Another form of living the second commandment of honoring the name of God and of the Saints may be carried out through a *vow*.

6. Vows

> A vow is a deliberate and free promise made to God, concerning some good which is possible and better. The virtue of religion requires that it be fulfilled (*CIC*, 1191; cf. *CCC*, 2101-2102).

The validity of a vow depends on the completion of the conditions that define it. They are the following:

a. Promise.

Promise is the intention before God to complete what is being promised. We must distinguish between a vow and a promise. A vow is a firm will, while a promise is the equivalent of a *wish* or *intention* of doing something in honor of God or of the saints.

b. Deliberate.

A vow demands that the person who takes it has considered what he is doing and has decided on his commitment to God.

c. Free.

A vow cannot be imposed by anyone. It may only be taken as a condition of a determined state of life in the Church. For example, to be a member of a religious order the candidate is required to take vows. But the candidate in question must freely take them (cf. *CCC*, 2103).

d. Made to God.

This deals with honoring the name of God, so the vow is made to God. When someone makes a vow to the Most Holy Virgin or the saints, they are considering them as intercessors before God.

e. A good.

It is not permitted to make a vow to do something wrong.

f. Possible.

One cannot vow to do something that is impossible.

g. A better good than its contrary.

The goodness of a vow comes from the fact that the person who makes it is committing himself to doing something better than what he is omitting. For this reason, vows made by religious who renounce good things in order to dedicate themselves fully to God have great value.

There are several biblical examples that treasure the taking of vows by believers. Jacob takes vows (Gn 28, 20-22), and also Israel (Nb 21, 2).

Ecclesiastes urges everyone to fulfill vows made to God as soon as possible.

> When you vow a vow to God, do not delay in paying it; for he has no pleasure in fools. Pay what you vow. It is better that you should not vow than that you should vow and not pay (Ecc 5, 4-5).

In the New Testament, Jesus mentions the practice of making vows in the Jewish world (Mk 7, 11) and St. Paul carries out the vow he had made (Acts 18, cf. Supplementary Reading 1).

Occasionally what was promised in a vow cannot be carried out. *The Code of Canon Law* indicates six cases where the accomplishment of vows is not binding:

> A vow ceases by lapse of the time specified for the fulfillment of the obligation, or by a substantial change in the matter promised, or by cessation of a condition upon which the vow depended or of the purpose of the vow, or by dispensation, or by commutation (*CIC*, 1194).

On other occasions, when difficulties arise, a vow may be dispensed by proper ecclesiastical authority. The different cases are determined in the *Code of Canon Law* (cf. *CIC*, 1196-1197).

But besides guiding the right use of an oath and of a vow, the second commandment forbids some acts which go against the virtue of religion, such as the irreverent use of the name of God and above all, blasphemy.

7. The irreverent use of the name of God and of holy things

Jewish piety is summarized in this passage of the psalmist: "O LORD, our LORD, how majestic is thy name in all the earth!" (Ps 8, 9). Hence, the religious man of all times has used the name of God and everything related to him, as well as sacred places and holy objects used in worship, with reverence and love.

The fruits of this religious consideration are the use and language of a number of religious customs, such as the consecration of holy objects used in divine worship, the blessing before meals, of the house and of the common tools man uses in his profession. We also say thank you for all the good we have received with a "thank God," and we always try to accept his will saying, "thy will be done."

It's evident that this language is a living reality and changes over time, yet Christians should find ways to make the name of God heard more frequently and should always do it reverently. Believers must show signs of faith, which will contribute to giving Christian testimony in a society which renounces religious signs.

But, on the contrary, one should avoid certain secular expressions which mention God or things related to him and the saints, etc. without proper reverence. For this reason, interjections like "God," "Christ," or "Jesus" should be carefully avoided. "Oaths which misuse God's name, though without the intention of blasphemy, show lack of respect for the Lord (CCC, 2149)."

8. Blasphemy against God. Sacrilege against the Virgin Mary and the saints

Blasphemy is speaking contemptuously of God or his perfections. It may also be contempt directed toward the saints, and is particularly grievous when directed against the Most Holy Virgin Mary. St. Thomas Aquinas states this in these terms:

> Even as God is praised in his saints, in so far as praise is given to the works which God does in his saints, so does blasphemy against the saints, redound, as a consequence, against God (St. Thomas Aquinas, *Summa theologiae*, II-II, q. 13, a. 1 ad 2).

The Tradition of the Church has underlined the graveness of the sin of blasphemy and classifies it as an intrinsically evil act.

Improper use of the name of God leaves room for a wide variety of abuses. Blasphemy was punished with severe punishment in the Old Testament. Leviticus narrates that a son of an Egyptian and an Israelite 'blasphemed and cursed the Name.' When the boy was brought to Moses, God passed his sentence:

> "Bring out of the camp him who cursed; and let all who heard him lay their hands upon his head, and let all the congregation stone him. And say to the people of Israel, Whoever curses his God shall bear his sin. He who blasphemes the name of the LORD shall be put to death; all the congregation shall stone him; the sojourner as well as the native, when he blasphemes the Name, shall be put to death (Lv 24, 14-16).

With this act, God tries root out this grave sin which was quite common in neighboring towns (cf. 2 Mac 8, 4; 9, 28; Ezk 35, 12-15).

In the New Testament, the awareness of the serious nature of this sin continues. So, for example, the Jews try to stone Jesus to death by accusing him of blasphemy, since "It is not for a good work that we stone you but for blasphemy; because you, being a man, make yourself God" (Jn 10, 33).

St. Paul considers himself a blasphemer when he hunted down Christians (1 Tim 1, 13). Later, the Apostle laments that "The name of God is blasphemed among the Gentiles because of you" (Rm 2, 24). In the New Testament, the seriousness of blasphemy is shown by the fact that it appears in catalogues of sins that merit condemnation (cf. 2 Tim 3, 2; Col 3, 8).

The Catechism of the Catholic Church shows the diverse forms that blasphemy may take:

> *Blasphemy* is directly opposed to the second commandment. It consists in uttering against God—inwardly or outwardly—words of hatred, reproach, or defiance; in speaking ill of God; in failing in respect toward him in one's speech; in misusing God's name. St. James condemns those "who blaspheme that honorable name [of Jesus] by which you are called." [Jas 2, 7] The prohibition of blasphemy extends to language against Christ's Church, the saints, and sacred things. It is also blasphemous to make use of God's name to cover up criminal practices, to reduce peoples to servitude, to torture persons or put them to death. The misuse of God's name to commit a crime can provoke others to repudiate religion (CCC, 2148).

Besides blasphemous words and gestures there are also blasphemous attitudes: those that mock God and ridicule any manifestation of Christian signs. Those who laugh about divine things and despise everything to do with religious life increase this kind of blasphemy. Some antireligious attitudes remind us of what some authors call *diabolic blasphemies*.

St. Thomas Aquinas argues that blasphemy may be even more serious than murder.

> If we compare murder and blasphemy as regards the objects of those sins, it is clear that blasphemy, which is a sin committed directly against God, is more grave than murder, which is a sin against one's neighbor. On the other hand, if we compare them in respect of the harm wrought by them, murder is the graver sin, for murder does more harm to one's neighbor, than blasphemy does to God.

> Since, however, the gravity of a sin depends on the intention of the evil will, rather than on the effect of the deed, as was shown above (I-II, 73, 8), it follows that, as the blasphemer intends to do harm to God's honor, absolutely speaking, he sins more grievously than the murderer. Nevertheless murder takes precedence, as to punishment, among sins committed against our neighbor (Saint Thomas Aquinas, *Summa theologiae*, II-II, q. 13, a. 3, ad 1).

Besides personal sin, blasphemy includes the potential for giving serious scandal to others.

Until recently, almost all governments imposed severe punishments on those who blasphemed in public.

Conclusion

Since God is great, it is obvious that his name should be respected. Therefore, any use of God's name must be in the context of awe and respect. For this reason, many people have adopted the custom of making acts of reparation when they hear his name abused.

In a similar way, the use of his name when taking an oath or making a vow is so serious that it places the person in the presence of God in a special manner.

OUTLINE

I. Glossary

ASSERTORY OATH;

A type of oath in which God is called upon as a witness to the truth of what is being said, as when a person takes an oath in court.

BLASPHEMY:

Words or insulting gestures against God, the Virgin Mary, the saints or the Church.

OATH:

To take God as a witness to what is being said.

PERJURY:

To make a promise without any intention of completing it or to lie under oath.

PROMISSORY OATH:

A type of oath in which God is called upon as a witness to something that will happen in the future, as when a public official solemnly swears to fulfill the duties of his office.

SACRILEGE:

The violation of sacred persons, places, things.

VOW:

A promise made freely and deliberately to God concerning something which is better than its contrary.

II. Summary of Principles

1. The second commandment obliges us to honor the name of God and to pay due respect to his person and everything related to him.

2. Everything consecrated to God—people, places, things— merits this special respect.

3. To reverently invoke the Name of God, Jesus Christ, the Virgin Mary and the saints is an act of religion.

4. Oaths and vows are solemn ways to honor the name of God.

5. "False oaths call on God to be witness to a lie. Perjury is a grave offense against the Lord, who is always faithful to his promises" (CCC, 2163).

6. A promissory oath obliges one to perform a certain action. An assertory oath calls on God to witness an affirmation.

7. It is sinful to promise under oath something evil in itself. The sin is grave if what is being sworn is seriously evil.

8. When an oath is taken about something illicit, there is no obligation to carry it out. The obligation, rather, is not to carry it out.

9. The obligation to stand by an oath is removed when the circumstances have notably changed or when it would impede the accomplishment of a greater good.

10. The virtue of religion requires valid vows to be fulfilled.

11. Blasphemy is intrinsically evil.

SUPPLEMENTARY READINGS

1. In many circumstances, the Christian is called to make *promises* to God. Baptism and Confirmation, Matrimony and Holy Orders always entail promises. Out of personal devotion, the Christian may also promise to God this action, that prayer, this alms-giving, that pilgrimage, and so forth. Fidelity to promises made to God is a sign of the respect owed to the divine majesty and of love for a faithful God.

"A *vow* is a deliberate and free promise made to God concerning a possible and better good which must be fulfilled by reason of the virtue of religion." [CIC, 1191§1] A vow is an act of *devotion* in which the Christian dedicates himself to God or promises him some good work. By fulfilling his vows he renders to God what has been promised and consecrated to him. The *Acts of the Apostles* shows us St. Paul concerned to fulfill the vows he had made.

(CCC, 2101-2102; cf. Acts 18, 18; 21, 23-24)

2. . . . [A]s you have now made the vow, as you have now bound yourself, you are not free to do anything else. Before you incurred the obligation of the vow, you were free to choose the less perfect way, although such liberty deserves no credit when what is not owed is paid, to one's own gain. But, now that your promise binds you before God, I do not invite you to great perfection, I warn you to avoid a great sin. If you do not keep what you have vowed, you will not be the same as you would have been if you had not made the vow. For, in that case, you will have been less perfect, not worse; whereas now—which God forbid!—you will be as much worse off if you break your word to God as you will be more blessed if you keep it. So then, do not regret having made the vow; rather, rejoice that you are no longer free to do what you might have done to your own great harm. Go forward boldly, then, and turn your words into deeds; he who inspired your vow will help you. Happy the necessity which forces us to better things!

(St. Augustine, *Letters*, 127, 8)

QUESTIONS

1. What is an oath?

2. What are the two kinds of oaths?

3. Does God swear oaths?

4. What are the limitations on using oaths?

5. List the necessary conditions for an oath.

6. What is Jesus' admonition in regard to oaths?

7. What is a vow?

8. List the necessary conditions for a vow.

9. What is blasphemy?

10. What is meant by the phrase "blasphemous attitudes?"

PRACTICAL EXERCISES

1. In the following cases, to what degree do the oaths or vows taken oblige, and why?

   a. Mark's sister Carrie, a successful and important figure in the local business community, recently married Allen, her boyfriend of four years. Things appeared to have been going well until Mark accidentally discovered one day that Allen had concealed from his sister the fact that he had been previously married and is the father of a six year old child. The situation is further complicated when Mark discovers that Allen has not obtained a legal divorce or a declaration of nullity from the Church! This means that his sister's marriage is invalid. When Mark confronted Allen about this information, Allen denied the charges and a terrible argument ensued. The next morning, Allen was gone. Mark feels that his family's honor has been destroyed by Allen's actions, and has personally vowed to take revenge on him. Does this vow bind Mark? Why or why not?

   b. Laura and her sister Theresa have not spoken to one another for seven years as a result of a fight over some antiques that their grandmother left behind when she died. Because he was angry with Laura at the time of her argument with Theresa, Laura's father supported Theresa and gave all of the property to her, an action he later deeply regretted. Although he apologized to Laura and asked Theresa to share the property with her sister, she refused to do so, resulting in the rift between the sisters. Laura's father recently decided to rewrite his will, and Laura demanded that he swear to name her as his sole heir, leaving her sister out of his will. Because he still feels guilty about what occurred before, her father has done so, but his conscience is bothering him. Must he do what he swore to do?

   c. Peter promised to give his friend Sara a ring which he won in a contest and which she liked very much. Although he believed the ring to be of little value, he later discovered that it is actually worth quite a lot of money. Now he doesn't want to give Sara the ring. Must he?

   d. Because he had been only an average student for the first three years of high school, David had found it difficult to be accepted to the extremely competitive premedical program at the college he had chosen at the beginning of his senior year. His family was poor and could not afford to send him to the school, and it wasn't very likely that he was going to get a scholarship because of his past academic performance. But David had thought and prayed a lot about it, and he wanted to be a doctor. He worked hard during his senior year, and had succeeded in earning straight A's both semesters. In addition, he had gone to a local community college for one year, where he had also earned straight A's. All the time he was working on his lately-developed dream of attending medical school, he had prayed to God to help him and to grant him the favor of becoming a doctor. At one point, after careful consideration, he had even vowed that if God would help him gain admittance to medical school, he would devote his first two years as a doctor to serving as a missionary doctor with a lay volunteer program in a poor country in Asia or Africa. Now that he has graduated at the top of his class from medical school, David has been offered a position at one of the most prestigious research hospitals in the U.S. He remembers the vow that he made, but this is a chance that he may not get again for a long time. What should he do?

2. It is an easy matter to think of popular words, phrases and expressions which are blasphemous or sacrilegious in nature. List instead common expressions, popular and solemn practices which indicate the respect had for God and his name.

3. Read the following Scripture passages about the punishment which befalls blasphemers: 1 K 21, 13-16; 2 K 19, 4-6; Tb 1, 18. Why do you think that God punished so severely those who blasphemed his name among the People of Israel?

4. The *Catechism of the Catholic Church* explains the importance of the imposition on the baptized of the name "Christian":

> In Baptism, the Lord's name sanctifies man, and the Christian receives his name in the Church. This can be the name of a saint, that is, of a disciple who has lived a life of exemplary fidelity to the Lord. The patron saint provides a model of charity; we are assured of his intercession. The "baptismal name" can also express a Christian mystery or Christian virtue (*CCC*, 2156).

Reflect on this text, and justify the reasons the Church gives for reserving the name "Christian" for the baptized. What specifically makes a person Christian?

CHAPTER XI
The Third Commandment:
Remember to Keep Holy the Sabbath Day

Lawrence, a practicing Catholic, hires a company to do some work on his ranch. He hires Paul, a contractor, who agrees to complete the work in a specified period of time. Paul, also a Catholic, says he will do all that is needed to fulfill his end of the agreement; he proposes to use workers overtime and even on Sundays.

Lawrence does not like the idea of working on Sunday, but he thinks that perhaps it will be necessary. Desiring to finish the project as soon as possible, he signs a contract with Paul. One Sunday Lawrence inspects the construction site, and finds men at work. He begins to doubt the morality of his contract with Paul.

- What obligations does faithful observance of the Third Commandment place on Christians in modern society?

- How should Christians resolve the conflicts which sometimes arise between the demands of this commandment and their other obligations?

Introduction

On the universal calendar, Sunday has always been highlighted in such a way that it constitutes an obligatory reference point for all social activities.

It's true that some non-Christian religions have their own day for worship: Saturday for Jews, Friday for Muslims. But in Western culture, Sunday is the day of rest and, for believers, a day of worship.

The fulfillment of the virtue of religion reaches its highest point in the worship of God in the Eucharist. To adore God belongs to the essence of religion itself. In every religion, there are many different forms of worship.

In the Old Testament God himself dictated the norms which people should follow to worship him. A very detailed law was established which included the institution of a priesthood, construction of temples, principal feasts, practices of worship, and above all the celebration of the Sabbath.

The Sabbath day, which had an enormous importance throughout the religious experience of Israel, became the Christian Sunday in the New Testament. The redeeming death of Jesus Christ and his Resurrection on the first day of the week were so decisive for the faith that the day of Christian worship was transferred to Sunday.

1. The Importance of the Sabbath in the Old Testament

From the very first page of the Bible, one can see the importance of the *seventh day*. Furthermore, it is widely believed that the narration of the Creation happening in seven days is done to highlight the importance of the seventh day and the obligation to dedicate this day to divine worship. With this, the sacred writer certainly underlines the power of God in his creative action. But above all he wants to highlight that God's power should be recognized by man through worship:

> Thus the heavens and the earth were finished, and all the host of them. And on the seventh day God finished his work which he had done, and he rested on the seventh day from all his work which he had done. So God blessed the seventh day and hallowed it, because on it God rested from all his work which he had done in creation (Gn 2, 1-3).

Later, when God had made the Israelites his people, he made laws concerning the observance of the Sabbath:

> Remember the Sabbath day, to keep it holy. Six days you shall labor, and do all your work; but the seventh day is a Sabbath to the LORD your God; in it you shall not do any work, you, or your son, or your daughter, your manservant, or your maidservant, or your cattle, or the sojourner who is within your gates; for in six days the LORD made heaven and earth, the sea, and all that is in them, and rested the seventh day; therefore the LORD blessed the Sabbath day and hallowed it (Ex 20, 8-11).

In this passage, we see the obligation to rest as primary, and the obligation of divine worship as secondary. But soon after, Scripture gave Saturday a double end: it was also a day consecrated to God. Leviticus prescribed:

> Six days shall work be done; but on the seventh day is a Sabbath of solemn rest, a holy convocation; you shall do

no work; it is a Sabbath to the LORD in all your dwellings (Lv 23, 3).

According to the Pentateuch, on Saturday the bread of proposition would be renewed (Lv. 24, 8) and sacrifices were to be celebrated:

> This shall be yours of the most holy things, reserved from the fire; every offering of theirs, every cereal offering of theirs and every sin offering of theirs and every guilt offering of theirs, which they render to me, shall be most holy to you and to your sons. In a most holy place shall you eat of it; every male may eat of it; it is holy to you (Nb 18, 9-10).

Consequently, from the beginning, the Sabbath included rest and the obligation of sacrifices. Both requirements showed the recognition of the power of God over his entire creation and over all men.

Gradually, the sacrificial rites together with the tasks which were forbidden became regulated. In this way, for example, on the Sabbath it was forbidden to cook food (Ex 16, 23), to light a fire (Ex 35, 3), to collect firewood (Nb 15, 32-36), to carry heavy objects on your shoulders (Jr 17, 21-22), to travel and to do business (Is 58, 13). In this way, slowly, a casuistic and at times ridiculous morality set in that was strongly denounced and condemned by Jesus Christ (cf. CCC, 2168-2173).

The Gospels retell the arguments between Jesus and the religious authorities of Israel in relation to the observance of the Sabbath. Jesus declared that the care of the sick comes before the Sabbath (Lk 13, 10-16; 14, 1-5; Jn 9-10). The true meaning of the Sabbath was proclaimed by Jesus with these words: "The Sabbath was made for man, not man for the Sabbath" (Mk 2, 27).

2. The Lord's day in the New Testament

The Resurrection of the LORD on the first day of the week introduced notable changes in the practice of divine worship. But this did not come about immediately. In fact, we know that the first Christians practiced the Jewish form of worship and the Christian liturgy simultaneously. The women delayed their visit to the sepulcher to fulfill the sabbatical precept (Mt 28, 1; Mk 15, 42). Peter and John likewise went up to the temple at the customary hour of prayer, while at the same time, they celebrated the Eucharist (Acts 2, 46). In addition, they already talked about the "Lord's Day" (Rv 1, 10).

Likewise, "the first day of the week" they "gathered together to break bread" (Acts 20, 7). On that day the Church in Corinth also celebrates the "breaking of the bread" (1 Cor 11, 17-34). And on that same day, they took up a collection for the poor (1 Cor 16, 2).

At the beginning of the second century, St. Ignatius, bishop of Antioch, tried to lay the foundations for transferring the Lord's Day from Saturday to Sunday:

> If then they who walked in ancient customs came to a new hope, no longer living for the Sabbath, but for the Lord's Day, on which also our life sprang up through him and his death,—though some deny him,—and by this mystery we received faith, and for this reason also we suffer, that we may be found disciples of Jesus Christ our only teacher (St. Ignatius of Antioch, *Letter to the Magnesians*, IX, 1).

The change of day also brought about a variation of name: "the Sabbath" was substituted by the "first day of the week" (Acts 20, 7) or "the eighth day" (Jn 20, 26), also the "day of the sun" (St. Justin) and more generally, "the Lord's Day."

3. The Christian Sunday

In the second century, the Eucharist was celebrated on Sundays. The *Didache*, an anonymous 2nd century text, and the *First Apologia*, written by the philosopher, St. Justin, relate the details of the celebration of Christian worship on the day of the LORD. These two writings even transmit some of the ceremonies which accompanied this celebration to us (cf. Supplementary Readings 1-2).

But these celebrations were private; Sunday lacked a public character until the year 321, a year after Emperor Constantine recognized the Christian religion. At the same time, servile works were forbidden. On July 3rd of that same year, the emperor forbade other public activities, such as the exercise of judicial action, and, gradually, all the rest of the liberal professions began to rest on that day. In this era, rest and Eucharistic worship went together. For that reason those acts which impeded attendance to the Eucharist were forbidden. Two councils of Orleans (in 511 and 538) engraved this on the conscience of the faithful so that they attended the Eucharist and made laws concerning the works which were not permitted on Sunday.

Together with Sundays, the custom of celebrating some solemnities, such as Christmas and other feasts that were used to "baptize" some pagan celebrations was very quickly introduced. Also the commemorative days of the martyrdom of saints were made solemnities. In this way, the Christian calendar was gradually formed.

In any case, above all feasts, Sunday stands out because it commemorates the death and Resurrection of Jesus Christ, just as the following passage taken from Vatican II reminds us:

> By a tradition handed down from the apostles which took its origin from the very day of Christ's resurrection, the Church celebrates the paschal mystery every eighth day; with good reason this, then, bears the name of the Lord's day or Sunday. For on this day Christ's faithful are bound to come together into one place so that; by hearing the word of God and taking part in the Eucharist, they may call to mind the passion, the resurrection and the glorification of the LORD Jesus, and may thank God who "has begotten them again, through the resurrection of Jesus Christ from the dead, unto a living hope." (1 Pet 1, 3) Hence the Lord's day is the original feast day, and it should be proposed to the piety of the faithful and taught to them so that it may become in fact a day of joy and of freedom from work. Other celebrations, unless they be truly of greatest importance, shall not have precedence over the Sunday which is the foundation and kernel of the whole liturgical year (*CSL*, 106).

4. The obligation of attending Holy Mass on Sundays and Holy Days of Obligation

The obligation to take part in the Sunday Eucharistic celebration has two origins:

a. The obligation of giving worship to God one day during the week, particularly on the Lord's Day.

b. The importance of the Eucharist, which actualizes and testifies to the death and resurrection of Jesus Christ, or renews the sacrifice of Christ.

Sunday is the day on which we celebrate the heart of the redemptive mission carried out by Jesus Christ. For this reason it occupies the center of the faith, or, as the Second Vatican Council teaches, the Eucharist is "the summit toward which the activity of the Church is directed; at the same time it is the font from which all her power flows" (*CSL*, 10).

Paul VI, in a document of exceptional importance, *Credo of the People of God*, teaches that:

> We believe that the Mass, celebrated by the priest representing the person of Christ by virtue of the power received through the sacrament of Orders, and offered by him in the name of Christ and the members of his Mystical Body, is the sacrifice of Calvary rendered sacramentally present on our altars. We believe that as the bread and wine consecrated by the LORD at the Last Supper were changed into his body and his blood which were to be offered for us on the cross, likewise the bread and wine consecrated by the priest are changed into the body and blood of Christ enthroned gloriously in heaven (*Credo of the People of God*, 24).

Therefore, given the real importance that the celebration of the Eucharist has for the Church, as well as for the life of the baptized, the Church requires the faithful to actively participate in its weekly celebration, since this is the way a Christian fulfills his obligation to worship God.

The *Code of Canon Law* declares the importance of Sunday in Christian life and, secondly, proclaims the obligation of Sunday Mass:

> Sunday, on which by apostolic tradition the paschal mystery is celebrated, is to be observed in the universal Church as the primary holy day of obligation (*CIC*, 1246).

The following canon declares the obligation to participate in the Holy Mass and to abstain from servile work:

> On Sundays and other holy days of obligation, the faithful are obliged to participate in the Mass. They are also to abstain from such work or business that would inhibit the worship to be given to God, the joy proper to the Lord's Day, or the due relaxation of mind and body (*CIC*, 1247).

Holy Days of Obligation, on the other hand, are days on which the Church commemorates important saints and events in her history, or one of the important mysteries of the Faith. Many of these feasts developed in response to particular historical circumstances and have since been retained by the Church because of their importance for reminding the faithful of certain truths which the Church proclaims. An example of one such feast is Corpus Christi, which was instituted to celebrate the Real Presence of Christ in the Eucharist.

Canon law lists ten days as holy days of obligation for the universal Church: *Christmas, Epiphany, the Body and Blood of Christ, the*

Ascension, Mary, Mother of God, the Immaculate Conception, the Assumption, St. Joseph, Sts. Peter and Paul and *All Saints Day.* However, not every one is a holy day of obligation in every country. The Code of Canon Law permits the Bishop's Conferences of individual nations, with the prior approval of the Holy See, to suppress certain holy days or to transfer their observance to a Sunday (cf. *CIC* 1246). In the United States of America, the solemnities that are holy days of obligation are six:

- Mary, the Mother of God (January 1)

- The Ascension of Jesus (40 days after Easter Sunday)

- The Assumption of Mary (August 15)

- The Feast of All Saints (November 1)

- The Immaculate Conception (December 8)

- Christmas Day (December 25)

The bishops of the United States have transferred the solemnities of the *Epiphany* and *the Body and Blood of Christ* to the Sundays which follow these feasts on the calendar, and have suppressed the solemnities of St. Joseph and Sts. Peter and Paul as holy days of obligation in the U.S. calendar.

5. Fulfillment of the precept of attending Mass

Fulfilling the precept to attend Mass is clearly a grave obligation; whoever does not fulfill this precept commits a mortal sin, except in situations where there is a serious reason to miss Mass, or in cases where it is impossible to be present at its celebration.

This same teaching is restated in the *Catechism of the Catholic Church*:

> For this reason the faithful are obliged to participate in the Eucharist on days of obligation, unless excused for a serious reason (for example, illness, the care of infants) or dispensed by their own pastor.[1] Those who deliberately fail in this obligation commit a grave sin (*CCC*, 2181).

The obligation to participate in the Eucharist on Saturday afternoon or evening or on Sunday is fulfilled in any Church. The Mass in the afternoon of the day before may be a wedding Mass or a funeral. The obligation of attending Mass on a Sunday or holy day of obligation is also fulfilled with Mass celebrated on the evening of the previous day (cf. *CIC, Relatio*, 277).

Since attending the Eucharist on Saturday evening is a universal norm (cf. *CIC*, 1248), one may opt for it whenever desired. But he ought to assure that the meaning of the day of the LORD, proper to Sunday, is not lost. For this reason, if the obligation is fulfilled on a Saturday, one should keep in mind that there is still the obligation to observe the rules regarding work on Sunday.

The fulfillment of the Sunday precept requires participation in the Mass. Some fall into the error of dealing with the Eucharist in a minimal way by arriving late or leaving early. The God who gave us his only Son should be treated in a better fashion.

A circumstance that excuses someone from attending the Sunday Eucharist is qualified in the law of the Church with the adjective "serious." Consequently, any cause for not attending Mass that is not serious is not a justified motive. The *Catechism* talks about a "serious reason," like "illness" or "the care of infants" (CCC, 2181). In other situations, the individual Catholic should consult a priest.

Finally, the obligation to attend the celebration of the Eucharist is limited to Saturday afternoons and evenings, Sundays, and holy days of obligation or vigils of these holy days. One cannot fulfill the precept on any other day of the week.

6. The obligation to rest

From the first paragraph of the book of Genesis (Gn 2, 2-3) and laws which govern the conduct required of the people of Israel (Ex 20, 8-11; Dt 5, 12-15), it is clear that the worship of God also included rest on the Sabbath day. There is a twofold reason for this:

a. Rest facilitates the worship of God by eliminating the obstacles that one's professional occupation might pose to celebrating divine worship.

b. The need for rest is a requirement of the human condition. Man is not a machine. The human person is in need of a combination of work and rest. Rest replaces lost energies and makes time for other activities which cultivate the human spirit.

In our day, in which work occupies a special place in social life and in which working schedules are irregular, it is not always possible to distinguish what works are forbidden on Sundays and holy days of obligation.

7. Works permitted on Sunday

Not all work inhibits the worship of God or the rest which human beings need in order to renew themselves, therefore there are some types of work which are permitted on Sundays and holy days of obligation. In trying to decide whether or not a particular activity violates the sacred character of Sunday, some general guidelines are helpful. Work should not be undertaken on Sunays and holy days of obligation if it:

a. impedes participation in the Eucharistic worship,

b. inhibits the festive happiness of Sunday,

c. or makes bodily or mental rest impossible.

Consequently, those works, including regular employment, which do not permit attendance at Sunday Mass or Mass on holy days of obligation should be avoided.

Also, those works which could be bothersome and could be an obstacle to living the festive character of Sunday are forbidden.

Likewise, those works which may tire or fatigue an individual, such works which are arduous in themselves or because they turn out to be such for the individual are also forbidden. In this way, for a person who busies himself with intellectual tasks, it may be restful to do some manual work like gardening. On the other hand, a manual worker may rest by studying or engaging in other intellectual tasks.

> Sanctifying Sundays and holy days requires a common effort. Every Christian should avoid making unnecessary demands on others that would hinder them from observing the Lord's Day.

> Traditional activities (sport, restaurants, etc.), and social necessities (public services, etc.), require some people to work on Sundays, but everyone should still take care to set aside sufficient time for leisure. With temperance and charity the faithful will see to it that they avoid the excesses and violence sometimes associated with popular leisure activities.

> In spite of economic constraints, public authorities should ensure citizens a time intended for rest and divine worship. Employers have a similar obligation toward their employees (CCC, 2187).

It is necessary to recover the festive dimension of Christian existence, and to this end Sunday represents the moment of returning the abundance of joy to the rest of the week. Besides, a Christian should proclaim happiness in the face of serious problems that surround the people of our times. In a word, Sunday should be converted into the true Christian Easter celebration.

In the case of a work which needs to be finished, one can secure permission to be excused from the obligation to rest. In such situations, however, it is necessary to keep in mind the serious obligation of avoiding scandal, (any word or deed which, either by commission or omission, is evil or has the appearance of evil and provides an occasion of sin to another). Canon law indicates:

> . . . [A] parish priest, in individual cases, for a just reason and in accordance with the prescriptions of the diocesan bishop, can give a dispensation from the obligation of observing a holy day or day of penance, or commute the obligation into some other pious works (CIC, 1245).

Conclusion

A Christian has a serious obligation to take an active part in the Eucharistic celebration on Sundays and Holy Days of Obligation and ought to abstain from works which impede proper rest. Obviously, the precept of attending Mass is more serious, but the obligation to refrain from unnecessary work also binds in conscience.

Furthermore, not fulfilling the Sunday obligation has certain implications in regard to the whole Christian community because of the potential for scandal.

Breaking the Sunday precept, besides being a grave sin, puts a certain distance between God and man, diminishes the sense of adoration which accompanies faith, and reduces one's sense of belonging to the Church and one's moral sense.

The worship that man gives God on a determined day and in an official and specific way corresponds to a principle which is written on man's conscience:

The celebration of Sunday observes the moral commandment inscribed by nature in the human heart to render to God an outward, visible, public, and regular worship "as a sign of his universal beneficence to all." [St. Thomas Aquinas, *Summa theologiae*, II-II, 122, 4] Sunday worship fulfills the moral command of the Old Covenant, taking up its rhythm and spirit in the weekly celebration of the Creator and Redeemer of his people (*CCC*, 2176).

One cannot avoid this moral duty written on man's heart and go on unaffected. When a Catholic stops going to Sunday Mass, his conscience soon becomes deadened.

OUTLINE

I. Glossary

DIOCESE:

A division of the Catholic Church, usually comprised of all the Catholics living within a particular geographic territory.

HOLY DAYS OF OBLIGATION:

Feast days of such importance in the Church's calendar that attendance at Mass is required.

MASS OR EUCHARIST:

The memorial of the death and Resurrection of the LORD, in which the sacrifice of the cross is renewed and the People of God are united (cf. *CIC*, 897). The richness of the Mass is also seen in the different names given to it (cf. *CCC*, 1328-1332).

PARISH:

A definite community of Catholics within a diocese, established by the bishop and entrusted to the care of a pastor.

SABBATH:

The seventh day of the Jewish week, set aside for rest and the worship of God. For Christians, Sunday is the Sabbath day in commemoration of Christ's resurrection.

SCANDAL:

Any word or deed (whether of omission or commission) that is evil in itself or has the appearance of evil and provides an occasion of sin to another.

II. Summary of Principles

1. The Lord's command to observe the Sabbath was changed from Saturday to Sunday in the early Church.

2. Man is obliged to dedicate one day of the week to God. In this way, he recognizes the lordship of God over all creation and over his own life.

3. It is a duty of natural law to dedicate some time to divine worship.

4. The Sunday precept is the Church's legislative specification of the divine precept to worship God on the seventh day.

5. Rest of mind and body is a natural requirement for man.

6. Free time offers the opportunity to form one's personality and to reach a spiritual equilibrium. At the same time it facilitates the gatherings of family and friends.

SUPPLEMENTARY READINGS

1. At the Eucharist, offer the eucharistic prayer in this way. Begin with the chalice: 'We give thanks to thee, our Father, for the holy Vine of thy servant David, which thou hast made known to us through thy servant Jesus.' *'Glory be to thee, world without end.'*

Then over the particles of bread: 'We give thanks to thee, our Father, for the life and knowledge thou hast made known to us through thy servant Jesus.' *'Glory be to thee, world without end.'*

'As this broken bread, once dispersed over the hills, was brought together and became one loaf, so may thy Church be brought from the ends of the earth into thy kingdom.'

Assemble on the Lord's Day, and break bread and offer the Eucharist; but first make confession of your faults, so that your sacrifice may be a pure one.

(*Didache*, 9 &14)

2. And on the day called Sunday, all who live in cities or in the country gather together to one place, and the memoirs of the apostles or the writings of the prophets are read, as long as time permits; then, when the reader has ceased, the president verbally instructs, and exhorts to the imitations of these good things. Then we all rise together and pray, and, as we before said, when our prayer is ended, bread and wine and water are brought, and the president in like manner offers prayers and thanksgiving, according to his ability, and the people assent, saying Amen.

(St. Justin, *The First Apology*, Chapter 67)

3. In respecting religious liberty and the common good of all, Christians should seek recognition of Sundays and the Church's holy days as legal holidays. They have to give everyone a public example of prayer, respect, and joy and defend their traditions as a precious contribution to the spiritual life of society. If a country's legislation or other reasons require work on Sunday, the day should nevertheless be lived as the day of our deliverance which lets us share in this "festal gathering," this "assembly of the firstborn who are enrolled in heaven."

(CCC, 2188; cf. Heb 12, 22-23)

4. There are nowadays many opportunities favorable to the development of a universal culture, thanks especially to the boom in book publication and new techniques of cultural and social communications. Shorter working hours are becoming the general rule everywhere and provide greater opportunities for large numbers of people. May this leisure time be properly employed to refresh the spirit and strengthen the health of mind and body—by means of voluntary activity and study; of tourism to broaden the mind and enrich man with understanding of others; by means of physical exercise and sport, which help to create harmony of feeling even on the level of the community as well as fostering friendly relations between men of all classes, countries, and races. Christians, therefore, should cooperate in the cultural framework and collective activity characteristic of our times, to humanize them and imbue them with a Christian spirit.

(GS, 61)

QUESTIONS

1. Who gave the Jews their guidelines for the worship of God in the Old Testament?

2. What was included in this law?

3. What two requirements of the Sabbath show the Jews recognized the dominion of God?

4. What effect did the resurrection have on Saturday as a day of worship?

5. Why was the Eucharistic celebration changed from Saturday to Sunday by the early Church?

6. In what terms does the *Constitution on the Liturgy* of Vatican II refer to the Eucharist?

7. Explain clearly and in detail the causes which excuse the obligation to attend Sunday Mass.

8. What is required in order to properly fulfill the Sunday precept of rest?.

PRACTICAL EXERCISES

1. Compare how the two texts, Ex 20, 8-11 and Dt 5, 12-15, formulate the prescriptions of the Mosaic law concerning fulfillment of the Sabbath. How extensive was the prohibition against working on the Sabbath? What do you think was the responsibility of the head of the household in regard to this commandment in view of the fact that God forbad even servants, slaves and beasts of burden from working on the Sabbath?

2. Sunday Mass has the character of a community experience which strengthens the life of faith. Comment on these words of St. John Chrysostom, which speak to the importance of these benefits: "You cannot pray in the home as in the Church, where many are assembled, where the cry of all is elevated to God as from one heart. There is in this something more: the union of spirit and

mind, the harmony of souls, the bond of charity, the prayers of the priests" (St. John Chrysostom, *Incomprehens* 3, 6). Using this passage, formulate a response to the common objections "I don't want go to Mass every Sunday because I don't get anything out of it," and "I think that a person can pray just as well at home as in Church." What is it about prayer and the worship of God at Mass which is superior to the prayer and worship of an individual in his or her home according to St. John Chrysostom?

3. Read Jesus' words about the correct spirit in which the observance of the Sabbath is to be kept in Mt 12, 9-14, Mk 3, 1-6, and Lk 6, 1-11. In the following cases, determine whether or not, in your opinion, the following individuals have failed to keep the Third Commandment. Be sure to offer specific reasons for your conclusions.

   a. Miguel and Francisco are brothers who always go together to Mass on Sundays. Last Sunday they went on spring break and they decided to attend a Mass celebrated in a parish at nine o'clock at night. It's the last Mass in that city. That day an unusual traffic jam caused by crowds of other college students made them arrive late and miss the entire Mass. When they got home, they talked about what happened that day. Miguel said that he didn't feel guilty about anything, since he had the intention of going to Mass as always and the traffic jam was unforeseeable. Francisco, on the other hand, felt guilty. They both go to confession regularly. In his next confession, Miguel doesn't plan to mention that he missed Mass last Sunday. Francisco plans to confess that he missed Mass. Who is right, Miguel or Francisco?

   b. Jennie is scheduled to take a trip with a group of friends. Their flight leaves early Sunday morning, so Jennie planned to go to the anticipated Mass on Saturday evening. On Saturday morning, Jennie's employer calls her and asks her to work the 1:00-9:00 p.m. shift at the restaurant, because another waitress called in to say that she couldn't make it in to work. Jennie prides herself in being flexible and willing to help people out when they are in a tight spot, but if she agrees, she won't have another opportunity to attend Sunday Mass. Jennie also recently had a disagreement with her employer and is afraid that if she doesn't agree, her employer might view her as uncooperative and give her a lower rating in her next job evaluation. What do you think she should do?

c. Every Sunday Perry sits in the back of church and talks about the weekend with his friends. When challenged by his parents he justifies what he is doing by stating, "The Church says I have to attend Mass on Sunday; that doesn't mean I have to pay attention." Is Perry fulfilling the obligation of attendance at Mass? Why or why not?

d. Brandy and her father, who is a doctor in a nursing home, live in a small town where the local Catholic church has only one Mass on Sunday morning. On this particular Sunday morning, her father is working the morning shift. On her way out the door to go to Mass, the telephone rings. It is her elderly grandfather. He is not feeling well and has run out of the medication that his doctor has prescribed for him. He asks if she can come over, pick up his prescription, have it refilled and stay with him until her father comes home from work. Brandy agrees, but feels guilty about having missed Mass. Do you think she should? How would you explain your answer to her?

4. Discuss and explain the problems which surround the Sunday rest. What can be done on Sundays and what ought to be avoided? In your opinion, does modern culture facilitate or inhibit the Christian observance of Sundays? Provide examples to support your statements.

CHAPTER XII
THE FOURTH COMMANDMENT:
HONOR YOUR FATHER AND MOTHER

Jack, a fifteen year old, arrived home one night with his eyes blurry and his balance obviously affected. It was clear that he had been drinking. His family had never seen him like this before and were very concerned. Jack's older brother, Mike, was as worried as his mother. Mike knew what the problem was. He had been a bad example, and Jack was simply imitating him. Mike knew he had not given a specific bad example in drinking to excess, but he suspected he had undermined the authority of his parents by his actions and attitudes.

Mike had returned home after finishing college at the beginning of the summer. He had come with an attitude that he didn't have to obey as he had to before he went to college. But because he was living at home his parents laid down the rules of the house. Mike's parents wanted him to come home at a certain time, to not smoke in the house, and to do chores around the house. Mike had grown accustomed to living with his roommates at college where he didn't have to do chores, and where he could come and go as he pleased. So Mike stayed out late many nights and, at times, smoked in the house around Jack and his other brothers and sisters. Mike's parents warned him that he was giving a bad example to the rest of the family. They had begun to notice that Jack especially had begun to disregard their authority by neglecting his homework and chores around the house.

The night Jack came home drunk it hit Mike like a bad dream. He had been an influence for the worse in his disregard for his parents' rules. He realized that even as an adult he had to abide by the rules established by his parents in their home, and, more importantly, that his example as the eldest could influence his brothers and sisters who were still dependent on their parents' guidance and direction.

- How does the Fourth Commandment protect the integrity of familial relationships?

- What are some of the specific obligations which are enjoined upon parents and children by this commandment?

- What obligations does the Fourth Commandment entail for human relations outside the family?

Introduction

After studying the commandments regarding God in the preceding chapters, this chapter begins the study of the commandments which regulate the moral links in family life and society. This includes an investigation of the relationship between husbands and wives, of parents with their children, and of children with their parents and with their brothers and sisters. Besides, this commandment also includes the study of moral duties (derived from family life) toward grandparents and other relatives, other relationships, such as those between students and teachers, and between citizens and governments.

1. Love, the foundation of the family

> Love is true when it creates the good of persons and of communities; it creates the good and gives it to others. Only one who is able to be demanding with himself in the name of love can give love to others. Love is demanding. It makes demands in all human situations. It is even more demanding in the case of those who are open to the gospel. Is this not what Christ proclaims in "his" commandment?
>
> Nowadays, people need to rediscover this demanding love, for it is truly the firm foundation of the family, a foundation able to "endure all things". . . .At work within it is the power and strength of God himself who "is love." At work, also, within it is the power and strength of Christ, the Redeemer of man and the Savior of the world" (FC, 14).

Among the many commitments contained in love for one's neighbor, love between spouses is primary, followed by parent-child relationships, because children's closest neighbors are their parents. The most elemental biology ties members of the same family together in such a way that moral conduct between parents and children (and vice versa) and among brothers and sisters is absolutely demanded.

We can even say more. Christian morality is the morality of charity. This *supernatural love* begins and grows in family life, and is reflected in the most intimate bonds of matrimony. At the same time, it is the love between a husband and wife that gives origin to children and is also the love that comes forth from a common origin joining brothers and sisters together—all fruit of the love of their parents. Therefore, ethically condemnable conduct in the bosom of a family is often called *unnatural* and even *monstrous*. In effect, it is "inhumane," for example, for a father to abandon his son, or for a son to hate his parents and not to attend to their needs.

All of these relationships are understood in the fourth commandment. The *Catechism of the Catholic Church* says:

> The fourth commandment is addressed expressly to children in their relationship to their father and mother, because this relationship is the most universal. It likewise concerns the ties of kinship between members of the extended family. It requires honor, affection, and gratitude toward elders and ancestors. Finally, it extends to the duties of pupils to teachers, employees to employers, subordinates to leaders, citizens to their country, and to those who administer or govern it.
>
> This commandment includes and presupposes the duties of parents, instructors, teachers, leaders, magistrates, those who govern, all who exercise authority over others or over a community of persons (*CCC*, 2199).
>
> The relationships within the family bring an affinity of feelings, affections and interests, arising above all from the members' respect for one another. The family is a privileged community called to achieve a "sharing of thought and common deliberation by the spouses as well as their eager cooperation as parents in the children's upbringing" (*GS*, 52).

2. Biblical facts about the fourth commandment

There are several places in the Old Testament where the Fourth Commandment is repeated. Two of these formulas are presented in the book of Exodus and in Deuteronomy:

> "Honor your father and your mother, that your days may be long in the land which the LORD your God gives you" (Ex 20, 12).
>
> "Honor your father and your mother, as the LORD your God commanded you; that your days may be prolonged, and that it may go well with you, in the land which the LORD your God gives you" (Dt 5, 16).

The words of Deuteronomy shed a new light, which conditions happiness on the observance of this precept.

New additions to these ethical minimums appeared with other teachings of the Old Testament that introduce additional moral demands. In this way, Leviticus insists:

> "Every one of you shall revere his mother and his father, and you shall keep my Sabbaths: I am the LORD your God" (Lv 19, 3).

In addition, the book of Proverbs offers this program of love and obedience to one's parents:

> My son, keep your father's commandment, and forsake not your mother's teaching. Bind them upon your heart always; tie them about your neck. When you walk, they will lead you; when you lie down, they will watch over you; and when you awake, they will talk with you (Pr 6, 20-22).

The book of Sirach also makes the following consideration:

> With all your heart honor your father, and do not forget the birth pangs of your mother. Remember that through your parents you were born; and what can you give back to them that equals their gift to you? (Sir 7, 27-28).

This book, which contains religious moral doctrine concerning human behavior, makes this profound reflection:

> Listen to me, your father, O children; and act accordingly, that you may be kept in safety. For the LORD honored the father above the children, and he confirmed the right of the mother over her sons.
>
> Whoever honors his father atones for sins, and whoever glorifies his mother is like one who lays up treasure. Whoever honors his father will be gladdened by his own children, and when he prays he will be heard. Whoever glorifies his father will have long life, and whoever obeys the LORD will refresh his mother; he will serve his parents as his masters.
>
> Honor your father by work and deed, that a blessing from him may come upon you. For a father's blessing strengthens the houses of the children, but a mother's curse uproots their foundations. Do not glorify yourself by dishonoring your father, for your father's dishonor is no glory to you. For a man's glory comes from honoring his father, and it is a disgrace for children not to respect their mother.
>
> O son, help your father in his old age, and do not grieve him as long as he lives; even if he is lacking in understanding,

show forbearance; in all your strength do not despise him. For kindness to a father will not be forgotten, and against your sins it will be credited to you; in the day of your affliction it will be remembered in your favor; as frost in fair weather, your sins will melt away. Whoever forsakes his father is like a blasphemer, and whoever angers his mother is cursed by the LORD (Sir 3, 1-16).

3. Relationship between the spouses

Among other precepts which regulate the relationship between husbands and wives, St. Paul teaches us a doctrine which has become classical for raising the relations between a wife and her husband to a very high ethical level:

> Wives, be subject to your husbands, as to the LORD. For the husband is the head of the wife as Christ is the head of the church, his body, and is himself its Savior. Husbands, love your wives, as Christ loved the church and gave himself up for her, that he might sanctify her, ... that she might be holy and without blemish (Eph 5, 22-25, 27).

There are many profound commentaries about this text, but here we will limit ourselves to the following notes:

a. The customs of the time regarding the role of woman must be taken into account. It is never legitimate to read a part of scripture taking it out of the context in which it was written.

b. In the ordinary course of family life, a woman often defers to her husband in the matter of decision-making. On the other hand, a husband is expected to consider the opinion and advice of his wife in his decisions.

c. St. Paul's entire teaching depends upon his parallel between man and woman and the union of Christ and the Church. Not only is matrimony in general described in this comparison, but also a woman with respect to her husband is situated.

d. For St. Paul, there is a certain identification between the Church and Jesus. The Church is the "Mystical Body" of Jesus Christ. That is, the Church is the "mysterious" body. Just as Jesus had a body of flesh and bones during his life, after the Ascension, the Church is just like his spiritual body. Paul deduces this identity of Christ and the Church from his first meeting with the LORD. When he was going to Damascus to persecute the Church, Christ told him: "I am Jesus, whom you are persecuting" (Acts 9, 5). Jesus directly identified himself with the Church.

e. According to this analogy, the relation of man and woman has a certain mysterious character similar to Christ's relation with his Church. Naturally, in keeping with the customs of the times, St. Paul discusses the authority of a husband (cf. Col 3, 18-19; 1 P 3, 1-7), but understanding that the nature of authority is to serve he adds that a husband should love his wife like his own body, "because no one ever hates his own flesh." Furthermore, he should love her "as Christ loves his Church." For matrimony unites a man and a woman in such way that they "become one flesh" (Gn 2, 24).

f. In this context, husband and wife should love each other mutually. The husband should love his wife "as himself" and vice versa, the woman her husband.

g. We should note that this passage, when talking about "loving," always uses (six times) the Greek term *agapan*, that is, "to appreciate" or, even better, "to have a great esteem for." This same term is used to talk about the "love"—*agape*—of God for man. Consequently, husband and wife should love each other with that supernatural love, which includes, of course, human love.

In summary, the family, born of the sacrament of Matrimony, should be a privileged place for love between the spouses, in equality of dignities and differences of functions. In that climate of love, children should be born and grow, and they must, in turn, contribute to that climate of love in everyday family life.

4. Parents' relations with their children

After a brief look at St. Paul's writings on love, the Apostle also gives advice to parents with respect to the education of their children: "Fathers, do not provoke your children to anger, but bring them up in the discipline and instruction of the LORD" (Eph 6, 4).

In this mandate, the love of parents for their children is presupposed and another three items of interest are added: that parents educate their children with discipline; that they not be excessively rigorous; and that they form them in the teachings of Jesus Christ.

That parents should correct their children is a law of nature. The child is born with immense possibilities for good and for evil. For this reason, parents should guide them in good moral behavior. The letter to the Hebrews proposes a comparison between correction that God makes to man and that which parents carry out with their children:

> And have you forgotten the exhortation which addresses you as sons? — "My son, do not regard lightly the discipline of the LORD, nor lose courage when you are punished by him. For the LORD disciplines him whom he loves, and chastises every son whom he receives.

> "It is for discipline that you have to endure. God is treating you as sons; for what son is there whom his father does not discipline? If you are left without discipline, in which all have participated, then you are illegitimate children and not sons.

> Besides this, we have had earthly fathers to discipline us and we respected them. Shall we not much more be subject to the Father of spirits and live? For they disciplined us for a short time at their pleasure, but he disciplines us for our good, that we may share his holiness. For the moment all discipline seems painful rather than pleasant; later it yields the peaceful fruit of righteousness to those who have been trained by it (Heb 12, 5-11).

Parents have the grave obligation of educating their children, and this education includes the whole person. Children have the serious obligation to obey in return. This is more urgent today, inasmuch as in the present culture, children tend to reject the direction of their parents, and parents, out of fear, slowly begin to abandon this serious obligation.

In the area of education, parents have the duty to educate their children in the faith; this is a task that parents cannot ignore, even when they defer to other people or an institution to complement their children's education, for example, school and catechism class (cf. CCC, 1656-1657; 2223-2229).

The child should be taught simple prayers to be said at bedtime with the parent participating. As the child grows, the child should be instructed in the Catechism in a minimal way. Children's *Lives of the Saints* books should be employed as well. Although both parents must attend to this especially grave obligation, studies have shown that fathers play an especially important part in forming their children's religious habits.

The obligation of parents to correct their children is at least as serious as the obligation which binds them in relation to their children's intellectual education.

5. Children's relations with their parents

Besides honoring their parents, children are also expected to obey them. The Apostle adds a Christian motive for obedience: it is desired by Christ. St. Paul writes to the Colossians:

> "Children, obey your parents in everything, for this pleases the LORD" (Col 3, 20).

The same thing is repeated in his letter to the Ephesians, explaining a passage from the Old Testament, but complementing it with these words:

> Children, obey your parents in the LORD, for this is right. "Honor your father and mother" (this is the first commandment with a promise), "that it may be well with you and that you may live long on the earth" (Eph 6, 1-3).

Parents are called to conduct themselves so as to be worthy of honor.

> You parents, the divine precept seems to say, should act in such a way that your life will merit the honor (and the love) of your children. Do not let the divine command that you be honored fall into a moral vacuum! Ultimately, then, we are speaking of mutual honor.
>
> The commandment "honor your father and your mother" indirectly tells parents: Honor your sons and daughters. They deserve this because they are alive, because they are who they are, and this is true from the first moment of conception.
>
> The fourth commandment then, by expressing the intimate bonds uniting the family highlights the basis of its inner unity (*FC*, 15).

It is good to keep in mind that when a parent does not act in an honorable way, his position as parent requires respect even when his conduct would appear to indicate otherwise.

6. Relations with other members of the family

The ties of blood do not end with parent-children relationships. They also extend to all those who belong to the extended family: grandparents, uncles, aunts, cousins.

The structure of the family in modern society has changed noticeably in recent years. In previous centuries, western society was largely agricultural. In that agricultural society, in the country as well as in the city, it was frequent to see family clans that sheltered two or three generations, from grandparents to grandchildren. In the early industrial era, the family home served grandparents and single aunts and uncles. Today, the immediate family lives alone.

Even in such diverse circumstances, morality postulates the duty to love in a special way those who are joined by blood ties. Undoubtedly, grandparents occupy a special place, because they may be in more need of the presence of their children and grandchildren. Those relatives who are in more need certainly must receive proper love. In fact, there should never be a family member who would not expect to be helped by the rest of the family. Non-family members should supply that service only when there is no family member to take care of the person in need.

The family should live in such a way that its members care and take responsibility for the young, the old, the sick, the handicapped, and the poor. There are some families who are at times incapable of providing this help. Only then does this responsibility devolve onto other persons, other families, and, in a subsidiary way, society to provide for their needs.

7. Obligations of civil authority

Given the social character of the human person, social life is essential. As a result, just as particular moral obligations arise in family life, ethical obligations and rights also arise in social life. Just as parents have obligations to their children, in a similar way, the civil authority must meet certain moral demands with society and with each citizen.

a. Citizens' obligations to government.

According to Biblical teachings, authority comes from God, so legitimate authority should always be obeyed. Regarding this subject, we should note that the Apostle's teachings are very demanding, and he was speaking about the authorities of the Roman Empire, who far from being models, were persecuting Christians.

> Let every person be subject to the governing authorities. For there is no authority except from God, and those that exist have been instituted by God.
>
> Therefore he who resists the authorities resists what God has appointed, and those who resist will incur judgment. For rulers are not a terror to good conduct, but to bad. Would you have no fear of him who is in authority? Then do what is good, and you will receive his approval, for he is God's servant for your good. But if you do wrong, be afraid, for he does not bear the sword in vain; he is the servant of God to execute his wrath on the wrongdoer.
>
> Therefore one must be subject, not only to avoid God's wrath but also for the sake of conscience. For the same reason you also pay taxes, for the authorities are ministers of God, attending to this very thing. Pay all of them their dues, taxes to whom taxes are due, revenue to whom revenue is due, respect to whom respect is due, honor to whom honor is due (Rm 13, 1-7).

The clarity and richness of this testimony inspired the early Christian moral doctrine concerning the duties of Christian citizens toward the legitimately established authority. The following affirmations are included in this doctrine:

- Authority, as the power of direction of the community, comes from God. That is, the natural necessity of authority in society and *not the particular form of exercising it*, is derived from God.

- Since authority has a divine origin, the Christian has the obligation in conscience of obeying whoever lawfully exercises it.

- Authority may never require one to act immorally.

- If one does not obey the authorities, one may be legitimately punished by the authorities.

- Taxes should be paid to the legitimate authority. Later, moral theology determined the conditions which make tax laws just. But, if it is just, it obliges in conscience.

- Finally, respect is due to those who govern.

All of these principles, though not mentioned by name, are included in the following passage from St. Peter, written in the era in which Christians lived under the disastrous reign of a cruel and tyrannical emperor, Nero:

> Be subject for the Lord's sake to every human institution, whether it be to the emperor as supreme, or to governors as sent by him to punish those who do wrong and to praise those who do right. For it is God's will that by doing right you should put to silence the ignorance of foolish men. Live as free men, yet without using your freedom as a pretext for evil; but live as servants of God. Honor all men. Love the brotherhood. Fear God. Honor the emperor (1 P 2, 13-17).

But moral theology, confronted with arbitrary and even tyrannical authorities, determined that a Christian can oppose and, in certain circumstances, overthrow illegitimate governments and unjust laws:

> The citizen is obliged in conscience not to follow the directives of civil authorities when they are contrary to the demands of the moral order, to the fundamental rights of persons or the teachings of the Gospel. *Refusing obedience* to civil authorities, when their demands are contrary to those of an upright conscience, finds its justification in the distinction between serving God and serving the political community. "Render therefore to Caesar the things that are Caesar's, and to God the things that are God's." "We must obey God rather than men" (*CCC*, 2242; cf. Mt 22, 21; Acts 5, 29).

b. Governments' obligations to citizens.

From the mentioned biblical texts, one can deduce that authority is a service to the common good of society and also a help to each one of its citizens. The nature of civil authority itself is not power, but rather service: the authority has *power* precisely because it must serve the community.

In effect, because society is necessary for the fulfillment of human nature, then authority is necessary in order for the common good of all in society.

The fundamental reality that limits the exercise of authority is the dignity of the human person. Therefore, laws, the institutions created in society and the state itself are justified in the degree that they facilitate dignified living conditions for their citizens. If the objective of the state is to obtain the common good, then it will only pursue the means to help its citizens reach and live according to their dignity.

Conclusion

The success of all societies is based on the success of the family. As each cell which makes up the parts of the body is crucial to the functioning of the whole body, so in like manner does the health of particular families contribute to the functioning of the body of society. It is necessary that all members of society make a concerted effort to promote the well being of the family. In this way the well being of society is promoted. The *Catechism of the Catholic Church* offers the following summary:

> The fourth commandment *illuminates other relationships in society*. In our brothers and sisters we see the children of our parents; in our cousins, the descendants of our ancestors; in our fellow citizens, the children of our country; in the baptized, the children of our mother the Church; in every human person, a son or daughter of the One who wants to be called "our Father." In this way our relationships with our neighbors are recognized as personal in character. The neighbor is not a "unit" in the human collective; he is "someone" who by his known origins deserves particular attention and respect.
>
> Human communities are *made up of persons*. Governing them well is not limited to guaranteeing rights and fulfilling duties such as honoring contracts. Right relations between employers and employees, between those who govern and citizens, presuppose a natural good will in keeping with

the dignity of human persons concerned for justice and fraternity (CCC, 2212-2213).

As taught by Jesus in the Parable of the Good Steward and reaffirmed in St. Paul's Letter to the Romans, the exercise of human authority is always a sharing in the authority of God. It is therefore necessary that this power be exercised with care for God will call all to account for its use or misuse (cf. Lk 12, 42-48; Rm 13, 1-5).

OUTLINE

I. Glossary

AGAPE:

A word derived from the Greek term *agapan* (to have great esteem for); it is used in the New Testament to describe both the relationship that exists between Christ and his Church, and the relationship that ought to exist between a husband and wife.

AUTHORITY:

The characteristic of government and those who represent it by which they are able to dictate laws or oblige the fulfillment of laws.

COMMON GOOD:

The true end and perfection of society and of each one of its members.

DEMOCRACY:

Derived from the Greek *demos* (people) and *kratos* (power); it means that form of government in which the people exercise sovereignty.

FAMILY:

A group of persons united by bonds of kinship. In the strict sense of the word, it is the community of a man and woman and any children born from their marriage.

POLITICS:

Art of governing and conserving order and ethically correct customs.

STATE:

Political body of a nation, director of the common good.

SOCIETY:

Natural or contracted association of individual persons who collaborate in common works and objectives.

II. Summary of Principles

1. By God's design, matrimony and family life are oriented to the procreation and education of children and the good of the spouses.

2. Parents are to honor their children by the good conduct of their lives.

3. Children's respect for and obedience to their parents is in accord with the nature of man and the will of God.

4. Individuals are obliged to satisfy the demands of social life.

5. Just human laws oblige in conscience.

6. Human authorities are obliged to assist individuals in their quest for full development in accord with the common good of society.

7. Government must respect the dynamics of society. For this reason it should not only allow but also promote private associations.

8. Since parents are the primary educators of their children they have a fundamental right to choose the education they consider most apt for their children.

9. Public authority must respect parents' rights regarding the education of their children.

10. The fundamental rights of man must be respected and supported by the laws of the state.

11. The hierarchy of the Church can, and on occasions does, issue moral judgments concerning concrete situations in social life.

In our days the State has come to be a formidable machine which works in a marvellous fashion, wonderfully efficient by reason of the quantity and precision of its means. Once it is set up in the midst of society, it is enough to touch a button for its enormous levers to start working and exercise their overwhelming power on any portion whatever of the social framework.

The contemporary State is the easiest seen and best-known product of civilization. And it is an interesting revelation when one takes note of the attitude that mass-man adopts before it. . . . Suppose that in the public life of a country some difficulty, conflict, or problem presents itself, the mass-man will tend to demand that the State intervene immediately and undertake a solution directly with its immense and unassailable resources.

This is the gravest danger that today threatens civilization: State intervention; the absorption of all spontaneous social effort by the State, that is to say, of spontaneous historical action, which in the long run sustains, nourishes, and impels human destinies. When the mass suffers any ill-fortune or simply feels some strong appetite, its great temptation is that permanent, sure possibility of obtaining everything—without effort, struggle, doubt, or risk—merely by touching a button and setting the mighty machine in motion. . . .

The result of this tendency will be fatal. Spontaneous social action will be broken up over and over again by State intervention; no new seed will be able to fructify. Society will have to live *for* the State, man *for* the governmental machine. And as, after all, it is only a machine whose existence and maintenance depend on the vital supports around it, the State, after sucking out the very marrow of society, will be left bloodless, a skeleton, dead with that rusty death of machinery, more gruesome than the death of a living organism.

(José Ortega y Gasset, *The Revolt of the Masses*, pp. 119-121)

The family, a communion of persons

"In matrimony and in the family a complex of interpersonal relationships is set up — married life, fatherhood, motherhood, filiation and fraternity— through which each human person is introduced into the 'human family' and into the 'family of God' which is the Church.

"Christian marriage and the Christian family build up the Church: for in the family the human person is not only brought into being and progressively introduced by means of education into the human community, but by means of the rebirth of Baptism and education in the faith the child is introduced into God's family, which is the Church.

"The human family, disunited by sin, is reconstituted in its unity by the redemptive power of the death and resurrection of Christ. Christian marriage, by participating in the salvific efficacy of this event, constitutes the natural setting in which the human person is introduced into the great family of the Church.

"The commandment to grow and multiply, given to man and woman in the beginning, in this way reaches its whole truth and full realization. The Church thus finds in the family, born from the sacrament, the cradle and the setting in which she can enter the human generations, and where these in turn can enter the Church" (*FC*, 15).

"The Family finds in the plan of God, the Creator and Redeemer, not only its *identity*, what it *is*, but also its *mission*, what it can and should *do*" (*FC*, 17).

"The family, which is founded and given life by love, is a community of persons . . . Its first task is to live with fidelity the reality of communion in a constant effort to develop an authentic community of persons. The inner principle of that task, its permanent power and its final goal is love: without love the family is not a community of persons and, in the same way, *without love the family cannot live, grow and perfect itself as a community of persons*. What I wrote in the encyclical *Redemptor hominis* applies primarily to and especially within the family as such: 'Man cannot live without love. He remains a being that is incomprehensible to himself, his life is senseless, if love is not revealed to him, if he does not encounter love, if he does not experience and make it his own, if he does not participate intimately in it (*FC*, 18; cf. also *RH*, 10).

"The church is deeply convinced that only by the acceptance of the Gospel are the hopes that man legitimately places in marriage and the family capable of being fulfilled. Willed by God in the very act of creation, marriage and the family are ordained to fulfillment in Christ and have need of his graces in order to be healed from the wounds of sin and restored to their 'beginning,' that is, to full understanding and the full realization of God's plan" (*FC*, 3).

QUESTIONS

1. Why does the Church insist that love is the foundation of the family?
2. What is the key to loving properly?
3. What is the Old Testament attitude toward parents?
4. What does the statement "St. Paul's entire teaching depends upon his parallel between man and woman and the union of Christ and the Church" mean?
5. What does "revering your parents" mean?
6. List the obligations that parents have toward the children.
7. List the obligations that children have toward their parents.
8. What practical steps can be taken to deal appropriately with a child's anger toward his parents or a parent's anger toward his children while maintaining the nature of the parent-child relationship required by the fourth commandment?
9. Relations between siblings are often difficult. Suggest some ways in which this might be remedied
10. Why is the required love of family life called supernatural?
11. Why must one obey the civil authorities? Are there any exceptions?
12. List the six affirmations in the doctrine of obedience to authority.
13. What is the nature of civil authority?

PRACTICAL EXERCISES

1. The period of betrothal or engagement is a natural preparation for marriage. In light of this chapter, write an essay which explains your understanding of what engagement is and how an engaged couple can best prepare themselves for their eventual marriage during this period.

2. Explain the meaning of this text from Vatican II: "The well-being of the individual person and of human and Christian society is intimately linked with the healthy condition of that community produced by marriage and family" (GS, 47).

3. Discuss some of the material benefits possessed by families in modern western civilization and the positive and negative effects which you think they have on family life. In view of your answer, do you think family life in countries that do not enjoy as many material benefits as ours is generally better, or do you think that things are generally the same every where? Support your answer with specific examples.

4. Comment on each of the following situations, evaluating each person's attitude, actions or decisions in light of the Fourth Commandment:

   a. Susan says she should be allowed to live by her own rules at home since she is eighteen years of age.

   b. Peter's dad arrives at home drunk on a regular basis, and starts screaming at the family members. Peter plans to throw his father out of the house on the next occasion.

   c. Dante doesn't want to tell his parents his brother has been hanging out with kids who are known to sell drugs at school because he doesn't want to be a squealer.

5. You are a parent with four children. Discuss steps which can be taken to avoid or reduce sibling disagreements.

CHAPTER XIII
THE FIFTH COMMANDMENT:
YOU SHALL NOT KILL

Now Abel was a keeper of sheep, and Cain a tiller of the ground. In the course of time Cain brought to the LORD an offering of the fruit of the ground, and Abel brought of the firstlings of his flock and of their fat portions. And the LORD had regard for Abel and his offering, but for Cain and his offering he had not regard. So Cain was very angry, and his countenance fell. The LORD said to Cain, "Why are you angry and why has your countenance fallen? If you do well, will you not be accepted? And if you do not do well, sin is crouching at the door; its desire is for you, but you must master it."

Cain said to Abel his brother, "Let us go out to the field." And when they were in the field, Cain rose up against his brother Abel, and killed him. Then the LORD said to Cain, "Where is Abel your brother?" He said, "I do not know; am I my brother's keeper?" And the LORD said, "What have you done? The voice of your brother's blood is crying to me from the ground. And now you are cursed from the ground, which has opened its mouth to receive your brother's blood from your hand. When you till the ground, it shall no longer yield to you its strength; you shall be a fugitive and a wanderer on the earth."

Cain said to the LORD, "My punishment is greater than I can bear. Behold, you have driven me this day away from the ground; and from your face I shall be hidden; and I shall be a fugitive and a wanderer on the earth, and whoever finds me will slay me." Then the LORD said to him, "Not so! If anyone slays Cain, vengeance shall be taken on him sevenfold." And the LORD put a mark on Cain, lest any who came upon him should kill him. Then Cain went away from the presence of the LORD, and dwelt in the land of Nod, east of Eden (Gn 4, 2-16).

The story of Cain and Abel is one of the most dramatic and instructive in Scripture. Along with the Decalogue, it forms the biblical foundation for the Church's absolute insistence on the inviolability and sacredness of human life. In light of this story, we may ask ourselves the following questions:

- Does God's revelation forbid all killing, or only some types of killing?

- What is the meaning of human suffering?

- Can the desire to prevent suffering ever justify taking someone's life?

- In light of the biblical prohibition against murder, can war ever be truly justifiable?

- Why does the Church teach that man's stewardship over his own life does not include the right to end it?

Introduction

God did not give man absolute dominion over his life, but rather gives him the duty of guarding his own life and the lives of those around him. This is how it is expressed in Deuteronomy: "See now that I, even I, am he, and there is no god beside me; I kill and I make alive; I wound and I heal; and there is none that can deliver out of my hand" (Dt 32, 39).

> God proclaims that he is absolute LORD of the life of man, who is formed in his image and likeness (cf. Gn 1, 26-28). Human life is thus given a sacred and inviolable character, which reflects the inviolability of the Creator himself. Precisely for this reason God will severely judge every violation of the commandment "You shall not kill," the commandment which is at the basis of all life together in society. He is the "goel," the defender of the innocent (cf. Gn 4, 9-15; Is 41,14; Jr 50, 34; Ps 19, 14). God thus shows that he does not delight in the death of the living (cf. Wis 1,13). Only Satan can delight therein: for through his envy death entered the world (cf. Wis 2, 24). He who is "a murderer from the beginning," is also "a liar and the father of lies" (Jn 8, 44). By deceiving man he leads him to projects of sin and death, making them appear as goals and fruits of life (*EV*, 53.3).

This teaching supposes, besides the simple acceptance of the existence of God, a specifically Christian understanding of God as all-powerful and paternal. Human life has its origin in him and one's life depends on him. Therefore, the atheist and agnostic ideologies—and even some religions—will not accept some of Christianity's moral teachings about the value and meaning of life. Many philosophies view human beings as dependent only on themselves—the absolute masters of their own lives and destinies. But Christianity, in regarding the life and the conduct of man, rejects *autonomy*, dependence on one's self, and *heteronomy*, dependence on someone else, and only accepts *theonomy*, dependence on God. Such dependence is precisely the glory and salvation of humanity. The human person can only find the fullness of being and the guarantee of existence in God.

1.   All life belongs to God. Respect for human life

The Catholic doctrine concerning the value of life is based on the fifth commandment: "You shall not kill." God commands everyone to respect his own life and the lives of others. This commandment deals with protecting the most fundamental human right: the right to existence itself. For that reason, God reminds humanity in the Old Testament that he is the only owner of life and that, when creating man, he gave him the personal right to defend it. No one can deny this right, and therefore to attempt to take one's own life or that of another is especially serious.

This commandment was completed and brought to perfection by Jesus Christ. In the Sermon on the Mount, he enriched it with these words:

> You have heard that it was said to the men of old, "You shall not kill; and whoever kills shall be liable to judgment." But I say to you that every one who is angry with his brother shall be liable to judgment; whoever insults his brother shall be liable to the council, and whoever says, "You fool!" shall be liable to the hell of fire.
>
> So if you are offering your gift at the altar, and there remember that your brother has something against you, leave your gift there before the altar and go; first be reconciled to your brother, and then come and offer your gift (Mt 5, 21-24).

In these words, Jesus introduces two new elements to the fifth commandment:

- He commands that not only should one respect the life of another, but also that one must value his own dignity, in such a way that any offense which violates any person's dignity is condemned.

- He specifies that no one can direct himself to God when he holds his fellow men to be enemies. Christ demands that one should be reconciled with his enemies before talking with God. This shows the importance of love for one's fellow men which is included in the generic and negative formula of "not killing."

This same doctrinal development regarding respect for life demands the defense of all human life, including the unborn and those whose lives are considered useless.

But the "novelty" of the fifth commandment, as reinterpreted by Jesus Christ, is enriched with the proclamation of the commandment of love. In this way, the precept of not killing is converted into the new commandment of Jesus Christ: "This is my commandment, that you love one another as I have loved you" (Jn 15, 12). The commandment of charity enriches the primitive formulation of the fifth commandment of the Mosaic law.

2. Conservation of existing life

> For the greatest personal possession of the natural order is life itself, since it is the necessary condition for the enjoyment of all other blessings, even those that are spiritual. To deprive someone of life is to inflict upon him the greatest harm of the natural order . . . a sin that is obviously all the more serious because it is completely irreparable. When someone is murdered, he stays murdered; a murderer cannot restore life (*Responding to God*, Richard Butler, O. P.).

Only God is the absolute owner of human life, and man must try to live his life to the best of his abilities. For this reason, one is seriously obliged to take care of life as a good steward whose life is on loan from God.

a. The duty to conserve one's own life.

To protect one's own life, each person is permitted to defend himself when under attack, even if the consequences are the unintended death of an unjust aggressor for self-defense permits the force necessary to repel an unjust attacker.

Legitimate self-defense is moral (cf. *CCC*, 2263-2267). However, no one can end one's own life; therefore, suicide (*CCC*, 2259-2262) and mutilation (*CCC*, 2297-2298) are forbidden. Furthermore, because of the unique value of each life, one has the serious duty of taking care of one's health. The use of illegal drugs and the excessive use of alcohol are therefore immoral (*CCC*, 2288-2291).

b. Respect for the life of others.

If man is not the owner of his own life, he certainly cannot dispose of the life of others. Taking the life of an innocent person—murder or homicide—is a serious offense against God and the moral order (cf. *CCC*, 2268-2269). Kidnapping, torture, and terrorism are also forbidden (cf. *CCC*, 2297-2298). The death penalty is permitted only rarely, in cases of extreme gravity (cf. *CCC*, 2266-2267).

c. **Abortion and the rights of the unborn.**

> "...From the time that the ovum is fertilized, a life is begun which is neither that of the father nor of the mother; it is rather the life of a new human being with its own growth. It would never be made human if it were not human already. . .Right from the fertilization the adventure of new life begins, and each of its capacities requires time— a rather lengthy time—to find its place and to be in a position to act...." (*CHCW*, 35).

Abortion causes the death of a child before he can survive outside the mother's womb. It can be *spontaneous* or *procured*, depending on whether it occurs naturally or is brought about through the intervention of man.

The study of *spontaneous abortion or miscarriages* is purely a concern of medicine which studies ways to avoid it. On the other hand, *procured* abortion involves medicine, law, politics and, in a special way, morality.

In this wide discussion, one can distinguish three classes of induced abortion: *eugenic abortion* because of a malformation of the fetus; *therapeutic abortion* for medical reasons as in cases of rape and *psychological* or *psychosocial abortion*, when one wishes to terminate an undesired pregnancy for psychological motives, economic circumstances or for social reasons.

The Magisterium of the Church has consistently proclaimed the gravely sinful nature of abortion. The Fathers of the Church condemned it to combat the frequent practice in the Greco-Roman world. This condemnation is found in the *Didache*, a first century Church text (ca. A.D. 80) which told Christians "You shall not procure abortion. You shall not destroy a newborn child."

This condemnation was repeated in Vatican Council II and, since the Council, Paul VI and John Paul II have reiterated this condemnation.

> Some people try to justify abortion by claiming that the result of conception, at least up to a certain number of days,

cannot yet be considered a personal human life. But in fact, 'from the time that the ovum is fertilized, a life is begun which is neither that of the father nor the mother; it is rather the life of a new human being with his own growth. It would never be made human if it were not human already.

This has always been clear, and . . . modern genetic science offers clear confirmation. It has demonstrated that from the first instant there is established the program of what this living being will be: a person, this individual person with his characteristic aspects already well determined. . . .' (cf. *DPA*, 12-13).

Even if the presence of a spiritual soul cannot be ascertained by empirical data, the results themselves of scientific research on the human embryo provide 'a valuable indication for discerning by the use of reason a personal presence at the moment of the first appearance of a human life: how could a human individual not be a human person?' (*EV*, 60; cf. also *DV*, 1, 1).

Furthermore, what is at stake is so important that, from the standpoint of moral obligation, the mere probability that a human person is involved would suffice to justify an absolutely clear prohibition of any intervention aimed at killing a human embryo. Precisely for this reason, over and above all scientific debates and those philosophical affirmations to which the magisterium has not expressly committed itself, the Church has always taught and continues to teach that the result of human procreation, from the first moment of its existence, must be guaranteed that unconditional respect which is morally due to the human being in his or her totality and unity as body and spirit .... (ibid.).

Pope John Paul II states clearly the gravity of the sin of abortion in the following words:

> . . . Therefore, by the authority which Christ conferred upon Peter and his Successors, in communion with the Bishops— who on various occasions have condemned abortion and who in the aforementioned consultation, albeit dispersed throughout the world, have shown unanimous agreement concerning this doctrine—*I declare that direct abortion, that is, abortion willed as an end or as a means, always constitutes a grave moral disorder*, since it is the deliberate killing of an innocent human being. This doctrine is based upon the

natural law and upon the written Word of God, is transmitted by the Church's Tradition and taught by the ordinary and universal magisterium ....(ibid., 62).

Such condemnation becomes even more serious with the punishment of excommunication (exclusion of a baptized person
from participation in the ritual and sacramental life of the
Church), which the *Code of Canon Law* imposes: "A person
who actually procures an abortion incurs an automatic excommunication" (*CIC*, 1398). One who knows that abortion
is condemned is automatically excommunicated from the
Church. If a person does not know that this sin is cause for
excommunication, he is not excommunicated. All those who
cooperate in the abortion are also subject to excommunication: "Formal cooperation in an abortion constitutes a grave
offense" (*CCC*, 2272).

The insensitivity of today's culture that defends abortion is
inexplicable. It is possible that in the future people may look
back at our times and be scandalized in the same way that
we cannot explain how it was possible that slavery was practiced in America.

c. **The error of a pro-choice Catholic (i.e for a free choice)**

Some Catholics defend what they call a "pro-choice position."
According to them a woman has the freedom to *choose* to abort
her baby under the "right to privacy," and this right can not
be superseded. Abortion then is not considered as a life-death
issue but as a rights-choice issue. They eliminate the unpleasant and potentially painful notion of the principal pro-life
argument: abortion is murder. They refuse to acknowledge
that there is a human being in the womb. Since the pro-
choicers deny personhood to the unborn, they present abortion as something akin to the removal of a tumor.

Other Catholics while maintaining that they are personally
opposed to the practice of abortion, believe that is morally
wrong for them (or for the Church as an social institution)
to attempt to prohibit its practice. They insist that it would
be wrong for them to allow their personal religious convictions to influence their political decisions.

John Paul rejects these pro-choice positions:

... we have what appear to be two diametrically opposed tendencies. On the one hand, individuals claim for themselves in the moral sphere the most complete freedom of choice and demand that the State should not adopt or impose any ethical position but limit itself to guaranteeing maximum space for the freedom of each individual, with the sole limitation of not infringing on the freedom and rights of any other citizen. On the other hand, it is held that, in the exercise of public and professional duties, respect for other people's freedom of choice requires that each one should set aside his or her own convictions in order to satisfy every demand of the citizens which is recognized and guaranteed by law; in carrying out one's duties, the only moral criterion should be what is laid down by the law itself. Individual responsibility is thus turned over to the civil law, with a renouncing of personal conscience, at least in the public sphere.

At the basis of all these tendencies lies the *ethical relativism* which characterizes much of present-day culture. There are those who consider such relativism an essential condition of democracy, inasmuch as it alone is held to guarantee tolerance, mutual respect between people and acceptance of the decisions of the majority, whereas moral norms considered to be objective and binding are held to lead to authoritarianism and intolerance (*EV*, 69-70).

3. The problem of pain and suffering

The subject of pain and suffering has been one of the great questions of man throughout history. Philosophical systems as well as religions have always asked: Why do humans suffer? What is the origin of suffering? Why do honorable, innocent human beings suffer?

These questions are even more disturbing if one takes into account that no one is free from suffering, that pain is widespread and common, and that suffering is often profound and severe. It is also possible to exaggerate the apparent senselessness of pain if one thinks about "useless," or "unjust" pain and especially the pain of innocent people.

This is why a shout of desperation is lifted up against God; one of the causes of atheism in our times has been the enigma of pain. Vatican II, when talking about the numerous causes of atheism in our time, teaches: "atheism results not rarely from a violent protest against the evil in this world" (*GS*, 19).

Suffering is certainly part of the mystery of man. Perhaps suffering is not wrapped up as much as man is by this mystery, which is an especially impenetrable one. The Second Vatican Council expressed this truth that . . . only in the mystery of the Incarnate Word does the mystery of man take on light. In fact . . . , Christ, the final Adam, by the revelation of the mystery of the Father and his love, *fully reveals man to himself* and makes his supreme calling clear.' If these words refer to everything that concerns the mystery of man, then they certainly refer in a very special way *to human suffering*. Precisely at this point the 'revealing of man to himself and making his supreme vocation clear' is particularly *indispensable*. It also happens—as experience proves—that this can be particularly *dramatic*. But when it is completely accomplished and becomes the light of human life, it is particularly *blessed*. Through Christ and in Christ, the riddles of sorrow and death grow meaningful.

The mystery of the Redemption of the world is in an amazing way *rooted in suffering*, and this suffering in turn finds in the mystery of the Redemption its supreme and surest point of reference (*SD*, 31; cf. 1 P 4, 13; Col. 1, 24; *GS*, 22).

Christians are called to join their sufferings to the suffering of Jesus Christ, who died on the Cross for the sins of the world. In this way, human suffering assumes a meaning and purpose which transcends our ordinary understanding; it can become an offering to God in reparation for sin.

4. The meaning of death and euthanasia

The origin of death is sin. St. Paul tells us: "But then what return did you get from the things of which you are now ashamed? The end of those things is death" (Rm 6, 21), and "sin, working death in me through what is good, in order that sin might be shown to be sin, and through the commandment might become sinful beyond measure" (Rm 7, 13), since "this perishable nature must put on the imperishable, and this mortal nature must put on immortality" (1 Cor 15, 53). For the Christian, however, death is not the end but rather a beginning.

In relation to death, the most urgent ethical problem is euthanasia. The word euthanasia comes from the Greek *eu* (good) and *thanatos* (death), so it means good or sweet death. The choice of this word reflects the fact that those involved in the revolution to change

ideas usually begin by changing the language. By any name this act
is still murder.

> By euthanasia is understood an action or an omission which
> of itself or by intention causes death, in order that all suf-
> fering may in this way be eliminated. Euthanasia's terms
> of reference, therefore, are to be found in the intention of
> the will and in the methods used (*IOE*, 14).

While the Church condemns euthanasia, it also recognizes there
exists a right to end unnecessary medical treatment in particular
circumstances (*see appendix no. 1*).

> Euthanasia must be distinguished from the decision to forego
> so-called 'aggressive medical treatment', in other words,
> medical procedures which no longer correspond to the real
> situation of the patient, either because they are by now dis-
> proportionate to any expected results or because they impose
> an excessive burden on the patient and his family. In such
> situations, when death is clearly imminent and inevitable, one
> can in conscience 'refuse forms of treatment that would only
> secure a precarious and burdensome prolongation of life, so
> long as the normal care due to the sick person in similar cases
> is not interrupted. . . .'(cf. *IOE*, IV).

> To forego extraordinary or disproportionate means is not the
> equivalent of suicide or euthanasia; it rather expresses accep-
> tance of the human condition in the face of death. . . . (*EV*, 65).

> . . . Taking into account these distinctions, in harmony with
> the magisterium of my Predecessors and in communion
> with the Bishops of the Catholic Church, *I confirm that
> euthanasia is a grave violation of the law of God,* since it is the
> deliberate and morally unacceptable killing of a human per-
> son. This doctrine is based upon the natural law and upon
> the written word of God, is transmitted by the Church's
> Tradition and taught by the ordinary and universal
> magisterium (ibid. 65).

From the foregoing, the following conclusions may be drawn:

* it is always wrong to take directly the life of a sick person;

* it is permissible to allow the imminent death of a person;

* extraordinary means are never required;

* in all cases ordinary means to sustain life are always required.

Psychological disorders and illnesses can be dealt with and treated through psychotherapy. Drugs may be administered for ethically legitimate reasons. The right of the patient to be informed as well as his right to refuse therapy must be considered while taking into account the ability of the patient to make these decisions

This moral doctrine is reasonable because it recognizes two principles: the right to die worthily as man and the right to life which is inherent to every human being.

5. Respect for the souls of others. Avoiding scandal

The Christian is obliged to lead a life which gives good example to others. Time and time again in the Gospels, Jesus reminds his followers that they will be judged by the fruits produced by their conduct (cf. Mt 7, 16-20), that they must be prepared to forgive one another if they wish to receive God's forgiveness (cf. Mt 6, 14-15), and that others will know that they are his followers by the love which they show toward one another (cf. Jn 13, 34-35).

In equally forceful terms, however, Jesus also warns his followers about the opposing sin of scandal:

> " . . . whoever causes one of these little ones who believe in me to sin, it would be better for him to have a great millstone fastened around his neck and to be drowned in the depth of the sea.
>
> Woe to the world for temptations to sin! For it is necessary that temptations come, but woe to the man by whom the temptation comes!" (cf. Mt 18, 6-7).

Scandal is an attitude or behavior which leads another to do evil. When a person does evil, he becomes the source of his neighbor's temptation. Not only does the person damage his own virtue and integrity, but may even draw his brother into sin and cause a break in his relationship with God through mortal sin. The sin of scandal is grave when it leads others to mortal sin whether by deed or omission (CCC, 2284). Those in authority have a particular responsibility to avoid scandal.

> Scandal takes on a particular gravity by reason of the authority of those who cause it or the weakness of those who are scandalized. It prompted our Lord to utter this curse: "Whoever causes one of these little ones who believe in me to sin, it would be better for him to have a great millstone

fastened around his neck and to be drowned in the depth of the sea."[1] Scandal is grave when given by those who by nature or office are obliged to teach and educate others (*CCC*, 2285).

Scandal can be provoked: by laws (abortion), institutions (slavery), fashions (immodest dress), entertainment (some TV shows and certain forms of popular music), parties, or opinions (racism).

6. Just war

War with all its horrors is never desirable. Nonetheless, "insofar as men are sinners, the threat of war hangs over them and will continue to do so until the coming of Christ" (*GS*, 78). Several criteria have been established by the Church to determine if an armed conflict is just.

- Any military action must be a last resort. All other avenues of peaceful settlement must be pursued, and must end in failure.

- The cause must be sufficiently grave and legitimate. Contrary to common belief, both offensive and defensive campaigns may be initiated for sufficient reason, whether it be resistance, pre-emptive or reactionary, to a foreign aggressor or prosecution of rights, e.g., territorial sovereignty, which no higher authority can protect.

- War must be declared and waged by proper authority. In other words, sovereign states in the person of recognized officials are the only agents capable of declaring and waging a just war.

- The goods obtained by military conflict must outweigh the tremendous evils which most certainly will come about as a result.

- Under no circumstances are non-combatants to be targeted by any military action. Political and military leaders, especially in modern times, must wield the awesome weapons provided by modern science with great care and discernment. On the other hand, they must have the courage to expeditiously prosecute war to a quick and decisive completion in order to avoid bloody and unsuccessful stalemates.

Along with the Church's teaching on just war, there is also her insistence on the respect which is due to the dignity of every human person, even when situations arise in which two nations may find themselves in conflict with one another. It is unfortunately true that hostilities between nations often bring violence and suffering to the innocent and the poor in the nations involved.

In such situations, everything possible must be done by those responsible for the conduct of the war to insure that the innocent are protected as far as is possible. Just as the Church condemns the targeting of civilian populations by military forces, so she also condemns *kidnapping, torture* and *terrorism* as gravely sinful and contrary to the moral law (cf. *CCC*, 2297-2298). These means can never be used because they involve violence directed against innocent persons.

War and violence are the sad result of sin, but if every individual strives to live with sincere fraternal love, then true peace will blossom in the world.

> Thus the message of the Gospel, which epitomizes the highest ideals and aspirations of mankind, shines anew in or times when it proclaims that the advocates of peace are blessed "for they shall be called sons of God."
>
> Accordingly, the Council proposes to outline the true and noble nature of peace, to condemn the savagery of war, and to earnestly exhort all Christians to cooperate with all in securing a peace based on justice and charity and in promoting the means necessary to attain it, under the help of Christ, the author of peace (*GS*, 77; cf. Mt 5, 9).

7. Respect for the body. Mutilation and organ transplants

The human body is a wonderful instance of God's majestic creation. As such, it should not be degraded or disfigured by mutilation or abuse. Any type of mutilation or disfigurement of the body is contrary to the moral law. As St. Paul pointed out, "Do you not know that your body is a temple of the Holy Spirit within you, which you have from God? You are not your own" (1 Cor 6, 19).

At certain times, however, it may become medically necessary to remove an organ or limb to save the life of a seriously ill person. Such action is morally permissible.

In recent years, organ transplants have been performed with increasing frequency. Organ transplants are permitted when both the donor and the recipient or those who speak for them give informed consent, when the physical and psychological dangers and risks are proportionate to the good sought and when the qualified surgical team and required equipment are present.

It is morally impermissible to bring about the disabling mutilation or the death of a human being, even in order to delay the death of another person (cf. *CCC*, 2292-2296).

"The brain and gonads may not be transplanted since they insure the personal and procreative identity, respectively" (*CHCW*, 88).

8. Cloning

Recent breakthroughs in scientific technology have added yet another dimension to the continuing debate over respect for the dignity of human life. The announcement in early 1997 of the successful cloning of a sheep by genetic scientists in Scotland has raised new moral and ethical concerns for the Church. As many as ten years before the successful completion of a cloning experiment, however, the Church, aware of the direction in which scientific research was proceeding, had condemned the procedure in the document *Donum Vitae* (See Supplementary Reading 5).

Cloning is gravely sinful and contrary to the moral law because it opposes the dignity of both the conjugal union between husband and wife and human procreation. Cloning, like artificial insemination, in vitro fertilization and the use of frozen embryos, is a technology which aims at producing human beings selected according to gender or other predetermined quality. It reduces human beings to objects which can be manufactured and manipulated according to the whim of the scientist controlling the reproduction, rather than respecting the integrity of the individual as a unique and irreplaceable creation of God, possessing his or her own integrity and identity.

9. Illicit drug use. Smoking and the abuse of alcohol

The use of illicit drugs and the abuse of alcohol are forbidden because, in addition to damaging the body, such activity reduces man to the levels of an animal by impairing his ability to think clearly. The human soul distinguishes man from the other animals, and to directly inhibit its faculties assaults the dignity of the human person.

> . . . From the moral viewpoint, "using drugs is always illicit, because it implies an unjustified and irrational refusal to think, will and act as free persons".

To say that drugs are illicit is not to condemn the drug user. That person experiences a *heavy slavery* from which he needs to be freed. The way to recovery cannot be that of ethical culpability or repressive law, but it must be by way of rehabilitation which, without condoning the possible fault of the person on drugs, promotes liberation from his condition and reintegration . . .

. . . Using drugs is anti-life. One cannot speak of the freedom to take drugs nor of the right to drugs, because a human being does not have the right to harm himself and he cannot and must not ever abdicate his personal dignity which is given to him by God, and even less does he have the right to make others pay for his choice. . . .

. . . With regard to tobacco also, the ethical unlawfulness is not in its use but in its abuse. At the present time it is established that excessive smoking damages the health and causes dependency. This leads to a progressive lowering of the threshold of abuse . . . .

. . . Unlike taking drugs, alcohol is not in itself illicit: *its moderate use as a drink is not contrary to moral law.* Within reasonable limits wine is a nourishment.

It is only the abuse that is reprehensible: alcoholism, which causes dependency, clouds the conscience and, in the chronic stage, produces serious harm to the body and the mind". . . . (*CHCW,* 94-99).

10. Sterilization

Sterilization is alteration of the reproductive organs, depriving a man or a woman of his or her procreative capability. Man has no authority to destroy his procreative faculties. Christian morality declares ethically condemnable voluntary sterilization seeking contraceptive ends.

One should distinguish between *direct* and *indirect sterilization.*

- *Direct sterilization* is intended to destroy the procreative capability. Direct sterilization is a sin against the fifth commandment, because it is not only mutilation of the body, but is also an attack on the integrity of the person. Practices such as the sterilization of a woman by means of tying the fallopian tubes or of a man by performing a vasectomy are examples of direct sterilization.

- *Indirect sterilization* is a secondary result of a different medical procedure or as a result of an accident. The Magisterium has accepted indirect sterilization as morally licit *only under necessary medical conditions,* as, for example, in the case of a woman whose ovaries must be removed because of ovarian cancer.

It is important to remember the distinction here—the sterilization of the woman in question is not a desired result of the surgery, but is tolerated as unavoidable if the woman's life is to be saved. On the other hand, the Magisterium has condemned direct sterilization which is carried out to avoid procreation.

This temptation to "play God" is very strong, particularly when human science discovers techniques to manipulate nature, but man must flee such temptation since experience shows that, in the long run, a lack of respect for nature results in the most serious moral disorders. Besides, the Christian should exercise faith and trust in God; man knows by experience that divine law is a light that guides human existence in the face of evil.

11. Physician-assisted suicide

A person's right to life extends from conception through natural death. Contrary to certain movements in contemporary society which maintain otherwise, this means that the terminally ill have a right to expect appropriate medical treatment which safeguards their dignity as a human being, while enabling them to cope with the pain that a serious or terminal illness often inevitably brings. Thus, the Church teaches that the terminally ill have "a right to die in total serenity, with human and Christian dignity" (cf. CDF, *Declaration on Euthanasia*).

But the right to die with dignity must not be interpreted as meaning that a person has the right to kill himself in order to avoid the "indignity" of the physical, emotional or psychological suffering that comes with a terminal illness. Nor does a person have the right to ask his physician to help him commit suicide. Yet this is precisely what many in society have begun to advocate. Understandably, this imagined "right" to suicide is often advocated by people who wish to avoid the danger of being victimized by overzealous medical personnel and technologies which can become unnecessarily intrusive, burdensome, or even abusive.

Contemporary medicine, in fact, has at its disposal methods which artificially delay death, without any real benefit to the patient.

It is merely keeping one alive or prolonging life for a time, at the cost of further, severe suffering. This is the so-called "therapeutic tyranny," which consists "in the use of methods which are particularly exhausting and painful for the patient, condemning him in fact to an artificially prolonged agony."

This is contrary to the dignity of the dying person and to the moral obligation of accepting death and allowing it at last to take its course. "Death is an inevitable fact of human life": it cannot be uselessly delayed, fleeing from it by every means.

> Aware that he is "neither the lord of life nor the conqueror of death," the health care worker, in evaluating means, "should make appropriate choices, that, relate to the patient and be guided by his real condition" (*CHCW*, 119-120).

The principle of "appropriate medical treatment" allows a physician, in the face of imminent death, to decide to end treatment which would only result in a dangerous and painful prolongation of the patient's life. At the same time, however, the physician must continue to provide the patient the normal treatment due to the patient in similar cases. Thus, for example, in the case of incurable pancreatic cancer, a doctor may forego the further application of chemotherapy because there is no hope for success and the pain that the patient suffers as a result of the treatment serves no good purpose, but he may not withhold from the patient food, liquids and the painkillers necessary to regulate the patient's discomfort. If he does this, he has acted correctly because he has done all that it is reasonable for him to do to care for his patient. Further, the administration of food and liquids, even artificially, is part of the normal treatment always due to the patient when this is not burdensome for him: their undue suspension could be real and properly so-called euthanasia.

> For the doctors and their assistants it is not a question of deciding the life or death of an individual. It is simply a question of being a doctor, that is, of posing the question and then deciding according to one's expertise and one's conscience regarding a respectful care of the living and the dying of the patient entrusted to him. This responsibility does not always and in all cases involve recourse to every means. It might also require renunciation of certain means to make way for a serene and Christian acceptance of death which is inherent in life. It might also mean respect for the wishes of the patient who refuses such means (*CHCW*, 121).

Conclusion

Life the preparation for Life in the hereafter. In God's plan man is seen as a steward over his soul and body, so it should be obvious that the God who gave both has requirements for the right use of both. This fact naturally includes requirements regarding relations with the souls and bodies of others. Since God shows responsibility for the origin of new life with man, there is a similar obligation to treat the sources of life as God wishes. In sum, man has an obligation to develop himself in body and soul while respecting the rights of others in all these matters.

OUTLINE

I. Glossary

ABORTION:

Procuring the expulsion or destruction of the fetus before it can live outside the mother's womb.

ASSISTED SUICIDE:

Any action, or omission of an action, which assists another person in bringing about his or her own death.

AUTONOMY:

The belief that man is entirely independent and is responsible only to himself for his actions and the direction of his life.

BIOETHICS:

Derived from the Greek words *bios* (life) and *ethos* (ethics), it is the science that studies the morality of the problems related to life, from birth till death.

CLONING:

The technique of of producing a genetically identical duplicate of an organism by replacing the nucleus of an unfertilized ovum with the nucleus of a body cell from the organism.

EUTHANASIA:

An action or omission of an action which, by itself or by intention, causes the death of a person in order to eliminate suffering.

EUGENICS:

The application of biological laws of heredity in order to perfect the human species.

EXTRAORDINARY MEANS

Those treatments which are beyond or out of the common order or method, not in the usual, customary or regular course, and exceeding the common degree.

HETERONOMY:

The belief that man is entirely dependent on others for happiness and meaning in his life.

JUST WAR:

The principle that war may be legitimately waged, under certain specific conditions, for the protection of a nation's rights.

MURDER:

To cause the death of an innocent person.

MUTILATION:

The disfigurement of the human body.

SCANDAL:

An attitude or behavior which leads another to do evil.

STERILIZATION:

The destruction of the procreative powers.

SUICIDE:

To voluntarily take one's own life.

THEONOMY:

The belief that man depends upon God for the meaning, direction and purpose of his life.

II. Summary of Principles

1. Man does not have absolute control over his life and destiny; he has been given by God the duty to guard both his own life and the lives of others.

2. Catholic teaching regarding the sacredness of all human life is founded upon the fifth commandment.

3. Man's natural obligation to respect human life was completed and brought to perfection by Jesus Christ.

4. Jesus not only repeated the prohibition against killing, but enjoined his followers to love their enemies.

5. The Christian is obliged to preserve his own life, and the lives of others. Self-defense is therefore permitted, while suicide, mutilation, sterilization, the use of illegal drugs and the abuse of alcohol are forbidden as grave sins against God.

6. Capital punishment is permitted only in the most extraordinary circumstances.

7. Murder, abortion, euthanasia, kidnapping, torture and terrorism are grave sins against God.

8. The Christian discovers the meaning of human suffering through faith in Jesus Christ, who suffered and died for the salvation of man.

9. Death is the result of Original Sin. As a consequence of the Redemption, the Christian believes that death is the beginning of eternal life.

10. Each person has a serious obligation to respect the souls of others by striving always to give good example. To lead another person into sin through scandal is a grave evil.

11. The Church accepts the principle of the just war waged for legitimate reasons and with proportionate means.

SUPPLEMENTARY READINGS

1. The Oath of Hippocrates.

> *Hippocrates was a medical doctor in the Golden Age of Hellenism. Remembered as the Father of Medicine, his writings comprised the first important compendium of clinical medicine in the Western world. Among his works is the famous "Hippocratic Oath" (hórkos) which has had a significant impact on the formulation of medical ethics. In former times, every doctor was required to swear this oath before undertaking the practice of medicine.*

I swear by Apollo, the Physician, the Aesculapius and health and all-heal and all the gods and goddesses that, according to my ability and judgment, I will keep this oath and stipulation:

To reckon him who taught me this art equally dear to me as my parents, to share my substance with him and relieve his necessities if required: to regard his offspring as on the same footing with my own brothers, and to teach them this art if they should wish to learn it, without fee or stipulation, and that by precept, lecture and every other mode of instruction, I will impart a knowledge of the art to my own sons and to those of my teachers, and to disciples bound by a stipulation and oath, according to the law of medicine, but to none others.

I will follow that method of treatment which, according to my ability and judgment, I consider to the benefit of my patients, and abstain from whatever is deleterious and mischievous. I will give no deadly medicine to anyone if asked, nor suggest any such counsel; furthermore, I will not give to a woman an instrument to produce abortion.

With purity and holiness I will pass my life and practice my art. I will not cut a person who is suffering with a stone, but will leave this to be done by practitioners of this work. Into whatever houses I enter, I will go into them for the benefit of the sick and will abstain from every voluntary act of mischief and corruption; and further from the seduction of females or males, bond or free.

Whatever, in connection with my professional practice, or not in connection with it, I may see or hear in the lives of men which ought not to be spoken abroad, I will not divulge, as reckoning that all such should be kept secret.

While I continue to keep this oath unviolated may it be granted to me to enjoy life and the practice of the art, respected by all men at all times but should I trespass and violate this oath, may the reverse be my lot.

2. A Letter to the U.S. Supreme Court.

> *Joseph Cardinal Bernardin was the Archbishop of Chicago, Illinois from 1982-1996. In 1995, he was diagnosed as having cancer. Thought to have been cured through treatment, he was diagnosed as suffering from pancreatic cancer early in 1996. Informed that summer that his cancer was terminal, Cardinal Bernardin chose to discontinue treatment for his illness in Au-*

gust 1996. Shortly before his death on November 18, 1996, Car-
dinal Bernardin wrote the following letter to the Justices of the
U.S. Supreme Court, who were preparing to meet to hear ar-
guments in a case favoring the "right" of terminally ill patients
to commit suicide with the assistance of their doctors.

Dear Honorable Justices:

I am at the end of my earthly life. There is much that I have con-
templated these last few months of my illness, but as one who
is dying I have especially come to appreciate the gift of life. I
know from my own experience that patients often face difficult
and deeply personal decisions about their care. However, I also
know that even a person who decides to forgo treatment does
not necessarily choose death. Rather, he chooses life without the
burden of disproportionate medical intervention.

In this case, the Court faces one of the most important issues of
our times. Physician-assisted suicide is a decidedly public matter.
It is not simply a decision made between patient and physician.
Because life affects every person, it is of primary public concern.

I have often remarked that I admire the writings of the late Father John Courtney Murray, who argued that an issue was related to public policy if it affects the public order of society. And
public order, in turn, encompassed three goods: public peace,
the essential protection of human rights, and commonly accepted
standards of moral behavior in the community.

Our legal and ethical tradition has held consistently that suicide,
assisted suicide, and euthanasia are wrong because they involve
a direct attack on innocent human life. And it is a matter of public
policy because it involves a violation of a fundamental human
good.

There can be no such thing as a "right to assisted suicide" because there can be no legal and moral order which tolerates the
killing of innocent human life, even if the agent of death is self-
administered. Creating a new "right" to assisted suicide will endanger society and send a false signal that a less than "perfect"
life is not worth living.

Physician-assisted suicide also directly affects the physician-pa-
tient relationship and, through that, the wider role of physicians
in our society. As has been noted by others, it introduces a deep
ambiguity into the very definition of medical care, if care comes to

involve killing. Beyond the physician, a move to assisted suicide and, perhaps beyond that, to euthanasia creates social ambiguity about the law. In civilized society, the law exists to protect life. When it begins to legitimate the taking of life as a policy, one has a right to ask what lies ahead for our life together as a society.

In order to protect patients from abuse, and to protect society from a dangerous erosion in its commitment to preserving human life, I urge the Court not to create any right to assisted suicide.

With cordial wishes, I am

Sincerely yours,

Joseph Cardinal Bernardin, Archbishop of Chicago

November 7, 1996

3. Man suffers in different ways, ways not always considered by medicine, not even in its most advanced specializations. Suffering is something which is *still wider* than sickness, more complex and at the same time still more deeply rooted in humanity itself. A certain idea of this problem comes to us from the distinction between physical suffering and moral suffering. This distinction is based upon the double dimension of the human being and indicates the bodily and spiritual element as the immediate or direct subject of suffering. Insofar as the words "suffering" and "pain" can, up to a certain degree, be used as synonyms, *physical suffering* is present when "the body is hurting" in some way, whereas *moral suffering* is "pain of the soul."

(*SD*, 5)

4. But I am not so discouraged by what has happened to me that I complain now of the attacks of wicked men against virtue; the reason for my surprise is that they have accomplished what they set out to do. The desire to do evil may be due to human weakness; but for the wicked to overcome the innocent in the sight of God— that is monstrous. I cannot blame that friend of yours who said, 'If there is a God, why is there evil? And if there is no God, how can there be good?.'

(Boethius, *Consolation of Philosophy*, Bk 1, Prose 4)

5. . . . All human beings, from their mothers' womb, belong to God who searches them and knows them, who forms them and knits them together with his own hands, who gazes on them when they are tiny shapeless embryos and already sees in them the adults

of tomorrow whose days are numbered and whose vocation is even now written in the 'book of life'. . . .

(EV, 61; cf. also Ps 139, 1; 13-16)

6. The political debate about abortion has produced much muddled thinking about the possibilities of conscientious dissent from the Church's teaching on the dignity of all human life. It is all too common for Catholic politicians to say they are "personally" opposed to abortion but will nevertheless vote to permit it, and even fund it, out of respect for the consciences of those who hold different views. This "respect" for another's conscience should never require abandoning one's own. Conscientious opposition to abortion, rooted in an understanding of the sanctity of human life, may not be sacrificed to the mistaken consciences of those who would unjustly take the life of an unborn baby.

(Bishop John J. Myers, Pastoral Statement, July 1990)

7. Techniques of fertilization in vitro can open the way to other forms of biological and genetic manipulation of human embryos, such as attempts or plans for fertilization between human and animal gametes and the gestation of human embryos in the uterus of animals, or the hypothesis or project of constructing artificial uteruses for the human embryo.

These procedures are contrary to the human dignity proper to the embryo, and at the same time they are contrary to the right of every person to be conceived and to be born within marriage and from marriage. Also, attempts or hypotheses for obtaining a human being without any connection with sexuality through "twin fission," cloning or parthenogenesis are to be considered contrary to the moral law, since they are in opposition to the dignity of both human procreation and of the conjugal union.

(DV, 1.6)

APPENDICES

1. Terminal illness: Appropriate medical treatment

According to the Pontifical Council for Pastoral Assistance, Charter for Health Care Workers, the issue of the terminally ill and their care is complex, and requires that a careful balance be maintained between the issue and principles involved in the discussion. These issues include:

- The question of appropriate types of medical treatment,

- The Christian understanding of the nature and value of human suffering,

- The obligation of the Christian to alleviate the sufferings of others,

- And the morality of discontinuing, refusing or withholding medical treatment in the case of terminally ill patients.

> "... The principle ... of *appropriate medical treatment in the remedies* can be specified and applied:

> —"In the absence of other remedies, it is lawful to have recourse, with the consent of the patient, to the means made available by the most advanced medicine, even if they are still at an experimental stage and not without some element of risk.

> —"It is lawful to interrupt the application of such means when the results disappoint the hopes placed in them," because there is no longer due proportion between "the investment of instruments and personnel" and "the foreseeable results" or because "the techniques used subject the patient to suffering and discomfort greater than the benefits to be had.

> —"It is always lawful to be satisfied with the normal means offered by medicine. No one can be obliged, therefore, to have recourse to a type of remedy which, although already in use, is still not without dangers or is too onerous." This refusal "is not the equivalent of suicide." Rather it might signify "either simple acceptance of the human condition, or the wish to avoid putting into effect a remedy disproportionate to the results that can be hoped for, or the desire not to place too great a burden on the family or on society" (*CHCW*, 65).

2. Discontinuing medical treatment

The right to life is specified in the terminally ill person as "a right to die in total serenity, with human and Christian dignity." This cannot be interpreted as the power to kill oneself or to give this power to others, but to experience dying in a human and Christian way and not flee from it "at any cost." This right is being explicitly expressed by people today in order to safeguard themselves at the point of death against "the use of techniques that run the risk of becoming abusive."

Contemporary medicine, in fact, has at its disposal methods which artificially delay death, without any real benefit to the patient. It is merely keeping one alive or prolonging life for a time, at the cost of further, severe suffering. This is the so-called "therapeutic tyranny," which consists "in the use of methods which are particularly exhausting and painful for the patient, condemning him in fact to an artificially prolonged agony."

This is contrary to the dignity of the dying person and to the moral obligation of accepting death and allowing it at last to take its course. "Death is an inevitable fact of human life": it cannot be uselessly delayed, fleeing from it by every means.

Aware that he is "neither the lord of life, nor the conqueror of death," the health care worker, in evaluating means, "should make appropriate choices, that is, relate to the patient and be guided by his real condition."

Here he will apply the principle—already stated—of *appropriate medical treatment*," which can be specified thus: "When inevitable death is imminent, despite the means used, it is lawful in conscience to decide to refuse treatment that would only secure a precarious and painful prolongation of life, but without interrupting the normal treatment due to the patient in similar cases. Hence the doctor need have no concern; it is not as if he had failed to assist the person in danger."

The administration of food and liquids, even artificially, is part of the normal treatment always due to the patient when this is not burdensome for him: their undue suspension could be real and properly so-called euthanasia.

For the doctors and their assistants it is not a question of deciding the life or death of an individual. It is simply a question of being a doctor, that is, of posing the question and then deciding according to one's expertise and one's conscience regarding a respectful care of the living and the dying of the patient entrusted to him. This responsibility does not always and in all cases involve recourse to every means. It might also require the renunciation of certain means to make way for a serene and Christian acceptance of death which is inherent in life. It might also mean respect for the wishes of the patient who refuses the use of such means (*CHCW*, 199-121).

"Discontinuing medical procedures that are burdensome, dangerous, extraordinary, or disproportionate to the expected outcome can be legitimate; it is the refusal of 'over-zealous' treatment. Here one does not will to cause death; one's inability to impede it is merely accepted. The decisions should be made by the patient if he is competent and able or, if not, by those legally entitled to act for the patient, whose reasonable will and legitimate interests must always be respected" (CCC, 2278).

3. The Christian meaning of suffering

In the messianic program of Christ, which is at the same time the program *of the kingdom of God*, suffering is present in the world in order to release love, in order to give birth to works of love towards neighbor, in order to transform the whole of human civilization into a 'civilization of love.' In this love the salvific meaning of suffering is completely accomplished and reaches its definitive dimension. Christ's words about the Final Judgment enable us to understand this in all the simplicity and clarity of the Gospel.

These words about love, about actions of love, acts linked with human suffering, enable us once more to discover, at the basis of all *human sufferings, the same redemptive suffering of Christ*. Christ said: 'You did it to me.' He himself is the one who in each individual experiences love; he himself is the one who receives help, when this is given to every suffering person without exception. He himself is present in this suffering person, since his salvific suffering has been opened once and for all to every human suffering. And all those who suffer have been called once and for all to become sharers 'in Christ's sufferings,' just as all have been called to 'complete' with their own suffering 'what is lacking in Christ's afflictions.' At one and the same time Christ has taught man *to do good by his sufering and to do good to those who suffer*. In this double aspect he has completely revealed the meaning of suffering.

This is the meaning of suffering, which is truly supernatural and at the same time human. It is *supernatural* because it is rooted in the divine mystery of the Redemption of the world, and it is likewise deeply *human* because in it the person discovers himself, his own humanity, his own dignity, his own mission (SD, 30-31).

4. More on the Christian meaning of suffering

"For the Christian, pain has a lofty penitential and salvific meaning. "It is, in fact, a sharing in Christ's Passion and a union with the redeeming sacrifice which he offered in obedience to the Father's will. Therefore, one must not be surprised if some Christians prefer to moderate their use of painkillers, in order to accept voluntarily at least part of their sufferings and thus associate themselves in a conscious way with the sufferings of Christ.

Acceptance of pain, motivated and supported by Christian ideals, must not lead to the conclusion that all suffering and all pain must be accepted, and that there should be no effort to alleviate them. On the contrary this is a way of humanizing pain. Christian charity itself requires of health care workers the alleviation of physical suffering.

In the long run pain is an obstacle to the attainment of higher goods and interests. It can produce harmful effects for the psychophysical integrity of the person. When suffering is too intense, it can diminish or impede the control of the spirit. Therefore it is legitimate, and beyond certain limits of endurance it is also a duty for the health care worker to prevent, alleviate and eliminate pain. It is morally correct and right that the researcher should try "to bring pain under human control."

Anesthetics like painkillers, by directly acting on the more aggressive and disturbing effects of pain, gives the person more control, so that suffering becomes a more human experience (*CHCW*, 69-70).

QUESTIONS

1. Why is human life sacred?

2. What is "theonomy"?

3. What new elements did Jesus introduce into the 5th commandment?

4. What is the difference between spontaneous and procured abortion?

5. Where is the earliest condemnation of abortion by the Church found?

6. What is euthanasia?

7. Explain the meaning and value of suffering from the Christian perspective.

8. Is permitting terminally ill people to die the same thing as euthanasia?

9. What is scandal? Why is giving scandal always a grave evil?

10. What are the conditions necessary for a just war?

11. Under what conditions may a person be the recipient of an organ transplant?

12. Explain the difference between two types of sterilization discussed in the chapter. Which of the two is morally permissible, when is it permissible, and why?

PRACTICAL EXERCISES

1. Karen is sixteen years old and has been dating a boy named Jim for three months. Because she has been raised by her parents to practice her faith, she knows that her parents would be very upset that she has involved herself in a sexual relationship with him. Karen is not even completely happy about her decision, because she knows that sexual relationships outside of marriage are contrary to God's commandments. Things are complicated still further when she finds out that she is pregnant. Now Karen is afraid and thinks that she wants to have an abortion so that her parents won't find out she is pregnant. When her friend Tiffany objects, Karen tries to rationalize her decision by saying, "It's all right because this doctor that I saw on TV said that it's not truly human for the first three months, anyway." However, even Karen doesn't sound very convinced by this argument. Imagine that you are Tiffany or another friend that Karen trusts. What arguments could you offer, drawing upon what you have learned in this chapter, to persuade Karen that deciding to have an abortion would be a terrible mistake?

2. Dan has been selling marijuana at school. When confronted by his friend Marco, he justifies his actions by arguing that marijuana is no more addictive than alcohol. Whether or not this is true, why is Dan's argument in defense of his actions irrelevant? Why is it still immoral for Dan to use and sell marijuana?

3. What are some of the moral problems arising out of drug use and the abuse of alcohol?

4. The editor of your local newspaper has written an editorial condemning the Catholic Church's teaching that euthanasia is immoral. In the editorial, he says that the Church's position is "outdated," and "insensitive to the suffering endured by the terminally ill and their families." He argues that it is cruel to allow someone to suffer needlessly and that people have a right to control their own lives, including the decision about when their lives are to end. Write a letter to him bdefending the Church's teaching and explain the reasons for the Church's position against euthanasia. Be sure to address his specific points in your response.

5. Summarize what the *Catechism of the Catholic Church* says about the death penalty (no. 2266). In light of the teaching contained in the Catechism, can the death penalty ever be legitimately used in the United States? Why or why not?

6. Javier and Melanie are young newlyweds, married for just over two years. They already have two children and have decided that they do not want to have any more. Since he is skeptical of other methods of contraception, Javier thinks that they should seek sterilization as a solution. Melanie objects, saying that this would be a sin. She proposes that they simply use Natural Family Planning to prevent the births of any more children, arguing that because it is a natural method and is approved by the Church, they will not be committing a sin. There are three problems with both Javier's and Melanie's dispositions and their reasoning according to Catholic moral teaching. What are they?

7. Bearing in mind what this chapter explains about the immorality of mutilation, what do you think of practices such as tattooing and body-piercing? Are these forms of mutilation, and therefore immoral? Why or why not?

8. Because Christians are obliged to preserve the lives of others, to protect their dignity and to do no harm, do you believe that there can ever be a good reason for an individual to fight with another person (i.e., in the case of a young man whose sister's reputation has been damaged by a lie)? Why or why not? Provide specific examples to support your argument.

CHAPTER XIV
THE SIXTH AND NINTH COMMANDMENTS:
YOU SHALL NOT COMMIT ADULTERY.
YOU SHALL NOT COVET YOUR
NEIGHBOR'S WIFE

Now when Jesus had finished these sayings, he went away from Galilee and entered the region of Judea beyond the Jordan; and large crowds followed him, and he healed them there.

And Pharisees came up to him and tested him by asking, "Is it lawful to divorce one's wife for any cause?"

He answered, "Have you not read that he who made them from the beginning made them male and female, and said, "For this reason a man shall leave his father and mother and be joined to his wife, and the two shall become one flesh"? So they are no longer two but one flesh. What therefore God has joined together, let not man put asunder."

They said to him, "Why then did Moses command one to give a certificate of divorce, and to put her away?"

He said to them, "For your hardness of heart Moses allowed you to divorce your wives, but from the beginning it was not so. And I say to you: whoever divorces his wife, except for unchastity, and marries another, commits adultery" (Mt 19, 1-9).

In the passage of Scripture presented here, Jesus strongly defends the dignity of marriage as created by God. Many people in Western societies today have begun to question even the value or necessity of marriage. In light of this, it is helpful to consider the following questions:

- What is the nature and purpose of marriage?

- Why do Christians view marriage as more than a social or legal contract?

- In what way does marriage as God created it provide for the good of children?

- Why does any use of our human sexuality outside marriage tend toward the loss of our personal dignity?

- How does the virtue of chastity protect both personal dignity and the integrity of marriage?

- What are some developments and trends of modern society which tend to undermine marriage?

Introduction

To understand the ultimate meaning of human sexuality one needs to put it inside the framework of marriage. Many errors arise from considering sexual intercourse only in itself, without any direct reference to the true meaning of love, matrimony and procreation.

Marriage is such a fundamental and natural part of human life that—as John Paul II teaches—man should be defined as "a betrothed being." There are only a few reasons—usually very elevated ones—for voluntarily and freely renouncing marriage, such as needing to give attention to one's existing family or for the noble motive of giving oneself to God in religious life, the priesthood or the apostolate of the faithful.

Regarding marriage, God created man and woman with natural sexual differences. Sex not only affects the constitution of one's body, but also one's very identity: Sexuality affects man at the most elementary level of personhood.

1. God created man and woman in a state of marriage

At the very beginning of the Bible, man and woman appear united as husband and wife. Genesis contains two complementary narratives of the appearance of the human couple:

a. The First Creation Story.

Chapter 1 describes the simultaneous creation of man and woman in these words:

> Then God said, "Let us make man in our image, after our likeness; and let them have dominion over the fish of the sea, and over the birds of the air, and over the cattle, and over all the earth, and over every creeping thing that creeps upon the earth." So God created man in his own image, in the image of God he created him; male and female he created them. And God blessed them, and God said to them, "Be fruitful and multiply, and fill the earth and subdue it; and have dominion over the fish of the sea and over the birds of the air and over every living thing that moves upon the earth" (Gn 1, 26-28).

b. The Second Creation Story.

Chapter 2 gives us a complementary story. The biblical writer relates the following words from the mouth of God:

"Then the LORD God said, 'It is not good that the man should be alone; I will make him a helper fit for him' (Gn 2, 18)." The narration shows the equality of man and woman through the creation of woman from the very body of man:

> . . . and the rib which the LORD God had taken from the man he made into a woman and brought her to the man. Then the man said, "This at last is bone of my bones and flesh of my flesh; she shall be called Woman, because she was taken out of Man." Therefore a man leaves his father and his mother and cleaves to his wife, and they become one flesh. And the man and his wife were both naked, and were not ashamed (Gn 2, 22-25).

If we consider these two narrations in parallel, one can deduce the following truths:

- Man and woman are equal in dignity: both were created by God in his image and likeness.

- Man and woman are destined to form a new social unit. For that reason, man and woman will leave their fathers and mothers to become a new family.

- That unity is so intimate that, in biblical language, it will form "one flesh": husband and wife will become "two in one."

- The man-woman relationship, united in marriage, has a procreative end. God directed his blessing precisely to this end:

> And God blessed them, and God said to them, "Be fruitful and multiply, and fill the earth and subdue it; and have dominion over the fish of the sea and over the birds of the air and over every living thing that moves upon the earth." (Gn 1, 28).

2. The procreation of human life in the family

According to the Bible and the teaching of the Church, the origin of a new human life should take place within marriage. From the first page of the Bible we can see that God creates man and woman united in marriage with the end of procreation (cf. Gn 1, 28).

This intention of God for marriage is so fundamental that all cultures have condemned procreation outside of matrimony. This same teaching is in the New Testament, with the condemnation of fornication and adultery (cf. Mt 15, 19; Mk 7, 21).

The reason is obvious: every human person has the right to be born of a known man and a known woman, whom he can call father and mother, and to carry out his normal existence in a home. This should be emphasized because man is born a helpless creature and needs the assistance of his parents for quite a long time. A human being not only materially but also spiritually needs the continuous and prolonged attention of his parents.

The family enjoys many rights, since it is the foundation of society. For its part, the Pontifical Council for the Family's *Letter on the Rights of the Family* recognizes that the family is founded on matrimony; therefore, a new life should only be procreated within matrimony:

> The family is founded on marriage, and is an intimate union of life, completed between a man and woman, that is constituted by the indissoluble bond of marriage, freely contracted, publicly affirmed, and that is open and to the transmission of life (*Preamble B*).

> Marriage is the natural institution that is exclusively entrusted with the mission of transmitting life (*Preamble C*).

A new life begun outside of matrimony should be protected and should share the same rights as a baby born inside marriage, since the child is not responsible for the illegitimacy and even less for the sin of his parents. Motherhood and childhood are entitled to special care and assistance.

3. Purposes of marriage

a. Good of the spouses.

The sexual union of a husband and wife in marriage is noble and honorable; the truly human performance of this act fosters their complete self-giving, deepens their love for one another, and is both the sign and cause of the perfect union with one another to which God calls them.

b. Procreation.

The structure of conjugal love and the conjugal donation of specific and intimate aspects of manhood and womanhood, taken as a whole, directly result in the procreation of new lives.

This doctrine is a constant in all teachings on Catholic morality.

> Marriage and conjugal love are by their nature ordained toward the begetting and educating of children. Children are really the supreme gift of marriage and contribute very substantially to the welfare of their parents. The God himself Who said, "it is not good for man to be alone," (Gn 2, 18) . . . wishing to share with man a certain special participation in his own creative work, blessed male and female, saying: "Increase and multiply" (Gn 1, 28).

> Hence, while not making the other purposes of matrimony of less account, the true practice of conjugal love, and the whole meaning of the family life which results from it, have this aim: that the couple be ready with stout hearts to cooperate with the love of the Creator and the Savior, who through them will enlarge and enrich his own family day by day (GS, 50).

Children are always a source of joy when they are born out of the parents' love for one another. The Church, following the testimony of Sacred Scripture, has traditionally viewed large families as a sign of God's blessing and the generosity of the parents (cf. CCC, 1652).

4. Properties of marriage

From this biblical teaching one can deduce that matrimony is characterized by two essential properties: unity and indissolubility.

a. Unity.

In matrimony, the spouses give what is specific and proper to each one of them. Therefore, if they communicate what is proper to their being, it directly follows that this cannot be shared with a third party. In this way, a man and woman love each other completely, which is radically opposed to one of them sharing his manhood or her womanhood with a third party.

Consequently, polygamy, having many wives, goes against the nature of matrimony. Interestingly, when society recognizes the dignity of women as being equal to that of man, polygamy disappears.

b. **Indissolubility.**

It is evident that marriage demands stability, distinguishing it from sporadic or occasional unions between man and woman. But natural morality and Christian revelation strongly state that this stability is permanent; the unit created through the matrimonial bond cannot be divided. We can adduce two arguments: First, if one gives everything, that totality is not complete if it is not total for life. Second, matrimony unites two people, but not only in isolated acts. Thus, this personal giving of oneself in his manhood or her womanhood demands permanency, for as long as they live.

If we take a deeper look at these arguments, we discover that they are conclusive. They are not derived from only the Christian faith, but rather from the very essence of the matrimonial union of man and woman.

A Christian also believes that a ratified and consummated marriage between a baptized man and a baptized woman is indissoluble by any human power or by a cause other than death. Jesus, who, when asked about divorce, categorically stated the indissolubility of matrimony with these words:

> "Is it lawful for a man to divorce his wife?" He answered them, "What did Moses command you?" They said, "Moses allowed a man to write a certificate of divorce, and to put her away." But Jesus said to them, "For your hardness of heart he wrote you this commandment. But from the beginning of creation, 'God made them male and female. For this reason a man shall leave his father and mother and be joined to his wife, and the two shall become one flesh.' So they are no longer two but one flesh. What therefore God has joined together, let not man put asunder" (Mk 10, 2-9).

Consequently, Jesus states that no human will, neither civil nor ecclesiastical—including the will of the two spouses—exists which has the power to break the link born of the spouses' self-giving in marriage. From this it should be clear that it is not accurate to say that the Church does not *grant* divorces (since it is not within her power to do so); rather, the Church does not *recognize* divorce (since it is impossible to break the sacramental union of a man and woman).

However, when no sacramental bond exists, a marriage may be *dissolved* under the following circumstances:

- When it is a natural—not sacramental—bond of a legitimate and consummated marriage of non-baptized parties. This is known as the *Pauline Privilege* (cf. *CIC*, 1143; 1 Cor 7, 12-15). The previous marriage is not dissolved by the Church but by the second marriage itself. The Church merely judges that the necessary conditions for the second marriage are present.

- When it is a natural—not sacramental—bond of a legitimate and consummated marriage between a baptized party and a non-baptized party. This is known as the *Petrine Privilege.*

- When it is a non-consummated marriage between baptized persons or between a baptized party and a non-baptized party. Such a marriage can only be dissolved for a just cause, at the request of both parties, or one of the parties if the other party is unwilling. A decision of this nature can only be made at the discretion of the Roman Pontiff (cf. *CIC*, 1142).

- In some exceptional cases, the Church, not the State, may also dissolve a *ratified*, though not *consummated*, marriage among Christians through a papal decision.

5. Joys of marriage

True conjugal love is not only exclusive and total, but it is also a fruitful love, both spiritually and physically. It is spiritually fruitful because marriage helps the married couple grow in holiness. It is physically fruitful because the marital act, when done as God wants, gives glory to God, and is needed to achieve the perfect union between spouses. Some may hold mistaken notions about the Church's teaching on the sacredness of the marital act. Far from believing sex to be tainted or somehow dirty, as some erroneously think, the Church upholds its dignity.

The acts in marriage, by which the intimate and chaste union of the spouses take place, are noble and honorable; the truly human performance of these acts fosters the self-giving they signify and enriches the spouses in joy and gratitude.

The Creator himself established that in the generative function, spouses should experience pleasure and enjoyment of the body and spirit. Therefore, the spouses do nothing evil in seeking this pleasure and enjoyment. They accept what the Creator has intended for them.

As Blessed Josemaría Escrivá wrote:

> When love is authentic, it demands faithfulness and rectitude in all marital relations. St. Thomas Aquinas comments that God has joined to the exercise of the different functions of human life a pleasure or satisfaction, which is something good. But if man, inverting the proper order of things, seeks satisfaction as an aim in itself, in contempt of the good to which it is joined and which is its aim, he perverts its true nature and converts it into a sin or an occasion of sin (Blessed Josemaría Escrivá, *Christ Is Passing By*, 25).

6. Annulment

There are obstacles which can prevent two people seeking to enter into the marital union from contracting a *valid* marriage. Generally speaking, these obstacles can arise from situations such as a lack of full, free, and voluntary consent, or an impediment such as a prior marriage, or it could be a deficiency in the form (two Catholics married before a judge). In such circumstances, the Church, after careful investigation by an ecclesiastical court, may issue a *declaration of nullity*. This is a declaration that no true marriage existed from the beginning.

Strictly speaking, therefore, the term annulment is incorrect since the Church cannot make a valid marriage null and void, but can only, after careful investigation, confirm that what was thought to be a valid marriage in fact never was because of some impediment which was not discovered at the time the couple first sought to enter into the marital state.

7. Meaning and value of the different dimensions of human sexuality

The reality of marriage and of family makes human sexuality very important. One should distinguish some of the diverse and complementary aspects of human sexuality.

a. Genital.

Sexuality obviously manifests itself in the male and female genitalia. Furthermore, sexual intercourse is the normative expression of human sexuality. From the diversity of male and female genitalia, one can deduce that the exercise of sexuality should be between a man and a woman. The complementarity of masculine and feminine genitalia verifies this same argument. This is one of the principal reasons why there cannot be marriage between persons of the same gender.

b. Human affection.

Human sexuality is not merely an instinct as in animals which is manifested in very defined cycles. Man's sexuality contains psychological components; that is, it is subject to the intellect and will. This is why man can control and direct it.

For this reason, the exercise of sexuality worthy of man should include affection between the husband and wife. The sexual exercise is considered a personal and loving "meeting" between husband and wife. This joining in love profoundly differs from other fleeting sexual relations, in which one looks to satisfy his instincts for temporal pleasure.

c. Pleasure.

The Creator himself established that in the generative function, spouses should experience pleasure and enjoyment of the body and spirit. Therefore, the spouses do nothing evil in seeking this pleasure and enjoyment. They accept what the Creator has intended for them. Nevertheless, spouses should know how to keep themselves within the just limits of moderation (GS, 49, and Pius XII, Discourse, October 29, 1951 and John Paul II, Address on November 26, 1993).

Sexual pleasure is total when sensual joy goes together with the love, affection, and sacrifice that cultivate this joining of the spouses. For this reason, if love is lacking or if one exclusively seeks to satisfy his passions without regard to the needs of his spouse, the exercise of sexual life could lead to a separation between the spouses.

d. Procreation.

Procreation synthesizes the three prior dimensions. The biology of the sexes demands procreation, and human affection demands love to be fertile. For that reason, spouses, who put up obstacles to biology and human affection so that the exercise of conjugal love becomes infertile, sin gravely.

Still, marriage and the exercise of sexuality carried out within marriage are not exclusively for having children. As the Second Vatican Council teaches:

> Marriage to be sure is not instituted solely for procreation; rather, its very nature as an unbreakable compact between persons, and the welfare of the children, both demand that the mutual love of the spouses be embodied in a rightly ordered manner, that it grow and ripen .Therefore, marriage persists as a whole manner and communion of life, and maintains its value and indissolubility, even when despite the often intense desire of the couple, offspring are lacking (GS, 50).

It is important to note that marriage gives the couple a right to the procreative act, but there is no right to children which requires God to make all marriages fertile.

In summary, a natural and human use of sex between adults includes the harmonious integration of the above four dimensions involved in human sexuality. If any of these four dimensions are lacking, the use of sex may lead to dissatisfaction, perversity, promiscuity, immorality and an inversion of the true meaning of love.

8. Catholic doctrine regarding sexuality

Catholic doctrine on human sexuality is in accord with the physiological and psychic nature of man. Christian morality respects human nature and does not debase man, but rather starts off with man's very being. In this sense, we should summarize Catholic doctrine with these three basic affirmations:

a. Positive value of sexuality.

Christian morality begins from this fundamental affirmation: Man and woman are destined and created by God for procreation. God desires and created the profound and positive meaning of sexuality. Catholic morality deduces the value of sexuality from biblical passages that tell us about the relationship between God and his people in terms of betrothed love: God is the bridegroom, madly in love with his people, the Church, who are in turn his bride.

For this reason the Church has always condemned those movements that doubted the value of sex. This positive judgment is continuously repeated throughout history to the present time. In recent years, when faced with devaluation of sexuality and the resultant proliferation of sexual sins, the Congregation for the Doctrine of the Faith published the Declaration *Persona Humana* which reaffirms the positive meaning of human sexuality.

b. Controlling sexuality.

Once the positive value of sexuality is strengthened, Christian morality maintains that man needs to control his sexual instincts.

The reason is obvious: if a person is to be master of all his energies—anywhere from physical strength, to will and emotions—he must control that profound and vital impulse which is the sexual instinct. It is necessary to be constantly aware that the force of passion is so strong and so instinctive that if man does not control it, he will be enslaved by it. This truth is obvious .

Therefore, it is important that one be educated in sexuality with the objective of self-control. Education is indispensable for all ages: the age of puberty, when the sexual instinct awakens; in adolescence, when the desire for closer and more intimate relations between a man and a woman begin; and even in marriage, with the goal of not following blind instincts in conjugal relations between the spouses, but rather controlling them rationally and with honest love. The *Catechism of the Catholic Church* devotes a large section to encouraging everyone in the "struggle against concupiscence of the flesh" (CCC, 2520; cf. 2520-2527).

c. Upright use of sexuality.

As we said before, the end of sexuality is not exclusively for pleasure, but also for procreation in marriage. To deny this is a disorder and in the long run brings about a perversion of sexuality. For this reason Catholic morality teaches that the only permissible use of sexuality takes place within marriage. Consequently, extra-marital, pre-marital, and solitary sexual acts are forbidden by Christian morality and constitute a grave sin.

9. Chastity as a virtue: purity of body and heart

Chastity is the moral virtue which moves a person to moderate the use of the sexual powers out of love for God and a desire to please him by avoiding anything that would harm the dignity of other people. As such, chastity is another expression of the virtue of temperance.

Without a genuine desire to love God and neighbor, chastity (or any other supernatural virtue) is impossible, because these virtues require the assistance of God's grace if a person is to be able to live them. Furthermore, chastity is also an expression of love for God and neighbor. Why? By chastity a man shows that he desires to please God by submitting his will to God's plan for human sexuality, and that he loves his neighbor by avoiding any kind of relationship which treats another person as an object or means to satisfy his own selfish desires.

However, it is necessary to emphasize that simply abstaining from sexual activity does not mean that a person is living a chaste life. It is important here to remember Jesus' teaching that the hidden thoughts and desires of the human heart are equally sinful as our actions, for it is from these sinful desires that sinful actions are born (cf. Mt 5, 27-30; 15, 16-20). The man who abstains from illicit sexual activity may be practicing the virtue of *continence,* but it cannot be said that he is living a truly chaste life if he still desires those activities.

The fact that the history of Christianity is filled with the examples of men and women who have lived lives of great virtue in regard to chastity is sufficient to prove that purity of body and heart is indeed possible. There is an even greater need today for heroism and self-sacrifice in a world where many have given themselves totally to pleasure. Young people especially need role models who are not afraid to be pure, and to demonstrate that purity is possible.

Much of the difficulty arises from the fact that few young people plan to live a life of purity. To be successful the correct means must be utilized. These include:

- regular reception of the sacraments of the Eucharist and Reconciliation,

- complete honesty in confession,

- establishing a prayerful relationship with Jesus and Mary,

- having friends who think and act pure,

- and keeping the eyes, mind and moods under control.

Acquiring or preserving the virtue of chastity isn't easy, but if a person truly wants to live a pure life, then he must be willing to take the necessary steps and to make the sacrifices required to possess this great virtue.

10. Sins against chastity.
Doctrine of the Old Testament

The goal of sexual life and the satisfaction that comes with it are only reached when the four previously mentioned dimensions of human sexuality are fulfilled. Outside of these aspects, one finds himself en route to evil and sin. Such prohibitions are not only formulated by Catholic moral theology, but are also in the Bible and Sacred Tradition.

The condemnation of the unjust use of sexuality is seen in many instances in the Old as well as the New Testament. The following is a list of the sins which are condemned in the Old Testament:

- Adultery is sexual relations between a married person and someone other than one's spouse. Exodus clearly formulates this principle: "You shall not commit adultery" (Ex 20, 14).

- Fornication or pre-marital sex is condemned in an extremely rigorous manner. Besides the moral fault, a fine was also included (Dt 22, 20-21, 28-29; Sir 41, 17-34).

- Onanism and masturbation are condemned because they involve the deliberate and solitary seeking of sexual pleasure outside of the conjugal act or preventing the natural completion of the act. In the Old Testament, onanism is also condemned because Onan's intent was contraceptive; he refused to provide offspring for his sister-in-law in his deceased brother's place, as was required by the custom of the time. Both masturbation and contraception are essentially selfish and disordered acts which lack the mutual self-giving and openness required by the nature of the sexual act (Gn 38, 4-10).

- Prostitution. The Old Testament warns against this sin which leads to the destruction of the life of men and women who engage in such activity.

- Bestiality. This vice is punished with death (Lv 20, 15-16; Ex 22, 19).

- Incest. It also includes the condemnation of relatives who engage in sexual activity among themselves (Lv 20, 11-12, 17).

- Homosexuality. Sexual relations between members of the same sex (Gn 19, 4-10).

A twentieth century writer has noted:

> An unchaste man wants above all something for himself; he is distracted by an objective "interest"; his constantly strained will-to-pleasure prevents him from confronting reality with that selfless detachment which alone makes genuine knowledge possible. St. Thomas here uses the comparison of a lion who, at the sight of a stag, is unable to perceive anything but the anticipated meal. In an unchaste heart, attention is not merely fixed upon a certain track, but the "window" of the soul has lost its "transparency," that is, its capacity for perceiving existence, as if a selfish interestedness had covered it, as it were, with a film of dust. . . .

> This kind of interest is altogether selfish, The abandonment of an unchaste heart to the sensual world has nothing in

common with the genuine dedication of a searcher for truth to the reality of being, of a lover to his beloved. Unchastity does not dedicate itself, it offers itself. It is selfishly intent upon the "prize," upon the reward of illicit lust. "Chaste," says St. Augustine, "is the heart that loves God without looking for reward." One further comment: For anyone whose function it is to lead and counsel young people, it is this selfishness which characterizes the inner nature of unchastity (as intemperance) (J. Pieper, *The Four Cardinal Virtues*, 161).

The book of Sirach includes the following prayer of the just man who wants to live a chaste life:

> O LORD, Father and God of my life, do not give me haughty eyes, and remove from me evil desire. Let neither gluttony nor lust overcome me, and do not surrender me to a shameless soul (Sir 23, 4-6).

11. Sins against chastity.
New Testament teachings

In light of the corruption of the pagan world, the apostles warned Christians about letting themselves be contaminated by the evil pagan customs. Regarding this subject, the Church clearly taught converts to live purity and to abandon the vices they had practiced before.

The best view of the corruption caused by pagan customs related to the abuse of sexuality is contained in St. Paul's description of the vices of the Romans:

> Therefore God gave them up in the lusts of their hearts to impurity, to the dishonoring of their bodies among themselves, because they exchanged the truth about God for a lie and worshiped and served the creature rather than the Creator, who is blessed for ever! Amen. For this reason God gave them up to dishonorable passions. Their women exchanged natural relations for unnatural, and the men likewise gave up natural relations with women and were consumed with passion for one another, men committing shameless acts with men and receiving in their own persons the due penalty for their error. And since they did not see fit to acknowledge God, God gave them up to a base mind and to improper conduct (Rm 1, 24-28).

In other writings, St. Paul warns against every kind of sin of impurity. Just a brief look at the commands he makes to Christians from Thessalonica is evidence of this:

> For this is the will of God, your sanctification: that you ab-
> stain from unchastity; that each one of you know how to
> take a wife for himself in holiness and honor, not in the
> passion of lust like heathens who do not know God; that
> no man transgress and wrong his brother in this matter,
> because the LORD is an avenger in all these things, as we
> solemnly forewarned you. For God has not called us for un-
> cleanness, but in holiness (1 Th 4, 3-7).

In the different catalogues of sins found in St. Paul's letters, one finds all the sins against the virtue of chastity (1 Cor 6, 9-11, 15-20; Gal 5, 19-24).

In the same way, Jesus condemns sins of desire: "every one who looks at a woman lustfully has already committed adultery with her in his heart" (Mt 5, 27-28). This reinforces the Old Testament state-ment prohibiting covetousness, and it contains a strong pedagogical force, due to the influence that thoughts, the will and the emotions have in the area of the virtue of purity (cf. *CCC*, 2514-2519; 2531-2533).

12. Sins against chastity.
Doctrine of sacred tradition

Following these biblical teachings, Christian tradition reminded converts that, in conformity with their new life, they should guide their sexual conduct in accord with the ethical norms established in the New Testament. At the beginning of the second century, in a letter addressed to Emperor Antoninus Pius, St. Justin highlights the differ-ence between Christians and pagans in living human sexuality:

> For our Master, not only are they sinners who contract a
> double marriage . . ., but also they who look at a woman with
> desire, since for him they should refuse not only to commit
> the act of adultery, but also to wish to commit it, just as the
> wish to be before God is evident not only in works, but also
> in desires. And among us there are many men and women
> who having become disciples of Christ as children, remain in-
> corrupt for sixty or seventy years, and I am amazed at the
> power of this demonstration to all races of man. And this

countless crowd of those who have converted after a dissolute life (St. Justin, 1 *Apologia* XV, 5-7).

13. Sins against chastity.
The teaching of the Magisterium

The Magisterium of the Church, confirming the teaching of the Old Testament, the New Testament and Sacred Tradition, has also urged these same teachings throughout history. They who sin against the sixth and ninth commandments are:

- Spouses who break their promise of fidelity for life, and do not freely and responsibly accept children by impeding conception with artificial means.

- Married persons who have sexual relations outside of marriage and unmarried persons who have pre-marital sexual relations.

- Those who seek pleasure through the use of sexuality with another member of the same sex.

- Those who seek sexual pleasure egotistically with themselves in acts of masturbation.

- Those who entertain or delight themselves with impure thoughts and desires (covetousness).

- Those who condone an atmosphere which disregards any norm regulating the upright use of sexuality and induce impure thoughts and desires through magazines, pornographic movies, conversations, etc.

Numerous Church documents attest to the consistent teaching of the Church in regard to matters of chastity. A brief sample of some of these documents may be found in the Supplementary Readings section which follows this chapter.

Finally, the *Catechism of the Catholic Church*, under the title of "Offenses against chastity," condemns lust, masturbation, fornication, pornography, prostitution, rape and homosexuality (*CCC*, 2351-2359; cf. *VS*, 47).

14. Chastity in Marriage: responsible parenthood and Natural Family Planning

Life itself is sacred, and because of this very fact, sexual intercourse, unlike other physical actions, is itself also sacred. By it, couples share God's creative power and fatherhood. Every married couple must be aware of their mission to *Responsible Parenthood* conforming their sexual activity to the creative intention of God. In the encyclical *Humanae Vitae,* Pope Paul VI stated that the Church teaches that each and every act of marriage must be open to life *(HV, 11).*

Nevertheless *responsible parenthood* is not incompatible with recourse to *Natural Family Planning* (NFP). NFP is the practice of using infertile times for expression of marital love and is available for those who for serious reasons need to postpone a new birth. It requires both the knowledge and respect of the biological laws which are part of the human person and the practice of self-denial on living chastity on the part of the spouses.

The lawful use of NFP involves the use of the temperature method, the ovulation method or the sympto-thermo method. They have to be used under the following conditions:

- Each and every conjugal act must be open to the transmission of life. Artificial birth control (IUD device, pill, withdrawal or condom), masturbation or voluntary sterilization are never allowed since they are grave transgressions of God's law.

- The judgment to use NFP should be made with an upright conscience—a conscience informed by the teachings of the Church.

- The serious motives must exist at the time when NFP is practiced.

- There should be no occasion of sin for either of the spouses like serious danger of infidelity due to long periods of continence.

- Any act for sexual pleasure that by its nature is not directed or destined for the procreating and uniting aspects of married love (like oral intercourse or self or mutual masturbation) will be a grave sin.

15. Contraception and the destruction of marriage

Contraception—action against conception—has as its goal the prevention of the transmission of life. This action is a misuse of the reproductive faculties, and it violates one of the purposes of marriage. It is a direct refusal or saying "no" to God's plan for your life and vocation to bring forth new life. It may lead to a loss of faith. Since God knows everyone intimately, he alone truly knows the number of children a couple can raise. Contraception is an act which says to God, "I do not trust You in this matter; I will decide for myself".

Artificial birth control can never conform to Church teaching, even in extreme cases. To impede the sources of life is intrinsically evil and a violation of the law of God, as well as a misuse of the gifts which God has granted to mankind. The use of contraception indicates that a person is moved by fear or selfishness rather than love. Ironically, spouses who use contraception experience less intimacy in the midst of more frequent sexual acts. Love is no longer authentic. Its use non-verbally communicates: I accept the part of you which brings pleasure but not the part which brings forth new life. The innate language of the marital act that expresses the total self-giving of husband and wife is overlaid, through contraception, by an objectively contradictory language, namely that of not giving oneself totally to the other. This leads not only to a positive refusal to be open to life, but also to a betrayal of the inner truth of conjugal love, which ought to be a gift of one's self in personal totality.

The Catholic Church prohibits the use of artificial birth control, such as the pill, withdrawal, IUD, condom, etc. They can never be used, for they contradict the purpose of marriage because they interfere with God's plan and purpose in creating new life. They are intrinsically evil. Conversely, when there is chastity in the love of married persons, their marital life is authentic; husband and wife are true to themselves, they understand each other and develop the union between themselves.

While some forms of artificial birth control have contraception as their goal, the actual result is abortion. Others, such as the IUD, the pill, or the morning-after (abortifacient) pills, e.g. RU-486, are always abortifacients by destroying the new life—the already fertilized egg. These abortifacient methods of "contraception" are especially immoral, because, as life begins at conception, they cause the abortion of a new human life. Life must be always guarded with greatest care: abortion and infanticide are unspeakable crimes. From the moment of conception man is already destined to eternity in God.

16. Assisted fertilization and artificial insemination

Today, advances in medicine and biology permit the conception of a human being by a means other than the sexual union of man and woman. These techniques are called artificial insemination or *artificial fertilization.*

Moral judgments concerning these new problems are not found in revelation because these methods were unknown then. The teachings of the Magisterium help us to make the correct judgments.

On February 2, 1987, the Congregation for the Doctrine of the Faith published a long document, called "The Gift of Life" (*Donum vitae*) which contains the moral doctrine concerning new techniques which assist in creating a human being.

It is clear that the intentions which may lead to the use of the techniques of artificial fertilization can be noble. Think, for example, about the objective of correcting some disease or fulfilling the wishes of parents who are denied the normal results of the conjugal act, that is, to have children.

But "the ends don't justify the means," so moral judgment must be directed toward the permissibility of the means used. Catholic ethical doctrine distinguishes four distinct situations:

a. Assisted fertilization.

The sexual act does not result in the desired fertilization because of natural causes, so medical techniques are used to help obtain the desired effect. In a case in which the conjugal act cannot be carried out, or once it has been carried out the union of the sperm and the egg is impossible, a doctor can use means to assist the conjugal act, as long as the procedure occurs in conjunction with it, either in order to facilitate its performance or in order to enable it to achieve its objective. The licitness of this assisted fertilization has always been accepted by the Magisterium. Pius XII gave this positive moral judgment:

The moral conscience does not prohibit the use of some artificial means destined exclusively to facilitate the conjugal act, to ensure that the natural act, realized in the normal way, reaches its proper end (Pius XII, *Discourse to the Fourth International Congress of Physicians*, September 29, 1949).

Donum vitae contains this same teaching.

b. Homologous artificial insemination.

This is the name for fertilization outside the conjugal act, but with the sperm of a woman's own husband. This can be done in two ways: inside the body of the woman or in the laboratory. The first kind is called *in vivo* and the second is called *in vitro*.

In vivo fertilization is frequently accomplished by using a needle to introduce the sperm into the uterus of the woman.

Catholic moral doctrine considers it illicit for two reasons. First, the usual means of obtaining semen from the man, masturbation, is immoral. Secondly, the Magisterium has often repeated the principle that according to God's design, the unitive and procreative ends of the conjugal act are inseparable. This doctrine surprises a lot of Catholics, especially when there is only one way to have the desired child. If medical science makes it possible, why is it considered illicit?

The answer is founded on the general principle: "not all that is technically possible is ethically good." For example, the use of nuclear weapons on civilian targets, while technically possible, is clearly immoral.

> Artificial insemination as a substitute for the conjugal act is prohibited by reason of the voluntarily achieved dissociation of the two meanings of the conjugal act. Masturbation, through which the sperm is normally obtained, is another sign of this dissociation. Even when it is done for the purpose of procreation, the act remains deprived of its unitive meaning: "It lacks the sexual relationship called for by the moral order, namely the relationship which realizes 'the full sense of mutual self-giving and human procreation in the context of true love'" (*DV*, 2,6; cf. Sacred Congregation for the Doctrine of the Faith, *Declaration on Certain Questions Concerning Sexual Ethics*, 86; *GS*, 51).

c. **Homologous *in vitro* artificial insemination.**

This procedure is carried out outside the mother's body. It is performed in the laboratory, and, once the egg has been fertilized, it is placed inside the womb of the woman. The Church judges these techniques to be morally evil because it separates the unitive and procreative ends of the conjugal act. In addition, the fertilized embryo, an unborn child, is often killed or frozen for future use, which clearly offends the dignity of that child, because it is murder in the first case, and in the second, the child is treated as a piece of property, and not as a person (cf. *DV,* p. 30-31).

d. **Heterologous artificial insemination.**

The fertilization of the egg is accomplished with the sperm of someone other than a woman's own husband. There are multiple forms, which could be *in vivo* or *in vitro*, with semen from a known or unknown man. As for the mother, it could be the wife herself, or a "surrogate mother," as in the case of a so-called "rented uterus" (cf. *DV, 2,1*).

The ethical judgment of Catholic morality is negative and coincides with many pieces of civil legislation which prohibit it. The Magisterium adds profound reasons to justify its condemnation.

The last reason for the disapproval of the Church is respect for the human person, specifically in the natural faculty of transmitting life. For that reason, the Magisterium often calls upon doctors to serve people and their dignity:

> The humanization of medicine, which is insisted upon today by everyone, requires respect for the integral dignity of the human person first of all in the act and at the moment in which the spouses transmit life to a new person (*DV*, 2,7).

Conclusion

When all the major elements of marriage are present, Christian matrimony is a "great sacrament" (Eph 5, 32). And, valuing the sacrament, the spouses will happily accept children and live the moral and ascetical demands of "responsible parenthood." Asceticism (self-discipline and sacrifice) in marriage means living a life in which everything that does not contribute to or interferes with the ultimate end in view-the salvation of the souls of each member of the family-is sacrificed. In a word, not only are spiritual sacrifices and prayer a part of marriage, but sacrifices of time and pleasures, as well, for the good of the family. Perhaps, the greatest sacrifice is subordination of the individual will to the common good.

OUTLINE

I. Glossary

ADULTERY:

A carnal act between a married person and someone to whom he or she is not married.

CHASTITY:

The virtue which consists in moderating the sexual appetite according to one's state in life. To live this virtue, one either abstains from all sexual relations or is moderate in its use, in conformity with the moral norms.

CONCUBINAGE:

Cohabitation, or "living together," between unmarried persons. It is often called trial marriage.

CONTINENCE:

Abstaining from any type of sexual act, as well as from those activities which excite the passions and incline a person to the sexual act.

DECLARATION OF NULLITY:

The finding of an ecclesiastical court that a valid marriage never existed from the beginning.

DIVORCE:

The authority given to a civil magistrate to separate spouses joined in civil matrimony.

EROTICISM:

Exaggeration of the passion for sex and sexual pleasure.

HEDONISM:

The philosophy which considers pleasure as the supreme end of life.

INDISSOLUBILITY:

A quality of matrimony such that the marital union can only be broken by the death of one of the spouses.

LUST:

An inordinate desire for sexual pleasure.

MASTURBATION:

The action through which one procures sexual pleasure for oneself.

MATRIMONY:

The bond between a man and a woman joined in a conjugal union for life. This bond is ordered through its very nature to the good of the spouses and the procreation and education of children. That alliance was elevated by Christ to the dignity of a sacrament (cf. *CIC*, 1055).

MODESTY:

The virtue which regulates dress and conduct in relation to the individual and society according to faith and right reason.

PORNOGRAPHY:

Any written or visual material that morbidly excites the sexual appetite.

SEXUALITY:

The group of anatomical and physiological conditions that characterize many organic beings and through which they are either male or female. In human beings, psychological conditions are also included in sexuality.

UNITY:

The quality derived from the essence of the marital contract itself that demands that marriage be carried out between one man and one woman.

II. Summary of Principles

1. "Love is therefore the fundamental and innate vocation of every human being" (*FC*, 11).

2. "The essential properties of marriage are unity and indissolubility; in Christian marriage they acquire a distinctive firmness by reason of the sacraments" (*CIC*, 1056).

3. The deliberate frustration of fertility deprives married life of its most excellent gift and is a gravely sinful abuse of sexuality.

4. The Tradition of the Church understands the sixth and ninth commandments to regulate all areas of human sexuality.

5. Chastity integrates sexuality in the unity of the person. It demands self-control.

6. "Chastity includes an *apprenticeship in self-mastery* which is a training in human freedom. The alternative is clear: either man governs his passions and finds peace, or he lets himself be dominated by them and becomes unhappy"[1] (*CCC*, 2339).

7. "Those who are *engaged to marry* are called to live chastity in continence. . . . They should reserve for marriage the expressions of affection that belong to married love" (*CCC*, 2350).

8. Polygamy, free union, adultery and divorce are grave offenses against the dignity of marriage.

9. Sensibly spacing the conception of children by means of natural family planning is one of the expressions of responsible fatherhood and motherhood.

10. "A sacramental marriage that is ratified and consummated cannot be dissolved by any human power or by any cause other than death" (*CIC*, 1141).

1. Exhortation before marriage:

   Dear friends in Christ: As you know, you are about to enter into a union which is most sacred and most serious, a union which was established by God himself. By it, he gave to man a share in the greatest work of creation, the work of the continuation of the human race. And in this way he sanctified human love and enabled man and woman to help each other live as children of God, by sharing a common life under his fatherly care.

   Because God himself is thus its author, marriage is of its very nature a holy institution, requiring of those who enter into it a complete and unreserved giving of self. But Christ our LORD added to the holiness of marriage an even deeper meaning and a higher beauty. He referred to the love of marriage to describe his own love for his Church, that is, for the people of God whom he redeemed by his own blood. And so he gave to Christians a new vision of what married life ought to be, a life of self-sacrificing love like his own. It is for this reason that his apostle, St. Paul, clearly states that marriage is now and for all time to be considered a great mystery, intimately bound up with the supernatural union of Christ and the Church, which union is also to be its pattern.

   This union then is most serious, because it will bind you together for life in a relationship so close and so intimate that it will profoundly influence your whole future. That future, with its hopes and disappointments, its successes and its failures, its pleasures and its pains, its joys and its sorrows, is hidden from your eyes. You know that these elements are mingled in every life and are to be expected in your own. And so, not knowing what is before you, you take each other for better or for worse, for richer or for poorer, in sickness and in health, until death.

   Truly, then, these words are most serious. It is a beautiful tribute to your undoubted faith in each other, that, recognizing their full import, you are nevertheless so willing and ready to pronounce them. And because these words involve such solemn obligations, it is most fitting that you rest the security of your wedded life upon the great principle of self-sacrifice. And so you begin your married life by the voluntary and complete surrender of your individual lives in the interest of that deeper and wider life which you are to have in common. Henceforth you belong entirely to each other; you will be one in mind, one in heart, and one in affections. And whatever sacrifices you may hereafter be required to make to preserve this common life, always make them generously. Sacrifice is usually difficult and irksome. Only love can make it easy; and perfect love can make it a joy. We are willing to give in proportion as we love. And when love is perfect, the sacrifice is complete. God so loved the world that he gave his only begotten Son, and the Son so loved us that he gave himself for our salvation. "Greater love than this no one has, that one lay down his life for his friends."

No greater blessing can come to your married life than pure conjugal love, loyal and true to the end. May, then, this love with which you join your hands and hearts today, never fail, but grow deeper and stronger as the years go on. And if true love and the unselfish spirit of perfect sacrifice guide your every action, you can expect the greatest measure of earthly happiness that may be allotted to man in this vale of tears. The rest is in the hands of God. [Nor will God be wanting to your needs; he will pledge you the lifelong support of his graces in the holy sacrament which you are now going to receive].

(Liturgikon, *Rite of Marriage*, Our Sunday Visitor, 1960)

2. According to contemporary scientific research, the human person is so profoundly affected by sexuality that it must be considered as one of the factors which give to each individual's life the principal traits that distinguish it. In fact it is from sex that the human person receives the characteristics which, on the biological, psychological and spiritual levels, make that person a man or a woman, and thereby largely condition his or her progress towards maturity and insertion into society. Hence sexual matters, as is obvious to everyone, today constitute a theme frequently and openly dealt with in books, reviews, magazines and other means of social communication.

(PH, 1)

3. . . . All is common among us—except our wives. At that point we dissolve our partnership, which is the one place where the rest of men make it effective. Not only do they use the wives of their friends, but also most patiently yield their own to their

friends. They follow (I take it) the example of those who went
before them, the wisest of men—Greek Socrates and Roman Cato,
who shared with their friends the wives they had taken in marriage, to bear children in other families too. And I don't know
whether the wives objected; for why would they care about a
chastity, which their husbands gave away so easily? O model of
Attic wisdom! O pattern of Roman dignity! The philosopher, a
panderer, and the censor, too!

(Tertullian, Apologia, XXXIX, 11-13)

4. Experience teaches us that love must find its safeguard in the stability of marriage, if sexual intercourse is truly to respond to the
requirements of its own finality and to those of human dignity.
These requirements call for a conjugal contract sanctioned and
guaranteed by society—a contract which establishes a state of life
of capital importance both for the exclusive union of the man and
the woman and for the good of their family and of the human
community. Most often, in fact, premarital relations exclude the
possibility of children. What is represented to be conjugal love is
not able, as it absolutely should be, to develop into paternal and
maternal love. Or, if it does happen to do so, this will be to the detriment of the children, who will be deprived of the stable environment in which they ought to develop in order to find in it the way
and the means of their insertion into society as a whole.

The consent given by people who wish to be united in marriage
must therefore be manifested externally and in a manner which
makes it valid in the eyes of society.

(PH, 7)

5. In the pastoral field, homosexuals must certainly be treated with
understanding and sustained in the hope of overcoming their personal difficulties and their inability to fit into society. Their culpability will be judged with prudence. But no pastoral method
can be employed which would give moral justification to these
acts on the grounds that they would be consonant with the condition of such people. For according to the objective moral order, homosexual relations are acts which lack an essential and
indispensable finality. In Sacred Scripture they are condemned
as a serious depravity and even presented as the sad consequence
of rejecting God. This judgment of Scripture does not of course
permit us to conclude that all those who suffer from this anomaly

are personally responsible for it, but it does attest to the fact that homosexual acts are intrinsically disordered and can in no case be approved of.

(PH, 8)

6. Whatever the force of certain arguments of a biological and philosophical nature, which have sometimes been used by theologians, in fact both the Magisterium of the Church—in the course of a constant tradition— and the moral sense of the faithful have declared without hesitation that masturbation is an intrinsically and seriously disordered act. The main reason is that, whatever the motive for acting this way, the deliberate use of the sexual faculty outside normal conjugal relations essentially contradicts the finality of the faculty. For it lacks the sexual relationship called for by the moral order, namely the relationship which realizes "the full sense of mutual self-giving and human procreation in the context of true love" [GS, 51]. All deliberate exercise of sexuality must be reserved to this regular relationship. Even if it cannot be proved that Scripture condemns this sin by name, the tradition of the Church has rightly understood it to be condemned in the New Testament when the latter speaks of "impurity," "unchasteness" and other vices contrary to chastity and continence.

(PH, 9)

7. For a Christian marriage is not just a social institution, much less a mere remedy for human weakness. It is a real supernatural calling. A great sacrament, in Christ and in the Church, says St. Paul. At the same time, it is a permanent contract between a man and a woman. Whether we like it or not, the sacrament of matrimony, instituted by Christ, cannot be dissolved. It is a permanent contract that sanctifies in cooperation with Jesus Christ. He fills the souls of husband and wife and invites them to follow him. He transforms their whole married life into an occasion for God's presence on earth.

(Blessed Josemaría Escrivá, Christ Is Passing By, 23)

8. ...conjugal love requires in husband and wife an awareness of their mission of "responsible parenthood," which today is rightly much insisted upon, and which also must be exactly understood. Consequently it is to be considered under aspects which are legitimate and connected with one another.

In relation to the biological processes, responsible parenthood means the knowledge and respect of their functions; human intellect discovers in the power of giving life biological laws which are part of the human person.

In relation to the tendencies of instinct or passion, responsible parenthood means that necessary dominion which reason and will must exercise over them.

In relation to physical, economic, psychological and social conditions, responsible parenthood is exercised, either by the deliberate and generous decision to raise a large family, or by the decision, made for grave motives and with due respect for the moral law, to avoid for the time being, or even for an indeterminate period, a new birth.

Responsible parenthood also and above all implies a more profound relationship to the objective moral order established by God, of which a right conscience is the faithful interpreter. The responsible exercise of parenthood implies, therefore, that husband and wife recognize fully their own duties towards God, towards themselves, towards the family and towards society, in a correct hierarchy of values.

In the task of transmitting life, therefore, they are not free to proceed completely at will, as if they could determine in a wholly autonomous way the honest path to follow; but they must conform their activity to the creative intention of God, expressed in the very nature of marriage and of its acts, and manifested by the constant teaching of the Church.

(HV, 10)

9. "...The Church has always been mindful of the relation between spirit and flesh; this has shown up in her definitions of the double nature of Christ, as well as in her care for what may seem to have nothing to do with religion—such as contraception. The Church is all of a piece. Her prohibition against the frustration of the marriage act has its true center perhaps in the doctrine of the resurrection of the body. This again is a *spiritual* doctrine, and beyond our comprehension. The Church doesn't say what this body will look like, but the doctrine proclaims the value of what is least about us, our flesh. We are told that it will be transfigured in Christ, that what is human will flower when it is united with the Spirit.

The Catholic can't think of birth control in relation to expediency but in relation to the nature of man under God. He has to find another solution to the problem..."

(Flannery O'Connor Collected Works,
Letter to Cecil Dawkins, 23 December 1959, p. 1117)

APPENDICES

1. Pre-marital sex

There is a time and a place for everything. For sex, the time and place is within marriage, which gives grace to the spouses to love each other in Christian charity.

Only within marriage does human sexuality achieve its full sense and perfection as a vehicle for a love that is mutual, exclusive, permanent and self-giving between a man and a woman. Sex cannot be a manifestation of love if it violates God's plan. Couples who approach the Church and request the sacrament of marriage are rejecting many of society's limited notions of sexuality.

When a society permits sexual behavior to be torn from its moorings in human love and marriage, when it treats sex as a mechanism for personal pleasure, it encourages a destructive mentality and diminishes the value of personal commitment and of human life itself.

The purpose of sex is procreation and the conjugal union between husband and wife. There is an inseparable connection, established by God, which man on his own initiative may not break, between the unifying and the procreative significance of the marriage act.

The marital act at the same time unites husband and wife in the closest intimacy, and together, makes them capable of generating new life. This union fosters the mutual self-giving of the spouses: by means of the reciprocal gift which is proper and exclusive to them, husband and wife tend toward that communion of their beings whereby they help each other toward personal perfection in order to collaborate with God in the begetting and rearing of new life.

The Church teaches that these two aspects of marital intercourse—the strengthening of interpersonal unity between spouses and the procreation of the new life—are two inseparable goods.

For these reasons, separation of sex from marriage is one of the great contemporary sins. Sex without marriage goes against the plan God made from the beginning. Only within marriage are husband and wife given the conditions and grace necessary to begin a family.

Sexuality, by means of which man and woman give themselves to one another through the acts which are proper and exclusive to spouses, is not simply biological, but concerns the innermost being of the human person. It is achieved in a truly human way only if it is an integral part of the love by which a man and a woman commit themselves totally to each other until death. The total physical self-giving would be a lie if it were not the sign and fruit of a total personal self-giving, in which the whole person, including the temporal dimension, is present: if the person were to withhold something or reserve the possibility of deciding otherwise in the future, by this very fact, he or she would not be giving totally.

Sex outside the bonds of marriage involves a selfishness contrary to the plan of God. Sex is seen, not as the giving of oneself exclusively and forever to another, but rather as a satisfaction of a momentary urge or need, no more significant nor important than the urge or need. This is obviously wrong. However, the sexual act between husband and wife, when done in accordance with the plan of God, is both sacred and holy. Used correctly, sex becomes a joyful affirmation of true love between husband and wife.

When there is impurity, love is stifled, blinded and questioned. Impurity is self-centered and a mere pursuit of pleasure without commitment or responsibility. Through concupiscence a person tends to treat as his own possession another human being, one who does not belong to him but to God. Signs of affection between unmarried persons are right and good when they are in keeping with the demands of modesty and are true signs of pure love. They must not be actions which arouse passions.

2. More on contraception

Considering God as the ultimate cause of all things, it should be kept in mind that at the origin of every human person there is a creative act of God. No man comes into existence by chance; he is always the object of God's creative love. From this fundamental truth of faith and reason it follows that the procreative capacity, inscribed in human sexuality, is, in its deepest truth, a cooperation with God's creative power. And it also follows that man and woman are neither the arbiters of this capacity, nor its masters. The biological phenomenon of human reproduction, wherein the human person finds his or her beginning, also has its end in the emergence of a new person, unique and unrepeatable, made in the image and likeness of God.

The use of contraception deprives the marital act of its sacred nature, saying "no" to the transmission and to the value of life. This "no" to life leads to selfishness in which each partner will increasingly tend to use the other to satisfy his or her sensual needs.

Furthermore, once the primary purpose of sexual relations is excluded, there is little to distinguish it from other sexual perversions such as pre-marital sex, masturbation, etc., which seek as their primary end sensual satisfaction, without openness to life

In the conjugal act, husband and wife are called to confirm in a responsible way the mutual gift of self which they have made to each other in the marriage covenant. The logic of the total gift of self to the other involves a potential openness to procreation: In this way the marriage is called to even greater fulfillment as a family. Certainly the mutual gift of husband and wife does not have the begetting of children as its only end, but is in itself a mutual communion of love and of life. The intimate truth of this gift must always be safeguarded. Intimate is not here synonymous with subjective. Rather, it means essentially in conformity with the objective truth of the man and woman who give themselves. The person can never be considered a means to an end; above all never a means of "pleasure." The person is and must be nothing other than the end of every act. Only then does the action correspond to the true dignity of the person.

QUESTIONS

1. How is one to understand the ultimate meaning of sexuality?

2. In what state were man and woman created?

3. List four truths about men and women which we learn from the biblical narrative of Adam and Eve.

4. What is the "image and likeness of God" in man?

5. What is the purpose for which God created marriage?

6. What are the properties of marriage?

7. What are the four circumstances under which a non-sacramental marriage may be legitimately dissolved?

8. In what sense can we talk about Christian matrimony as an "authentic supernatural vocation"?

9. List the three points of Catholic doctrine regarding sexuality.

10. Explain the ways in which married love is fruitful.

11. List several sins against the 6th and the 9th commandments condemned by the Old Testament.

12. How are these condemnations reflected in New Testament ?

13. Why is contraception wrong?

14. What is assisted fertilization?

15. Why is artificial insemination wrong? Is there any circumstance in which it can be morally permissible?

16. What is an abortifacient?

17. List the helps to purity.

18. What harm is caused by sex outside of marriage?

PRACTICAL EXERCISES

1. Comment on the following text defining matrimony contained in the *Code of Canon Law*:

> The marriage covenant, by which a man and a woman establish between themselves a partnership of their whole life, and which of its own very nature is ordered to the well-being of the spouses and to the procreation and upbringing of children, has, between the baptized, been raised by Christ the LORD to the dignity of a sacrament (*CIC*, 1055).

2. Analyze Supplementary Reading 8 and make an outline of the principle characteristics of "responsible parenthood," according to the encyclical *Humanae vitae*.

3. Give specific arguments to explain why the following statements and ideas are seriously erroneous:

   a. For me, premarital sex is not a sin, because I love my girlfriend/boyfriend and we are planning to get married someday.

   b. My wife and I don't intend to have any children. The world is overpopulated already, and it would be irresponsible to bring more children into such a situation.

   c. Masturbation is an unimportant issue because it is harmless and doesn't hurt anyone.

   d. If a person is not happy with his or her marriage, then he or she should get a divorce. It's stupid to stay with someone when you're unhappy.

   e. After his parents have gone to bed, Jerome calls the sex-talk numbers. He justifies it to himself on the basis that it they are just harmless fantasies, and he is not involved in sexual activity.

4. Keisha is engaged to Marcus and thinks they should discuss the number of children they will have. Whenever she brings up the subject, he says he doesn't want to think about children yet, and that they can decide after they are married. Should Keisha be concerned about his attitude? Explain. Do you think that this is a good approach to marriage in general? Why or why not?

5. Katie has been dating Matt for six months. She feels their necking has gone too far but is afraid to say anything out of fear of losing him. At the same time, she is afraid that he will soon ask her to go farther than simply necking, although she hopes that this won't happen. She has confided all this to you, and you can see that she is very uncertain about what to do. Do you see any danger signs in this relationship? What do you think are the chances that Matt will ask her to go too far? What would you advise her to do next?

6. Imagine that you and your boyfriend/girlfriend are double-dating with the following couples. How would you react to the following situations, and what would you say to the people involved?

a. You are at your senior prom with José and Marisa. José suggested they get a hotel room for the night and told Marisa, "Don't worry; there are two double beds in the room. You can sleep in one; I'll sleep in the other."

b. You and your boyfriend/girlfriend have gone to a party at a friend's house with Tino and Anne. Upon arrival, you discover that there is a lot of alcohol making its way around the party. You overhear Tino saying to Anne, "You can drink as much as you like; you're safe with me."

8. Steve likes to tell dirty jokes with his friends and, despite his parent's instructions to the contrary, watches R-rated movies on cable. He does these things even when his younger brother Dylan is around. His sister's fiance Geoffrey has criticized his behavior on several occasions, saying that he has a responsibility to set a good example for his kid brother. Steve responds by making fun of Geoff, calling him "uptight" and "preachy." Now Steve's parents have caught Dylan reading *Playboy,* and they have grounded him for three weeks. Steve still maintains that he is not at all responsible for Dylan's actions. What do you think, and why?

CHAPTER XV
THE SEVENTH AND TENTH COMMANDMENTS: YOU SHALL NOT STEAL; YOU SHALL NOT COVET YOUR NEIGHBOR'S GOODS

God destined the earth and all it contains for all men and all peoples so that all created things would be shared fairly by all mankind under the guidance of justice tempered by charity. No matter what the structures of property are in different peoples, according to various and changing circumstances and adapted to their lawful institutions, we must never lose sight of this universal destination of earthly goods. In his use of things man should regard the external goods he legitimately owns not merely as exclusive to himself but common to others also, in the sense that they can benefit others as well as himself (GS, 69).

Private property or some form of ownership of external goods assures a person a highly necessary sphere for the exercise of his personal and family autonomy and ought to be considered as an extension of human freedom (GS, 71).

Catholic teaching has always maintained the right of individuals to own private property. Yet because Original Sin distorts our perceptions, we should ask ourselves the following questions:

- What is the relationship of man to the material goods of this world?

- How does one maintain a balance between private ownership of goods and the demands of Christian charity?

Introduction

Catholic social teaching, from Pope Leo XIII through Pope John Paul II, has been a cry for justice in the wilderness of modern society. The Church has spoken time after time the truth that economic systems must serve the good of all men. Social progress is only possible on the basis of sound Christian morality. Both the human person and the family are prior to the state, with the latter existing to serve the former, not vice versa. Both society and the state have an obligation, in both justice and charity, to aid society's poorest and weakest members. While individual and private initiatives should be encouraged as the best way of producing wealth, morality must supersede pure competition in decisions concerning the ultimate distribution of the goods of this world. Private property is a fundamental human right.

Nevertheless, property must always be used in accordance with what best serves the common good. Wages paid to a breadwinner should be sufficient for the support of a family, so that women who so desire have the opportunity to dedicate themselves wholly to the rearing and education of their children. Human beings have a fundamental right to form and act through their own private associations (labor unions, for example) unobstructed by the power of the state. The resources of human labor must be recognized and protected as more valuable and more important than capital or material resources. Social actions should be carried out at the appropriate level—in other words, where possible, the individual acts on behalf of himself or others, through his work, the family, the local community and so on (this is called the Principle of Subsidiarity). The higher levels of government and the international arena are involved only where absolutely necessary.

In this chapter, we will explain the moral principles concerning the rights and duties of man and the injustices which keep him from achieving peace and social justice.

1. Biblical doctrine concerning the relation of man to material things

According to the Bible, God created the world with its multitude of things and variety of animals. And he gave everything to man, so that he may be lord over it. Man's dominion over creation is described in this way in Chapter 1 of Genesis:

> Then God said, "Let us make man in our image, after our likeness; and let them have dominion over the fish of the sea, and over the birds of the air, and over the cattle, and over all the earth, and over every creeping thing that creeps upon the earth" (Gn 1, 26).

Immediately following this, God explains the purpose of created things: they are destined for the use and service of man:

> And God said, "Behold, I have given you every plant yield-
> ing seed which is upon the face of all the earth, and every
> tree with seed in its fruit; you shall have them for food. . . ."
> (Gn 1, 29).

With figurative language, Chapter 2 of Genesis narrates the superiority and dominion of man over all creation:

> So out of the ground the LORD formed every beast of the
> field and every bird of the air, and brought them to the man
> to see what he would call them; and whatever the man
> called every living creature, that was its name. The man
> gave names to all cattle, and to the birds of the air, and to
> every beast of the field. . . . (Gn 2,19,20).

2. Universal destiny of created goods.

The passages of Genesis indicate the intimate relationship that God establishes between man and exterior reality. These texts contain at least four truths:

- The superiority of man over the rest of creation, indicated by the fact that man "gives them their names."

- The purpose of the world's material resources, vegetables and animals, is to serve man and he should have command over them.

- Man can be served by all things, but his dominion is not absolute: he can use them, but he must also protect and develop them.

- Biblical teachings highlight the fact that created goods are destined for all men and not only for some of them. This truth is more primary than the right to private property.

The *Catechism of the Catholic Church* formulates this biblical teaching in the following terms:

> In the beginning God entrusted the earth and its resources
> to the common stewardship of mankind to take care of
> them, master them by labor, and enjoy their fruits.[1] The
> goods of creation are destined for the whole human race
> (CCC, 2402).

3. Man possesses the right to property

In emphasizing that the goods of this world are intended for the assistance of all, the Bible also indicates that every man must have things necessary for living a human life. This is what is commonly called "the right to private property." That is, each person has the capability of possessing things as one's own. Property is a right of every person. This right is founded on human nature itself. These are the main reasons that justify it:

- Man, as a rational being, is able to plan his future. For this reason he needs the security that the possession of some things offer him. To deny him the right to possess is to present him with insecurity, which is what contradicts the desire to assure his life's future.

- Property is also demanded by the fact that man is a free being. Freedom demands that he possess things as his own. For, if he did not possess things, man would be excessively controlled by outside factors.

- Another justification of the right to private property comes from the family. Family life would be notably difficult if the family did not posses things in order to satisfy the innumerable and unforeseen needs that must be met.

- Finally, man's work needs to be equitably compensated. For that reason, he has the right and duty to claim the fruit of his work as his own.

This teaching is mentioned in the *Catechism of the Catholic Church*:

> However, the earth is divided up among men to assure the security of their lives, endangered by poverty and threatened by violence. The appropriation of property is legitimate for guaranteeing the freedom and dignity of persons and for helping each of them to meet his basic needs and the needs of those in his charge. It should allow for a natural solidarity to develop between men (CCC, 2402).

4. Relation between the universal destiny of goods and the right to private property

Catholic morality has always taught that, even affirming the natural right to private property, things which someone has in his possession do not lose their primary character of having been created by God to help every man. This condition of property is called the social function of property, and is a part of the common good.

One must then ask which of these two principles (that is, the particular right to own property or the social function of private property) is the more important.

Catholic moral doctrine teaches that the natural right to private property is subordinate to the social function of property, in such a way that, when there is a dispute between private property and its social function the social principle prevails over the private. The reason is obvious, because God created goods for the use of all men. Thus when only some possess many goods and make it impossible for the majority of men to live in dignity, God's plan is not fulfilled:

> The *universal destination of goods* remains primordial, even if the promotion of the common good requires respect for the right to private property and its exercise (CCC, 2403).

In addition, the state can intervene so that private property does not only not oppose the common good, but also has a positive repercussion for the good of society. In the same way, the state can claim some goods of special interest for the public, for instance, as in the right of eminent domain (the principle which states that a government can claim private property, with appropriate payment to the owner, because of a legitimate and overriding public concern, i.e., a farmer's land is needed for an interstate highway).

5. The social doctrine of the church

Moral theology has always studied the right use of goods, defending the possession of them and condemning their abuse. But at the beginning of the 19th century, with the start of industrialization, serious social problems appeared as a result of poor working conditions.

To address these problems, a new chapter of moral science was begun called the social doctrine of the Church; that is, the moral teaching of the Church on social problems brought about by an industrial society with new ways of life and the appearance of wage-earning masses.

Today one often hears about a century of the social doctrine of the Church. The encyclical *Rerum novarum* is normally considered the first piece of this new teaching. It was issued by Pope Leo XIII on January 15, 1891. The latest addition to this body of Church teaching is John

Paul II's encyclical *Centisimus annus*, published on May 1, 1991. The teaching of the Church regarding social life, economics and politics of all peoples continues to be the object of attention for moral theology.

The principle subjects which the social doctrine of the Church covers are work and its just wages; the right to private property and its social function; the right to belong to associations and labor unions; the defense of justice and the morality of strikes; the exercise of real freedoms, and the social function of economics and political life. In a word, everything related to the common good and to justice in social life (cf. *VS*, 99-100).

6. The duty of Christians to participate in public life

The social meaning of man and the universal character of the redemption of Jesus Christ oblige Christians to take an active part in social life.

The moral conduct of a Christian is not only concerned with purely individual acts. It also requires participation and collaboration in public activity so that the different dimensions of social life (for instance, politics, economics and law) are fulfilled and that they follow the ethical demands contained in the Gospel.

Frequently, men—including Christians—recognize their sins resulting from individual and interpersonal actions, but ignore the relation of their acts to society. This individualistic ethics has been rejected by the Second Vatican Council:

> Profound and rapid changes make it more necessary that no one ignoring the trend of events or drugged by laziness, contents himself with a merely individualistic morality. It grows increasingly true that the obligations of justice and love are fulfilled only if each person, contributing to the common good, according to his own abilities and the needs of others, also promotes and assists the public and private institutions dedicated to bettering the conditions of human life (*GS*, 30).

Other documents of the Church have re-emphasized this same teaching repeatedly. The Second Vatican Council reminds us that:

> The Church praises and esteems the work of those who for the good of men devote themselves to the service of the state and take on the burdens of this office (*GS*, 75).

The mission of Christians is to convey the spirit of the Gospel in public life. In civic life, ideally the Christian will avoid the many excesses which appear in the arena of political life.

7. International solidarity

Today's culture is characterized by its universalization. The rapidity of communication and the economic relations that exist among peoples and cultures cause the problems of one nation or continent to affect the rest of the world. For this reason, Catholic morality underlines the ethical rights and duties necessary for the international solidarity of different peoples and cultures.

> It is above all a question of *interdependence*, sensed as a *system determining* relationships in the contemporary world, in its economic, cultural, political and religious elements, and accepted as a *moral category*. When interdependence becomes recognized in this way, the correlative response as a moral and social attitude, as a "virtue," is *solidarity*. This then is not a feeling of vague compassion or shallow distress at the misfortunes of so many people, both near and far. On the contrary, it is *a firm and persevering determination* to commit oneself to the *common good*; that is to say to the good of all and of each individual, because we are *all* really responsible *for all*. This determination is based on the *solid* conviction that what is hindering full development is that desire for profit and that thirst for power already mentioned (*SRS*, 38).

The Catholic faith professes that all men have the same origin and are guided to the same end; that all are guilty of the same sins and that all have been redeemed by Jesus Christ; that the fatherhood of God includes all men. Consequently, we should note that no ideology nor religious confession enjoys so many universalizing elements as Christianity. That is why the very name of the Church is "Catholic," that is, "universal."

These reasons justify Pope Paul VI's concern for social problems that affect the entire world and John Paul II's words on the "new virtue of solidarity," which is characterized by the contemplation of the needs and problems of all humanity in light of the faith.

The *Catechism of the Catholic Church* devotes an entire section to "solidarity among the nations." It is not surprising that it analyzes the causes of unjust inequalities among diverse peoples and notes the reasons for living solidarity among different nations:

> *Rich nations* have a grave moral responsibility toward those which are unable to ensure the means of their development by themselves or have been prevented from doing so by tragic historical events. It is a duty in solidarity and charity; it is also an obligation in justice if the prosperity of the rich nations has come from resources that have not been paid for fairly (*CCC*, 2439).

8. Respect for nature. Ecology

Ecology is a term of Greek origin. It is derived from *oikos*, which means "hearth" or "patrimony" and *logos,* meaning "law" or "treaty". In the etymological sense, ecology is a treaty with nature, which should be considered as the "house" of all. Ecology, then, deals with protecting the residence in which human life is developed.

If one must respect another's goods, one must also respect nature and animals: this is a consequence of the universal destiny of goods for the use of men.

Today, we hear many stories which tell us about a deterioration of nature and an unmeasured and uncontrolled use of consumer goods, as well as the destruction of some species of animals. As should be obvious, ecology is a part of morality, which condemns these abuses of man.

This teaching is of such importance that it has been incorporated into the catechesis of the Catholic faith:

> The seventh commandment enjoins respect for the integrity of creation. Animals, like plants and inanimate beings, are by nature destined for the common good of past, present, and future humanity.[2] Use of mineral, animal, and vegetable resources of the universe cannot be divorced from the respect for moral imperatives. Man's dominion over inanimate and other living beings granted by the Creator is not absolute; it is limited by concern for the quality of life of his neighbor, including generations to come; it requires a religious respect for the integrity of creation[3] (*CCC*, 2415)

Since the *environment* is the world common to all men it should be respected. Nevertheless, some ecological interpretations are exaggerated since they forget a basic principle: mineral as well as plant and animal resources are at the service of humanity. For that reason, man can make use of them. What is forbidden is "abuse." Consequently, man cannot use things at his own caprice, destroying nature or mistreating animals. The dominion the Bible refers to is not a despotic dominion, because man is not an absolute lord, but an administrator.

9. "Do not steal." Respect for private property

In case of moral necessity, a starving man may take food if there is no one present to give it to him. Other than in a case of moral necessity, it is not licit to take someone else's goods against his reasonable will.

> . . . There is no theft if consent can be presumed or if the refusal is contrary to reason and the universal destination of goods. This is the case in obvious and urgent necessity when the only way to provide for immediate, essential needs (food, shelter, clothing . . .) is to put at one's disposal and use the property of others.[4] (CCC, 2408)

Stealing is the taking of another's goods against his reasonable wishes. For example, to do unjust damage to property, spray-painting property, to remove street signs, to refuse to pay just wages, to cheat others through pricing or the quantity of what is being sold, or to charge excessive rates of interest are all forms of stealing. One may also break the seventh commandment by not paying back what is owed, by spending more of someone else's money than is necessary, by not doing a day's work for a day's wage, or by failing to fulfill part or all of a business contract. Robbery, which is taking property by force, adds additional malice to stealing. One must discern carefully the multiple forms in which one can damage private property. The damage to goods may involve either private or state property, and all who effectively cooperate in doing damage to property are obliged to make restitution. The complexity of social life nowadays offers different ways of unjustly appropriating the goods of another. The *Catechism of the Catholic Church* proposes the following cases which are more frequent in today's social life:

> . . . [S]peculation in which one contrives to manipulate the price of goods artificially in order to gain an advantage to the detriment of others; corruption in which one influences the judgment of those who must make decisions according to law; appropriation and use for private purposes of

the common goods of an enterprise; work poorly done; tax evasion; forgery of checks and invoices; excessive expenses and waste. Willfully damaging private or public property is contrary to the moral law and requires reparation (*CCC*, 2409; cf. *VS*, 100).

Likewise, one "steals" from society when one neglects to contribute equally to the common good by not paying just taxes.

10. Restitution

The word restitution refers to the obligation to return things to the state in which they were before theft, damage, or robbery. Restitution must be made for all sins against justice. There is an obligation to make restitution for anything stolen as well as for any damage done to property. In difficult cases the best thing to do is to consult a priest in confession.

Conclusion

To speak about the seventh commandment is to talk about many complex obligations that arise from man's right to own property and his relations with his neighbor and the whole of society. The best solutions to these problems is to refer to the Church's continuing instruction on the ownership of property and the obligation to see it in light of the universal destiny of goods.

The social doctrine of the Church is a moral teaching, not a detailed technical response to problems in social life and politics. It is up to citizens, society and the state to find practical and specific solutions. The Church only offers the principles.

The reason that the Church proposes these teachings on human life is two-fold: the dignity of the human person and the social nature that characterizes man. The Church has always defended the dignity of man when it is not sufficiently recognized in the complexity of social life, economics and politics. Whenever the dignity of the human person is at risk, the Church emphasizes the scriptural basis for acknowledging man's dignity. Man was created in the image and likeness of God

OUTLINE

I. Glossary

JUSTICE:

The constant determination to give each his due.

PRINCIPLE OF SOLIDARITY:

The duty of cooperating and harmonizing all of the rights of the individual and the demands which are derived from the sociability of man. It represents the entire effort—a joint effort—to reach the good of the individual and of society.

PRINCIPLE OF SUBSIDIARITY:

"[A] community of a higher order should not interfere in the internal life of a community of a lower order, depriving the latter of its functions, but rather should support it in case of need and help to coordinate its activity with the activities of the rest of society, always with a view to the common good"[5] (CCC, 1883). With this principle, the Church opposes all forms of collectivism or nationalism.

PRINCIPLE OF THE COMMON GOOD:

The primacy of the common good over individual interests. That is, the effort to achieve a social good that makes possible the full development of man's own perfection.

PROPERTY:

Right of a person to possess things as his own.

RESTITUTION:

Reparation of an injustice committed, since, if the damage is not repaired, a permanent state of injustice is produced.

SOCIAL JUSTICE:

The justice which characterizes and regulates relations among individuals or among diverse groups and social classes in all areas of social interaction.

THEFT/ROBBERY:

To take away the goods of another against his reasonable will. When this is carried out with violence, it is called *robbery*.

II. Summary of Principles

1. Man has the right by nature to possess and use things as his own.

2. The right to private property is secondary in respect to the universal destiny of material goods for humanity in general.

3. In case of extreme necessity, man may possess and use another's goods (food, clothes, home), if it is the only means of securing those essential needs for existence.

4. A just social life supposes equitable relations between capital and labor.

5. Whenever one unjustly uses or takes the individual or social goods of another, he commits a sin against the seventh commandment.

6. When one takes something not one's own or when one unjustly injures another, he has the obligation to make full restitution or compensation for any damage done.

7. The hierarchy of the Church issues a moral judgment in economic or political matters when the dignity of the human person and the fundamental rights of man require it.

8. The center of social life, economy and politics is man, in his dignity as a person and a child of God.

SUPPLEMENTARY READINGS

1. In *Rerum Novarum,* Leo XIII strongly affirmed the natural character of the right to private property, using various arguments against the socialism of his time. This right, which is fundamental for the autonomy and development of the person, has always been defended by the Church up to our own day. At the same time, the Church teaches that the possession of material goods

is not an absolute right, and that its limits are inscribed in its very nature as a human right.

While the Pope proclaimed the right to private ownership, he affirmed with equal clarity that the "use" of goods, while marked by freedom, is subordinated to their original common destination as created goods, as well as to the will of Jesus Christ as expressed in the Gospel.

(*CA*, 30)

2. In the light of today's "new things," we have reread *the relationship between individual or private property and the universal destination of material wealth.* One fulfills oneself by using one's intelligence and freedom. In so doing a person utilizes the things of this world as objects and instruments and makes them his own. The foundation of the right to private initiative and ownership is to be found in this activity. By means of his work a person commits himself, not only for his own sake but also *for others* and *with others.* Each person collaborates in the work of others and for their good. One works in order to provide for the needs of one's family, one's community, one's nation, and ultimately all humanity.

(*CA*, 43)

3. It is well known how strong were the words used by the Fathers of the Church to describe the proper attitude of persons who possess anything towards persons in need. To quote Saint Ambrose: "You are not making a gift of your possessions to the poor person. You are handing over to him what is his. For what has been given in common for the use of all, you have arrogated to yourself. The world is given to all, and not only to the rich." [*De Nabuthe*, c. 12, n. 53; (P. L. 14, 747). Cf. J.-R. Palanque, Saint Ambrose et l'empire romain, Paris: de Boccard, 1933, pp. 336 f.] That is, private property does not constitute for anyone an absolute and unconditioned right. No one is justified in keeping for his exclusive use what he does not need, when others lack necessities. In a word, "according to the traditional doctrine as found in the Fathers of the Church and the great theologians, the right to property must never be exercised to the detriment of the common good". If there should arise a conflict "between acquired private rights and primary community exigencies," it is the responsibility of public authorities "to look for a solution, with the

active participation of individuals and social groups". [Letter to the 82nd Session of the French Social Weeks (Brest 1965), in L'homme et la revolution urbaine, Lyons Chronique sociale 1965, pp. 8 and 9. Cf. L'Osservatore Romano, July 10, i [965], Documentation catholique t. 62, Paris, 1965, col 1365].

(PP, 23)

4. God entrusted animals to the stewardship of those whom he created in his own image (cf. *Gn* 2, 19-20; 9, 1-4). Hence it is legitimate to use animals for food and clothing. They may be domesticated to help man in his work and leisure. Medical and scientific experimentation on animals is a morally acceptable practice if it remains within reasonable limits and contributes to caring for or saving human lives.

(CCC, 2417)

5. The permanent validity of the Catholic Church's social teaching admits of no doubt. This teaching rests on one basic principle: individual human beings are the foundation, the cause and the end of every social institution. That is necessarily so, for men are by nature social beings. This fact must be recognized, as also the fact that they are raised in the plan of Providence to an order of reality which is above nature.

On this basic principle, which guarantees the sacred dignity of the individual, the Church constructs her social teaching. She has formulated, particularly over the past hundred years, and through the efforts of a very well informed body of priests and laymen, a social doctrine which points out with clarity the sure way to social reconstruction. The principles she gives are of universal application, for they take human nature into account, and the varying conditions in which man's life is lived. They also take into account the principal characteristics of contemporary society, and are thus acceptable to all.

(MM, 218-220)

6. In order to achieve their task directed to the Christian animation of the temporal order, in the sense of serving persons and society, the lay faithful *are never to relinquish their participation in "public life,"* that is, in the many different economic, social, legislative, administrative and cultural areas which are intended to promote organically and institutionally the *common good.* The

Synod Fathers have repeatedly affirmed that every person has a right and duty to participate in public life, albeit in a diversity and complementarity of forms, levels, tasks and responsibilities. Charges of careerism, idolatry of power, egoism and corruption that are oftentimes directed at persons in government, parliaments, the ruling classes, or political parties, as well as the common opinion that participating in politics is an absolute moral danger, does not in the least justify either skepticism or an absence on the part of Christians in public life.

(CL, 42)

7. In the political sphere, it must be noted that truthfulness in the relations between those governing and those governed, openness in the relations between those governing and those governed, openness in public administration, impartiality in the service of the body politic, respect for the rights of political adversaries, safeguarding the rights of the accused against summary trials and convictions, the just and honest use of public funds, the rejection of equivocal or illicit means in order to gain, preserve or increase power at any cost—all these are principles which are primarily rooted in, and in fact derive their singular urgency from, the transcendent value of the person and the objective moral demands of the functioning of States. When these principles are not observed, the very basis of political coexistence is weakened and the life of society itself is gradually jeopardized, threatened and doomed to decay (cf. Ps. 14, 3-4; Rev 18, 2-3, 9-24). Today, when many countries have seen the fall of ideologies which bound politics to a totalitarian conception of the world—Marxism being the foremost of these—there is no less grave a danger that the fundamental rights of the human person will be denied and that the religious yearnings which arise in the heart of every human being will be absorbed once again into politics. This is *the risk of an alliance between democracy and ethical relativism*, which would remove any sure moral reference point from political and social life, and on a deeper level make the acknowledgment of truth impossible. Indeed, "if there is no ultimate truth to guide and direct political activity, then ideas and convictions can easily be manipulated for reasons of power. As history dem-

onstrates, a democracy without values easily turns into open or thinly disguised totalitarianism.

(*VS*, 101)

APPENDICES

Social justice and working for the common good

The moral virtue of justice is the constant and permanent determination to give to everyone what is his due. Justice that exists in the dealings of individual persons among themselves is called commutative justice. That which exists between the community and the subject is called distributive justice. That between the subject and the community is called legal justice.

Social justice is that justice which leads to the formulation of juridical and social norms that the common good demands for individuals. Social justice also means giving to all classes and groups in the nation their rights. When government laws and policies are directed to the benefit of only one group, or a few, but not for all the citizens of that society, then social justice is violated.

A good Catholic must also be a good citizen of his country and must work for the common good. He must therefore exercise his civic duties and practice the civic virtues. A good citizen loves his country, is sincerely interested in its welfare, and respects and obeys its lawful authority.

With regard to the Seventh Commandment of the Decalogue, a good citizen has to learn to value the things which are of common use (the *res publica*). He has to have a constant concern for the common good and the welfare of others.

The following text of Pope Pius XI in the Encyclical *Quadragesimo Anno* of 1931 is of capital importance as it equates the "requirements of the common good" to the "rules of social justice":

> "Since the present system of economy is founded chiefly upon ownership and labor, the principles of right reason, that is, of Christian social philosophy, must be kept in mind regarding ownership and labor and their association together, and must be put into actual practice.

"So as to avoid the reefs of individualism and collectivism, the twofold character, that is, individual and social, both of capital and of work or labor must be given due and rightful weight. Relations of one to the other must be made to conform to the laws of strictest justice—commutative justice, as it is called—with the support, however of Christian charity.

"Free competition, kept within definite and due limits, and still more, economic dictatorship, must be effectively brought under public authority in these matters which pertain to the latter's function. The public institutions themselves of nations, moreover, ought to make all human society conform to the needs of the common good; that is, to the norm of social justice."

QUESTIONS

1. Why is the Church concerned with property rights?

2. What is the universal destiny for which God created the goods of this world?

3. What does it mean to say that human beings have a "common stewardship" over created things?

4. Does property have a social function, or is personal property solely for the use of its owner?

5. What are the principle subjects covered by the Church's social doctrine?

6. What is the mission of the Christian in public life?

7. What obligations does man have towards the goods of creation found in nature?

328 OUR MORAL LIFE IN CHRIST

8. What is the difference between theft and robbery?

9. What is restitution? In what circumstances is restitution required?

PRACTICAL EXERCISES

1. Write an essay discussing the practical consequences for the social and political order that can be drawn from the following texts:

> a. Christian tradition has never upheld this right [of ownership or property] as absolute and untouchable. On the contrary, it has always understood this right within the broader context of the right common to all to use the goods of the whole of creation: The right to private property is subordinated to the right to common use, to the fact that goods are meant for everyone (*LE*, 14).

> b. The ownership of any property makes its holder a steward of Providence, with the task of making it fruitful and communicating its benefits to others, first of all his family (*CCC*, 2404).

2. Evaluate the morality of the individuals in the following cases in light of the Seventh and the Tenth Commandments.

   a. George's parents went out of town for the weekend and left the car keys home, so that George could use their car for necessary errands. George took the car one evening to go out with his friends, which his parents would almost certainly not have allowed. While they were out, he permitted his friend Katie to drive the car as well. Evaluate the morality of George's actions in light of the seventh commandment. Did he do anything wrong?

   b. Bart and Jim plan to "T-P" the rival football captain's house for homecoming. Is there a moral problem with a "harmless" act of vandalism like this? Why or why not?

   c. While Teresa was at college, she purchased a new wardrobe on a time payment plan. She used the information she learned in law school to file bankruptcy and kept the clothes. What she did was perfectly legal, but what is the moral nature of her actions? Can something be immoral if it is legal?

   d. Perry found a credit card and charged some sports equipment before destroying the card. Later, his conscience started to bother him, and he realized that he must make restitution. How do you think he should go about it?

3. Look for and comment on some passages of the New Testament which praise the spirit of poverty and condemn the anxiety for riches.

4. Resolve the following case: Margaret, Theresa and Ann went to California on the train. In the station Margaret found a wallet with $1000 in it, but there was no identification in the wallet. They decided to distribute the money among themselves. They considered this an extraordinary piece of luck, and proceeded to spend the money. Some days later, Ann told her mother about the incident, and her mother said she should not have spent the money. Ann told Theresa and Margaret about what her mother said and they started to worry. Should they have spent the money? If your answer is no, then what do you think they should do now?

CHAPTER XVI
THE EIGHTH COMMANDMENT:
YOU SHALL NOT BEAR FALSE WITNESS
AGAINST YOUR NEIGHBOR

Now, Peter was sitting outside in the courtyard. And a maid came up to him, and said, "you also were with Jesus the Galilean." But he denied it before them all, saying, "I do not know what you mean." And when he went out to the porch, another maid saw him, and she said to the bystanders, "This man was with Jesus of Nazareth. "And again he denied it with an oath, "I do not know the man." After a little while the bystanders came up and said to Peter, "Certainly you are also one of them, for your accent betrays you." Then he began to invoke a curse on himself and to swear, "I do not know the man." And immediately the cock crowed. And Peter remembered the saying of Jesus, "Before the cock crows, you will deny me three times." And he went out and wept bitterly (Mt 26, 69-75).

Dishonesty and falsehood are traits which no one appreciates in others. Beyond the personally offensive nature of such traits however, a deeper issue exists. Consider the following:

- Is there a relationship between personal freedom and truthfulness?

- What are the consequences of dishonesty for individuals and for society as a whole?

- Do Christians have particular obligations which surpass those of other people in regard to the truth?

Introduction

Ever since Greek philosophy claimed that reason distinguished man from all other creatures—man is a "rational animal"—the history of Europe has been characterized by a great enterprise to know the truth about reality. First, Greek and Roman and later all western philosophy has been marked by a desire to know what things are. Not only philosophy but also technological progress was included in the patrimony that the Greeks transmitted to the countries of Europe and America; for, as heirs to the emphasis on reason and the love of truth, the men of Europe and America have dedicated themselves to knowledge of the laws which govern matter and life.

Rational knowledge, with Roman Law and the monotheism of Israel, is the heart of the common legacy which the ancients passed down to Europe first, and through Europe to the rest of the world.

Not only the west, but any culture which has attained a certain maturity and pursues knowledge of the truth is characterized by a primacy of reason. Since man, as a rational being seeking to know what things are, desires to know and understand the truth about God, about humanity, and about the other realities surrounding him, there is placed within him an inclination toward his proper end.

1. Truth in the Old Testament

The wording of the eighth commandment is almost the same in Exodus and Deuteronomy, the two books that contain the Decalogue: "You shall not bear false witness against your neighbor" (Ex 20, 16; Dt 5, 20).

The moral content of this commandment should be understood in light of the seven previous ones. As our introduction noted, God establishes a minimum of moral demands in the Decalogue, which is why they are formulated negatively and only the most generic sins are condemned. In this way, besides polytheism and other things related to divine worship (first through third commandments), God forbids disobedience to one's parents (fourth commandment), to take innocent life (fifth commandment), adultery (sixth commandment), robbery (seventh commandment), and in the eighth, Yahweh condemns a lack of respect for the truth.

Evidently, the formulation of the eighth commandment is as generic as the rest of the Decalogue. It only points out an ethical minimum: protecting the dignity of the person, since social life would be impossible if truth is not respected as the foundation of social communication.

This natural attitude of the human person toward the truth is also characteristic of the message of the Bible. In fact, revelation is nothing more than the manifestation by God to man of the truth about God, about the meaning of human existence and about the value and end of all creation. God reveals himself precisely in order to manifest the saving truth to man. In the Old Testament Yahweh testifies that he tells the truth. God's revelation to Moses is accompanied by extraordinary signs—miracles—which illustrate the truth of what God has revealed (Ex 4, 1-17).

In the book of Numbers, Balach repeats the teaching of Yahweh who testifies to his truthfulness in everything he does and says: "God is not man, that he should lie, or a son of man, that he should repent. Has he said, and will he not do it? Or has he spoken, and will he not fulfill it?" (Nb 23, 19).

The book of Proverbs exults in the truthfulness of Yahweh and honors the man who seeks knowledge and the love of truth. When man acts in this way, he is on his way to reaching true wisdom:

> Hear, for I will speak noble things, and from my lips will come what is right; for my mouth will utter truth; wickedness is an abomination to my lips. All the words of my mouth are righteous; there is nothing twisted or crooked in them. They are all straight to him who understands and right to those who find knowledge. Take my instruction instead of silver, and knowledge rather than choice gold; for wisdom is better than jewels, and all that you may desire cannot compare with her. I, Wisdom, dwell in prudence, and I find knowledge and discretion (Pr 8, 6-12).

The Psalms poetically narrate the history of Israel and express the sentiments of the people. They worship God whose "truth lasts throughout the ages," given that "thy word is firmly fixed in the heavens. Thy faithfulness endures to all generations; thou hast established the earth, and it stands fast (Ps 119, 89-90)."

2. Truth in the New Testament

Truth is the correlation between the idea in the mind and the exterior reality. In order to present the truth with precision, force and love, it is necessary to go back to the definition of man as a rational animal. In effect, if man distinguishes himself from animals through his thought, the natural vocation of man is the desire to know the truth, profess it, defend it and communicate it. Therefore, man's relations with one another must be founded on truth, not on lies.

But the teaching of Jesus Christ is that which highlights the importance of honesty. The subject of truth is one of the characteristics of the Gospel of St. John. For example, when speaking of the person of Jesus, he states that "the Word became flesh and dwelt among us, full of grace and truth" (Jn 1, 14). Jesus speaks of himself: "I am the Truth" (Jn 14, 6). And he declares before Pilate that he has come "to bear witness to the truth. Every one who is of the truth hears my voice" (Jn 18, 37). But for those who follow him and those who believe in him, "the Spirit of Truth" (Jn 14, 16-17) will always accompany them. And it's not surprising that Jesus' prayer for his disciples is precisely that the Father "sanctify them in the truth; thy word is truth" (Jn 17, 17). And for this reason he asked "that they also may be consecrated in truth" (Jn 17, 19).

Finally, the action of the Holy Spirit on the apostles is that of a guide leading them "into all the truth" (Jn 16, 13). Consequently, to grow in faith is to grow in truth. Later tradition identifies revelation with truth. So to persevere in faith is to stay with the truth.

As in the rest of the Commandments, this is also enriched in the moral program of the New Testament with the teachings of Sacred Tradition and with the doctrine of the Magisterium. The richness of the eighth commandment is understood in Catholic morality as a precept of love and defense of the truth, not only regarding the good name of a person, but in all aspects and affairs of human life:

> The eighth commandment forbids misrepresenting the truth in our relations with others. This moral prescription flows from the vocation of the holy people to bear witness to their God who is the truth and wills the truth. Offenses against the truth express by word or deed a refusal to commit oneself to moral uprightness: they are fundamental infidelities to God and, in this sense, they undermine the foundations of the covenant (CCC, 2464).

3. Truth and freedom.
"The truth will set you free"

In conversations with the Jews, Jesus declared: "If you continue in my word, you are truly my disciples, and you will know the truth, and the truth will make you free" (Jn 8, 31-32). These words of Jesus contain two clear points.

First, Jesus gives a preview of what he will say on another occasion: that he "is the Truth" (Jn 14, 6). Moreover he tells us that the truth consists in following and accepting his doctrine. Consequently, a disciple of Christ is on the way to reaching the fullness of truth. This does not mean that a Christian has more knowledge of scientific truths, for example, but rather that he will possess the truth about life, about moral principles and, in general, about the meaning of human existence.

Secondly, the way to reach true freedom is the knowledge of truth. This is verified in everyday life. Ignorance, error, mistakes or falsehoods are dispositions that inhibit human freedom. If one really wishes to be free, he should profess love for the truth and seek it. This doctrine is explained at great length in the encyclical *Veritatis splendor* (cf. *VS*, 30-34; 84).

Consequently, all men are obliged to seek the truth. Therefore, it is not worthy of the human person to live contrary to the truth. One must develop his intelligence with the objective of being capable of discovering the truth in everything, from everyday life to the events that make up the entire human existence.

This search for the truth is even more obligatory regarding the truth about God. This principle is contained in the "principle of religious freedom," just as it was formulated in the Second Vatican Council:

> It is in accordance with their dignity as persons—that is, beings endowed with reason and free will and therefore privileged to bear personal responsibility—that all men should be at once impelled by nature and also bound by a moral obligation to seek the truth, especially religious truth. They are also bound to adhere to the truth, once it is known, and to order their whole lives in accord with the demands of truth. However, men cannot discharge these obligations in a manner in keeping with their own nature unless they enjoy immunity from external coercion as well as psychological freedom (*DH*, 2).

In this way, truth, freedom and the absence of coercion are joined together.

To conclude, one should remember the advice of St. Paul to Timothy: a Christian should not "be ashamed then of testifying to our LORD, nor of me his prisoner, but take your share in suffering for the gospel in the power of God" (2 Tim 1, 8). This is a good phrase which aptly sums up the study of the Ten Commandments, which guide the life of men down the correct moral route.

4. Spreading the truth

The principle which states that "good is diffusive" is fulfilled in the truth because truth is also a good. Consequently, it is not merely enough to speak truth, but it also must be *discussed and propagated*.

Truth should be affirmed in all circumstances, especially in the following:

- In the spreading of Christian truth. Christians have a serious obligation to talk about the teachings of revelation and the doctrine of the Magisterium concerning the many problems of life.

- To communicate the truth in social life. For example, information about drug-trafficking, terrorism or social fraud ought to be communicated to the legitimate authority.

- revelation of a secret if doing so obtains a social good proportional to the serious duty of keeping a secret. The exception to this guideline regards professional secrets. The duty to maintain a professional secret, except in cases of serious danger, must never be neglected.

- A special problem is presented in the case of the news media. Their purpose is to inform society, in regards to people and events on a daily basis. Often, when divulging the truth they violate the privacy of persons. It is true that being a public figure reduces the boundaries of private life. This is why a man or a woman who carries out public activities, as in politics or art, has less of a private life, depending on the extent of their public occupation. In any case, this margin—wide or narrow—should be respected.

> Everyone should observe an appropriate reserve concerning persons' private lives. Those in charge of communications should maintain a fair balance between the requirements of the common good and respect for individual rights. Interference by the media in the private lives of persons engaged in political or public activity is to be condemned to the extent that it infringes upon their privacy and freedom (CCC, 2492).

- In relation to the media, the individual must always possess a critical attitude toward the media, in such a way that he avoids falling into error, and worse, losing the meaning and love of truth.

Recognizing the importance of the media, the Magisterium not only values its use, but also emphasizes the ethical dimension of the professions involved in this field.

5. To tell the truth. Honesty versus dishonesty

Love for the truth should bring all men, and especially Christians, to tell the truth and to avoid falsehood. Jesus expressed this with this aphorism: "Let what you say be simply 'Yes' or 'No'; anything more than this comes from evil" (Mt 5, 37; cf. Jas 5, 12).

Jesus declares that he is the truth (Jn 14, 6). Lies come from the devil, the author and father of all lies:

> You are of your father the devil, and your will is to do your father's desires. He was a murderer from the beginning, and has nothing to do with the truth, because there is no truth in him. When he lies, he speaks according to his own nature, for he is a liar and the father of lies. But, because I tell the truth, you do not believe me (Jn 8, 44-45).

To lie is "to speak against the truth in order to induce a person entitled to it into error." According to this definition, to tell a lie requires the following conditions:

- To speak against the truth, that is, to say the contrary of what is thought or known.

- The intention of leading the listener into error.

One lies only when one says something false to someone who has the right to know the truth. For this reason, silence is permitted when the person one is dealing with does not have the right to know.

Since a lie is to say the contrary of what one thinks, a lie is an evil in itself, it is bad by its very nature. Besides, it also brings a series of evils with it. For example:

a. A lie causes damage to the one who tells it.

In effect, when one lies, one betrays one's self in thought and word. One should avoid lying because one's mind should reflect the truth which one possesses. Likewise, neither can one break his word, because it is expresses one's own integrity. Furthermore, on occasion, a lie connotes a weakness in personality if one lies because he lacks the fortitude to tell the truth and the responsibility to assume the consequences of professing the truth, whatever the cost.

b. It produces vice in human relations.

When one lies to his neighbor, one deceives him, and induces him into error and sows doubt and suspicion in social relations.

c. Dishonesty damages society.

Social and political life is directed toward solving the true problems in people's everyday life. Thus, the deceits of politicians are the cause of serious harm.

The *Catechism of the Catholic Church* enumerates these evils in the following terms:

> Since it violates the virtue of truthfulness, a lie does real violence to another. It affects his ability to know, which is a condition of every judgment and decision. It contains the seed of discord and all consequent evils. Lying is destructive of society; it undermines trust among men and tears apart the fabric of social relationships (*CCC*, 2486).

6. The gravity of a lie

Given that a lie is an evil in itself, it is always a sin. But it will be more or less serious in conformity with the following criteria which are cited in the *Catechism of the Catholic Church*:

> The *gravity of a lie* is measured against the nature of the truth it deforms, the circumstances, the intentions of the one who lies, and the harm suffered by its victims. If a lie in itself only constitutes a venial sin, it becomes mortal when it does grave injury to the virtues of justice and charity (*CCC*, 2484).

In summary, to judge the gravity of a lie one should take these four fundamental criteria into account:

a. The material related to the lie.

The object of a lie determines its gravity: a lie is a venial sin if the matter is less serious, or grave if the matter is serious. For example, calumny, when a serious defect is attributed to a person, would be a grave sin.

b. The intention.

The sin of lying can be more grave if the one who lies tries to cause serious damage, whether by deception or by distorting reality.

c. The circumstances which motivate lies.

A lie may cause serious evil depending on the circumstances. Such could be the case of a lie which unfavorably influences a person's professional life.

d. The effects of a lie.

Sometimes a lie may cause serious evils such as a lie concerning an important issue which causes social disturbances.

Even if the lie is not serious, it should be carefully refrained from because all dishonesty injures the trustworthiness of the person. Dishonesty goes against the dignity of man; dignity demands that a man be truthful.

7. Sins against another's reputation

Especially grave is the lie against the prestige, fame, good name and reputation of any person. There are three ways of violating the dignity of the person: calumny, detraction, and rash judgment, (cf. CCC, 2477).

a. Calumny.

Calumny is a lie told about someone, accusing him of something of which he is not guilty. Calumny is what is directly forbidden in the formulation of this precept in the Old Testament where it says: "You shall not bear false witness against your neighbor" (Ex 20, 16; Dt 5, 20).

Everyone has the right to fame and honor. *Fame* is the positive or negative opinion which is commonly held about another person. *Honor* is the testimony of the excellence of a man's character. The sin against a person's fame or honor is called *disparagement* or *slander*. Both are examples of calumny. In any case, when one disparages or slanders, he takes away someone's fame. For this reason, to defame or dishonor is to wound a person in himself: it damages his dignity. Calumny converts a worthy person into an undignified person who will be wrongly judged by the society in which he lives. Consequently, calumny is a sin against charity and against justice.

The sin of calumny is more or less serious depending on the importance of the object of the slanderous lie and also on the evils caused to the victim.

b. **Detraction.**

To detract from a person's good reputation is to declare the defects or faults of another without valid reason to a person who did not know them. It is allowed to reveal the faults of another only in situations when an evil could befall another person or grave harm could come to society. .

c. **Rash judgment.**

It is the interior or exterior judgment made about the reputation of a person, without sufficient reason, with which one attributes a moral defect his neighbor.

8. The duty to make restitution

Given that falsehood causes harm, one has the obligation to make restitution for it. This always happens in the case of calumny. In this instance, it is not sufficient to repent and it is not even enough to ask for forgiveness, one must make up for the harm committed. A lie may not only be a sin against truth or charity, but also against justice. And justice, by its very nature, demands reparation.

On occasion, reparation should be carried out publicly if the injury requires it. In other cases, it can be accomplished privately. Reparation may include restitution by means of economic compensation. This reparation—and in some cases, restitution—obliges in conscience. This means that there is no forgiveness of sins if one does not have the intention of making reparation or restitution.

The *Catechism of the Catholic Church* says:

> Every offense committed against justice and truth entails the *duty of reparation,* even if its author has been forgiven. When it is impossible publicly to make reparation for a wrong, it must be made secretly. If someone who has suffered harm cannot be directly compensated, he must be given moral satisfaction in the name of charity. This duty of reparation also concerns offenses against another's reputation. This reparation, moral and sometimes material, must be evaluated in terms of the extent of the damage inflicted. It obliges in conscience (CCC, 2487).

Conclusion

If society is to function with a minimum of problems, it should be obvious that the keystone of social interaction will be the truth. There can be no social relations where men cannot trust one another. All men have an obligation to speak the truth themselves, and to speak out in defense of the truth. It should be obvious to all that the truth is the glue which binds society together.

OUTLINE

I. Glossary

CALUMNY:

False accusation, done maliciously, to cause damage.

DETRACTION:

Revealing the hidden faults of another person to someone who has no right to know about them, thus damaging or destroying his good reputation.

FALSEHOOD:

A lack of correspondence between what one thinks and what one says.

HONOR:

Respect or good reputation which is acquired through the practice of virtue or heroic acts. The quality which brings man to be guided by the most elevated moral norms.

OBJECTIVE TRUTH:

Reality which exists outside of a person's intellect, and which is independent of his acknowledgment of its existence.

REALISM:

Theory of knowledge which justly values the role of reason and reality of objects in themselves, outside of the mind.

REPUTATION:

The good or bad opinion commonly held about another person.

RESTITUTION (REPARATION):

Compensation made to another for an injury inflicted upon him by one's sinful actions, i.e., repaying money stolen, replacing property damaged or stolen, or repairing the damage done to another's reputation or fame through sins of calumny, detraction, slander etc.

SLANDER:

Destroying the honor or fame of another by accusing him of something of which he is not guilty.

SUBJECTIVISM:

The doctrine concerning knowledge which exaggerates the function of reason, placing it above the objectivity of what is known.

TOLERANCE:

Respect for other people's ideas, though they may not be correct.

TRUTH:

The correlation between the interior idea and the external reality.

VERACITY:

Truthfulness; the disposition of a person to tell the truth.

II. Summary of Principles.

1. Every man has a natural right to have the truth told to him; but not every truth, only those that he has a legitimate interest in knowing.

2. Veracity is an act of justice among persons.

3. Every person has a natural right to privacy. On occasion, however, the private life of a public figure can be decisive in the decision to vote for him or not, granted that his beliefs and actions influence public life.

4. The media have a duty to inform the public with justice and veracity.

5. Unrestricted communication of one's intimate life can lead to emptiness and personal impoverishment.

6. Veracity exercises the honor of a person; the honorable man always tells the truth.

7. The way to true freedom is love for and practice of the truth.

SUPPLEMENTARY READINGS

1. Do you not know, I said, that the true lie, if such an expression may be allowed, is hated of gods and men?

What do you mean?, he said.

I mean that no one is willingly deceived in that which is the truest and highest part of himself, or about the truest and highest matters; there, above all, he is most afraid of a lie having possession of him.

Still, he said, I do not comprehend you.

The reason is, I replied, that you attribute some profound meaning to my words; but I am only saying that deception, or being deceived or uninformed about the highest realities in the highest part of themselves, which is the soul, and in that part of them to have and to hold the lie, is what mankind least like;—that, I say, is what they utterly detest.

There is nothing more hateful to them.

And, as I was just now remarking, this ignorance in the soul of him who is deceived may be called the true lie; for the lie in words is only a kind of imitation and shadowy image of a previous affection of the soul, not pure unadulterated falsehood. Am I not right?

Perfectly right.

The true lie is hated not only by the gods, but also by men?

Yes.

(Plato, *Republic* Bk. 2)

2. *Professional secrets*—for example, those of political office holders, soldiers, physicians, and lawyers—or confidential information given under the seal of secrecy must be kept, save in excep-

tional cases where keeping the secret is bound to cause very grave harm to the one who confided it, to the one who received it or to a third party, and where the very grave harm can be avoided only by divulging the truth. Even if not confided under the seal of secrecy, private information prejudicial to another is not to be divulged without a grave and proportionate reason.

(CCC, 2491)

3. It is essential that all those involved should form a correct conscience on the use of the media, especially with regard to certain issues which are particularly controversial today.

The first of these issues is information, or the search for news and its publication. Because of the progress of modern society and the increasing interdependence of its members on one another, it is obvious that information is very useful and, for the most part, essential. If news or facts and happenings is communicated publicly and without delay, every individual will have permanent access to sufficient information and thus will be enabled to contribute effectively to the common good. Further, all of them will more easily be able to contribute in unison to the prosperity and the progress of society as a whole.

There exists therefore in human society a right to information on the subjects that are of concern to men either as individuals or as members of society, according to each man's circumstances. The proper exercise of this right demands that the content of the communication be true and—within the limit set by justice and charity—complete. Further, it should be communicated honestly and properly. This means that in the gathering and in the publication of news the moral law and the legitimate rights and dignity of man should be upheld. All knowledge is not profitable, but on the other hand "love builds" (1 Cor 8, 1).

(IM, 5)

4. Those who receive the means of social communication—readers, viewers, audiences—do so of their own free choice. Special obligations rest on them in consequence. A properly motivated selectivity would be wholly in favor of whatever excels in virtue, culture and art. Likewise, it would never avoid whatever might be a cause or occasion of spiritual harm to the recipients or might be a source of danger to others through bad example; it would avoid whatever might hinder the communications of the good

and facilitate the communication of what is evil. This last usually occurs when financial help is given to those who exploit the media solely for profit.

If they are to obey the moral law, those who use the media ought to keep themselves informed in good time about assessments arrived at by the authorities with competence in this sphere and to conform to them as a right conscience would dictate. They should take appropriate steps to direct and form their consciences so that they may more readily resist less wholesome influences and profit more fully from the good.

(IM, 9)

5. The lie supposes such contempt, that when the greatness of God is affirmed, the grace of the deity is reduced, and the lowest things, elevated as the truth, are praised as noble.

(Leonardo da Vinci)

APPENDICES

1. The value of human reason and the meaning of truth

There has occasionally been a certain exaggeration of the value of reason in past times. The European rationalism of the eighteenth and nineteenth centuries was an overestimation of reason, and finally led to *Idealism*, which stresses the importance of what man conceives things to be, rather than of what things truly are. Rationalism represents a decay in rational knowledge, because it exposes itself to the caprice of men by only accepting what man is capable of knowing, which leaves Christian revelation outside the realm of rationalist thought, but not refuted by it.

On the other hand, in addition to the risk of rationalism or idealism, it is frequently said that modern culture has gone to the other extreme, that is, culture distrusts reason and no longer professes a love of the truth. Rather than the Truth, it is said, culture is enamored with "life". If this is actually the present situation, then not only the fall of the West but also the bankruptcy of man are certain. Hence, there it is very urgent that the importance of reason and the love of truth be re-acquired. In all times and in all cultures, the Christian must echo the Christ's promise that "the Truth will make you free" (Jn 8, 32).

2. Freedom and Truth

"Jesus therefore said to the Jews who had come to believe in him, 'If you abide in my word, you shall be my disciples, indeed and you shall know the truth, and the truth shall make you free.'" (Jn 8,31-32). Christ proposes here that knowing and living the truth is the way to an authentic freedom.

> According to Christian faith and the Church's teaching, *only the freedom which submits to the truth leads the human person to his true good. The good of the person is to be in the truth and to do the truth.*
>
> A comparison between the Church's teaching and today's social and cultural situation immediately makes clear the urgent need *for the Church herself to develop an intense pastoral effort precisely with regard to this fundamental question.* This essential bond between truth, the good and freedom has been largely lost sight of by present-day culture. As a result, helping man to rediscover it represents nowadays one of the specific requirements of the Church's mission, for the salvation of the world. Pilate's question: 'What is truth?' reflects the distressing perplexity of a man who often no longer knows *who he is, whence* he comes and *where* he is going.
>
> Hence we not infrequently witness the fearful plunging of the human person into situations of gradual self-destruction. According to some, it appears that one no longer need acknowledge the enduring absoluteness of any moral value (*VS*, 84-85).

Human persons must seek the truth and strive to live in that truth since freedom is bound to the truth. "If there is not transcendent truth there is no sure principle of guaranteeing just relation between the people (*CA, 44*).

> It is therefore urgently necessary, for the future of society and the development of a sound democracy, to rediscover those essential and innate human and moral values which flow from the very truth of the human being and express and safeguard the dignity of the person: values which no individual,

no majority and no State can ever create, modify or destroy, but must only acknowledge, respect and promote.

Consequently, there is a need to recover the *basic elements of a vision of the relationship between civil law and moral law*, which are put forward by the Church, but which are also part of the patrimony of the great juridical traditions of humanity (*EV*, 71).

The Church encourages political leaders to make decisions that will lead to the establishment of the moral values which come from the objective truth. Otherwise *ethical relativism* will undermine the foundation of freedom.

If there in no ultimate truth to guide and direct political activity, then ideas and convictions can easily be manipulated for reasons of power (*CA*, 46).

QUESTIONS

1. What does the statement that the commandments are "generically stated" mean?

2. What is revelation according to the chapter?

3. Define truth.

4. What is the foundation of man's relations with each other?

5. What is the main concern of St. John's gospel? What is the action of the Holy Spirit on the apostles?

6. What is a lie?

7. What conditions must be met for a person to be guilty of telling a lie?

8. Must the truth be told in all cases? Why or why not? Can you give a practical example of a situation in which a person would not be obligated to tell someone the truth?

9. List three effects of a lie.

10. List the four criteria for determining whether a lie is a venial or mortal sin.

11. What is the difference between calumny and detraction?

12. What is rash judgment?

PRACTICAL EXERCISES

1. Explain the following definition of St. Augustine: "A lie consists in saying something false with the intention of deceiving." Does this mean that it is permissible to say something which one knows is untrue, as long as there is no specific intention to deceive the person? Why or why not?

2. Comment on this maxim written by Goethe: "Every moral law and rule of conduct can be reduced to one: the truth." What does it mean to say that everything in the moral life can be reduced to the truth?

3. Based upon your understanding of the principles contained in this chapter, resolve the following questions:

   a. Anne is aware that her brother Jerry has been getting drunk on the weekend and is concerned about him. May she inform her parents?

   b. Terence's friend is dating a girl who had an abortion five years earlier. He knows they are talking about getting married. May he tell his friend that the girl had an abortion?

   c. Maria and her friend Teresa had a terrible argument. As a result, Maria told another person at the law firm where she and Teresa work that, while they were in college, Teresa had cheated on an important final exam, using information she had obtained illicitly. (The story is untrue, because although Teresa did have the opportunity to find out what was going to be on the exam before the test was administered, she never followed through. Her conscience would not permit her to do it.) As a result, Teresa's reputation at the firm has been severely damaged. One of the senior partners at the firm has even said that she is concerned about Teresa having access to confidential documents, because she is afraid that she will misuse the information. What is the specific nature of the sin of which Maria is guilty? What sort of restitution do you think Maria needs to make to Teresa for the damage that has been done to her reputation? How do you think she can do this?

   d. Ed arrived home after 3 a.m. Although he hadn't been drinking, he knows that his mother would disapprove of the hour at which he arrived home because he is only 16 years old. The next morning his mother asked him what time he came in. Does he have to tell the truth?

4. Comment on this quote: "Do not be afraid of the truth, even though the truth may bring you death" (Blessed Josemaría Escrivá).

5. Do you know of any instances in which the media has distorted or misrepresented the truth in their reporting of the news? What obligations does the media have with regard to the truth?

FOOTNOTES FOR CITED CATECHISM TEXTS

Chapter	Footnote # and reference

II
1. Gn 1, 27.
2. Gn 2, 7
3. Cf. Council of Vienne (1312): *DS* 902.
4. Rm 6, 11 and cf. 6, 5; cf. Col 2, 12.
5. Cf. *GS* 25 § 1.

III
1. Cf. Rm 6, 17.

V
1. Jn 15, 15; cf. Jas 1, 25; 2, 12; Gal 4, 1-7; 21-31; Rm 8, 15

VII
1. Gn 3, 5.
2. St. Augustine, *De civ. Dei* 14, 28: PL 41, 436.
3. Cf. Phil 2, 6-9.
4. *RP*, 16.

IX
1. Cf. Jn 13, 34.
2. Jn 13, 1.
3. Jn 15, 9; 12.
4. Cf. Gal 5, 20; Eph 5, 5.
5. Cf. Dt 18, 10; Jr 29, 8.
6. Roman Catechism 3, 2, 4.
7. Cf. 2 P 1, 4.

X
1. Cf. Mt 10, 32; 1 Tim 6, 12.
2. Cf. 2 Cor 1, 23; Gal 1, 20.

XI
1. Cf. *CIC*, can. 1245.

XIII
1. Mt 18, 6; Cf. 1 Cor 8, 10-13.

XIV
1. Cf. Sir 1, 22.

XV
1. Cf. Gn 1, 26-29.
2. Cf. Gn 1, 28-31.
3. Cf. *CA* 37-38.
4. Cf. *GS* 69 § 1.
5. *CA* 48 § 4; cf. Pius XI, *Quadragesimo anno I*, 184-186.

INDEX

Grace
  ethical requirements of Gospel and g. 6–7
  transformative power of g. 31

H

Habits, good 12
Happiness, Christian morality and 6
Health, personal 248
Heart
  h. as seat of conscience 75
  control of h. 12
Heaven 16
Hell 16
Heresy 170
Heteronomy 246
Hinduism 188
Holiness 15
Holy Spirit, truth and 334
Homosexuality 288
  same sex marriages and h. 94
Hope 187
  definition of h. 170
  h. as exercise in worship of God 170–171
Horoscopes 177

I

Idealism 345
Idolatry 175, 179
Ignorance 54, 56, 69, 73
Illness, terminal
  appropriate medical treatment of t. i. 268–269
  discontinuing medical treatment in t. i. 269–270
Imputability, diminished 54
Incest 288
Indifference 172
Indissolubility of marriage 280–281
Ingratitude 172
Intelligence, moral responsibility and 51
Irreligion 178

J

Jesus
  See also **Christ**
  call of J. 8
  fulfillment of Ten Commandments in J. 163
  J. brings fifth commandment to perfection 247
  J. fulfills love of neighbor 12
  J. fulfills precepts of law 15
  imitating the life of J. 8–9
  morality of J. 16
  name of God and J. 194

  truth and J. 333, 337
  willingness of J. to forgive sins 140
Judgment
  j. of conscience 72-73
  Last J. 14
  moral j. 56
  prudent j. 96
  rash j. 15, 340
Justice
  j. as condition for a legitimate oath 198
  social j. 326

K

Knowledge
  k. as a requirement for human act 52
  k. as condition for morality 53
  full k. 53
  partial k. 53

L

Law
  conscience and l. 15
  civil l. and moral law 347
  civil l., conscience and 77
  civil l., meaning and purpose of 92–93, 102
  civil l. must guarantee right to life 102
  civil l. must use natural law as a basis 90
  common good and l. 86
  conscience and l., conflicts between 94–95
  conscience and l., relationship between 77
  definition of l. 86
  divine l. as supreme rule of life 92
  divine l., conscience and 77
  divine l., freedom and 101
  divisions and kinds of l. 86–92
  eternal l. 87
  eternal l., sin and 130
  Evangelical l. (*see* also **Law,** new) 91–92
  excessive stress on l. 77
  freedom and l. 59–60
  Jesus fulfills precepts of L. 15
  just l. 93–94
  knowledge of l., conscience and 74
  l. as ordinance of reason 86
  l. does not enslave the conscience 94
  legal positivism and l. 100
  l. of retaliation (*lex talionis*) 30
  moral l. 148
  moral l. and civil law 347
  moral l. and conscience 77
  moral l. can be universally applied 112
  moral l. contradicted by situation ethics 112
  moral l., democracy must depend upon 148
  moral l. presupposes the rational order 87

natural l. 88–90, 148
natural l. and legitimate authority 100
natural l. and Magisterium 89
natural l. as human expression of eternal law 88
natural l. basis for common good of society 90
natural l., immutability of 89
natural l. must form basis of civil law 90
natural l., self evident character of 89
natural l. and Ten Commandments 160–161
natural l. universality of 89
new l. 91–92. See also **Law**, evangelical
new l. and Beatitudes 92
new l. and law of the Spirit 91, 94
positive l. 90–91
purpose of l. 85
unjust l., examples of 94
unjust l. not binding in conscience 95

Laws
l. of nature distinct from natural law 90
l. show man path to salvation 16
Legality, confusion of morality and 135
Liberty, religious 185–186
Lie, seriousness of 338–339
Life
Christian moral l. 10
interior l. as moral battleground 12
moral l. and freedom 16
obligation to protect l. 248–252
obligation to respect l. 248
procreation of l. in family 277–280
respect for l. 247
Love
Christian morality centered on l. 18
command to l. God and neighbor 18, 74, 173–174
l. as foundation of the family 228–229
l. as merely an emotion or a sentiment 44
l. as practical exercise in worship of God 171
l. of God 171–172
l. of neighbor 172–173
l. of self 173
new commandment of l. 18, 30
"new morality" and l. 44
self-sacrifice and l. 44
Lukewarmness 172

M
Magic 177
Magisterium 35
formation of conscience and M. 71, 78–79
M. as interpreter of the Word of God 34
M. defines truth and morals 34–35
natural law and M. 89
sin and M. 133

Man
ability of m. to choose good and evil 51–52
Christian concept of m. 27–30
concept of m. determines moral conduct 27
creation of m. 276–277, 278–279
harmony of m. and natural law 88
lordship of m. over creation 101, 312, 318
m. as living image of God 101
m. made in the image of God 28
m. responsible for his free acts 60
material things and m. in Bible 312–313
right to property and m. 314
unity of body and soul in m. 28–29
Marriage
conditions for dissolution of m. 281
joys of m. 281–282
man and woman created in a state of m. 276–277
properties of m. 279–281, 281–283
purposes of m. 278–279, 280–281
Mass, fulfillment of precept for attending 217–218
Masturbation 288
Media, obligation to truth 336
Monism 189
Moral categories, subjective 110–111
Moral choice
components of m. c. 106–107
prayer and m. c. 72
Moral concepts, conscience and 71
Moral conduct
concept of man and m. c. 27
effect of m. c. on man 51
errors of judgment in m. c. 78
Moral judgments 71
Moral life
importance of m. l. 51
rational principles of m. l. 50
Moral relativism.
See **Relativism**, moral
Moral theology
ancillary sciences of m. t. 35–36
goals of m. t. 26
Magisterium and m. t. 34–35
Sacred Scripture and m. t. 33
Sacred Tradition and m. t. 34
sources of m. t. 32–35
worship and m. t. 167
Moral truth 37
Morality
autonomous m. 77
Catholic m. and civil ethics 43–44